Praise for Ma

and *Creating a Life That Matters*

"Manis Friedman is one of a handful of original thinkers that miraculously appear in each generation. This wonderful book synthesizes his answers to life's most profound questions. It is hard to imagine the person who would not greatly benefit from reading *Creating a Life That Matters.*"

—Dennis Prager, nationally syndicated radio talk show host, founder of Prager University, and author of *The Rational Bible*

"Rabbi Manis Friedman has succeeded in making the profound teachings of Chabad Chassidic philosophy relevant and accessible to an entire generation. Most remarkably, he has done so without diluting or compromising their integrity, bringing these core truths—the essence of these age-old wellsprings of knowledge—to diverse audiences throughout the world.... This book is truly a modern guide to the perplexed that will benefit the scholarly and the uninitiated alike."

—Rabbi Mordechai Abergel, Chief Rabbi of Singapore

"A rising superstar... eloquent and witty."

—*New York Times Magazine*

"One of the great social philosophers of contemporary America."

—Oxford University

"A most unusual man who is saying what needs to be said.... Provocative and inspiring."

—Bob Grant, New York City radio talk show host

"Friedman is an energetic and entertaining speaker and writer, exploring with careful wit and compassion the gamut of human behavior."

—*The Hungry Mind*

Praise for *Doesn't Anyone Blush Anymore?*

"Anyone who is either married or thinking of getting married would do well to read [Friedman's] book."

—Bob Dylan

"Every page is valuable.... Gentle, sensitive, wise, and sometimes crack-up funny."

—*Lifestyles in Recovery*

"The message in Manis Friedman's folksy and fascinating book... is simple. It's good to be good."

—*Seventeen Magazine*

"I recommend that every person in America go out and buy [Friedman's] book."

—Paul Harvey, nationally syndicated radio commentator

"Very simply: Friedman is good."

—*Miami Jewish Herald*

"If a copy of Friedman's remarkable book could be presented to every young American on reaching marriageable age, millions would escape the anguish of divorce, failed relationships, and marital strife."

—Don Feder, *The Boston Herald*

"With wit and originality, Manis Friedman makes us take a fresh look at our own morality."

—*Guideposts*

Praise for *The Joy of Intimacy*

"Essential reading not only for couples who want to regain intimacy, but for singles seeking relationship wisdom in a culture of meaningless hook-ups.... He provides the antidote for the ills that plague today's relationships."

—Miriam Grossman, MD, author of *Unprotected* and *You're Teaching My Child What?*

Creating a Life That Matters

Creating a Life That Matters

How to Live and Love with Meaning and Purpose

MANIS FRIEDMAN

and

RIVKA GOLDSTEIN

It's Good to Know Publishing

New York

Copyright © 2021 Manis Friedman and Rivka Goldstein. All rights reserved. Printed in the United States of America. No part of this book may be used, reproduced, translated, electronically stored, or transmitted in any manner whatsoever without prior written permission from the publisher, except by reviewers, who may quote brief passages in their reviews.

For information, contact:

It's Good to Know Publishing
Brooklyn, New York
ItsGoodToKnowPublishing.com
Email: info@itsgoodtoknowpublishing.com
AskDodaRivka.com
rivkag@post.harvard.edu

Library of Congress Control Number: 2021904567
ISBN: 978-0-9862770-5-4 (trade paperback)
ISBN: 978-0-9862770-6-1 (hardcover)
ISBN: 978-0-9862770-7-8 (e-book)

10 9 8 7 6 5 4 3 2

Cover design: Alison Forner
Interior design: Alan Barnett

Note to the reader: The stories and examples in this book reflect the issues and questions that have recurred during many years of Rabbi Manis Friedman's public classes and private counseling sessions. However, the characters described and the details of their lives are composites, and resemblance to any particular person or event is purely accidental and unintentional. Names and details have been changed.

The information and insights in this book are solely the opinion of the authors and should not be considered as a form of therapy, advice, direction, diagnosis, and/or treatment of any kind. This information is not a substitute for medical, psychological, or other professional advice, counseling, or care. All matters pertaining to your individual health should be supervised by a physician or appropriate health-care practitioner. Neither the publisher nor the authors assume any responsibility or liability whatsoever on behalf of any purchaser or reader.

Todd M. Morgan, a great supporter of this project and of Rabbi Friedman's incredible work and wisdom, dedicates this book to his family—his wife, Rosanna; his children, Tammy Ratner and Josh Morgan; his grandchildren, Emily, Charlie, and Billy Ratner; and his brothers, Richard and Tommy Morgan.

The Toberman Family Charitable Foundation dedicates this book to William R. Skolnick; his wife, Fran; his children, Lisa and Scott Gad, Andrea and Alexander Douglas; and his grandchildren, Shira and Avi Gad.

Gary Carmell dedicates this book to the blessed memory of his beautiful wife, Roneet, and to his children, Jacob and Ariella, who he hopes will learn from Rabbi Friedman's extraordinary wisdom to help repair the world in their own unique ways. He also dedicates the book to Heather Nalle, an avid student of Rabbi Friedman's, who has been a blessing to Gary in countless ways since they first met.

. . . and Your righteousness to our children
Rotem Jale & Ilay Hillel Ibrahimzadeh,
that they may serve Your people
with righteousness & loving kindness . . .

Contents

PART THREE

Fathers & Mothers & Daughters & Sons

Foreword

Rivka Goldstein and I first met more than a decade ago at a women's event in Miami, where I was the guest speaker. It quickly became evident to me that this Harvard graduate has far more on the ball than just an aptitude for book learning and academic achievement. Rivka's enthusiasm for life and commitment to growth is unlike any I have ever seen.

After these many years, Rivka continues to astound me as to how wonderfully she embraces her diverse roles as wife, mother, teacher, relationship and life coach, matchmaker, and pivotal member of the community. Anyone who knows her will attest to her warmth, kindness, generosity, and nurturing nature. Even after she moved back to her native land of Singapore, we kept in close contact.

While she was living at the southernmost tip of continental Asia, on a resort island just off the coast of Singapore, Rivka's unquenchable thirst for knowledge and for truth led her to the works of Rabbi Manis Friedman, one of America's best-known rabbis and a world-renowned author, educator, counselor, lecturer, and philosopher who has devoted his life to teaching spiritual topics to the broadest imaginable audience. Combining ancient wisdom with captivating wit and insight, his popular books, seminars, and online offerings draw diverse audiences from around the world.

I have had the privilege of knowing and learning from Rabbi Friedman since the early 1970s, when I left my experimental community deep in the Colorado Rockies to become a student and later a teacher of Torah. I have witnessed his brilliance and his fame grow exponentially as his name seems to pop up everywhere, from international public affairs media and talk shows to the lecture halls of Oxford University, from such unlikely venues as *Rolling Stone* and *Seventeen* magazines to private conversations with celebrated individuals such as Nobel Prize-winning singer-songwriter Bob Dylan. Rabbi Friedman's talks shed light on a gamut of topics that include dating, intimacy, marriage, parenting, current affairs, and much more. He transports Chassidic philosophy from its profound intellectual heights to down-to-earth delights that are readily digestible, making him YouTube's most popular rabbi.

After meeting with Rabbi Friedman, Rivka spent hundreds of hours listening to and transcribing his talks with great diligence and enthusiasm. She then began to assemble and compile all she had learned. Over the course of more than four years, Rivka collaborated with Rabbi Friedman to create the manuscript that would eventually become the book you are holding in your hands.

Rivka describes her experience of absorbing, internalizing, and shaping this compendium of lectures as a challenge and a gift that defies description. "Words are limiting; they are barely adequate to convey the Torah's timeless teachings on the inner essence of a human being's relationship with God," she says. "Yet Rabbi Friedman manages to keep it real and relevant."

The synchronicity of time, space, and soul became complete when my husband, Simcha Gottlieb, was invited to refine and edit Rivka's manuscript. Simcha has spent much of his career writing, producing, and editing books, films, articles, and educational media. Having known Rabbi Friedman for more than four decades and having worked with him on a number of previous projects, Simcha embraced the opportunity as an honor and a privilege.

It has been a fascinating and rewarding experience for us both to watch the dynamic interaction between the perceptive teacher and the astute chronicler of his works, each so extraordinary in their own right.

There are waters of wisdom flowing on every page of this magnum opus. You're invited in for a drink. *L'chaim*.

Frumma Rosenberg-Gottlieb
Coauthor of *Age Well Now*

Preface

The book you are holding in your hands is of little cultural significance per se. Nor does it contain much explicit spiritual or religious content. And you will find no familiar pop psychology notions anywhere in these pages. The perspectives presented herein are simple truths, not limited to any particular cultural setting, undiluted with trendy theories, and unconstrained by religious dogma.

In a sense, these ideas—though far from prophetic and lacking all that thunder and lightning—are not unlike the Ten Commandments given at Mount Sinai. The Decalogue makes no mention of religion, heaven and hell, or reward and punishment. The Commandments are entirely free of psychological considerations or cultural idiosyncrasies; they speak of simple, unadorned principles of right and wrong, true and false, what is noble and what is not. Yet this ancient wisdom is as universally relevant today as the day it was revealed.

As you read these brief chapters on a variety of life's issues and challenges, you might find yourself wondering, "Why didn't I think of that?" Or occasionally, we hope, "Well! That explains everything." These teachings are derived, whether directly or indirectly, from the Chabad Chassidic wisdom tradition in which I was raised and trained—which, while somewhat mystical, emphasizes down-to-earth, practical action based on love of humanity.

I absorbed these ideas over the years from teachers and mentors who wholeheartedly embodied the philosophy and who articulated its principles with diligence and brilliance. My fellow students and I, otherwise rambunctious teenagers with more energy than sense, sat quietly mesmerized by the beauty and elegance of a selfless view of life that appealed to our youthful idealism. We were humbled by deep insights into the properties of the human soul, the relationship between Creator and creation, the blessings of love and intimacy, the purpose of life. We reviewed these heavenly topics again and again, debated them, wrestled with them, struggled to fathom their inner meaning and to internalize their implications. We were swimming in a sea of emotional intelligence, and grateful for it.

Then came the challenge. As wide-eyed adolescence reluctantly released its grip and we stepped forward as young adults, the Rebbe of our generation, the seventh leader of the international Chabad Chassidic community, urged each of us to take the learning we had imbibed and turn it outward—to relocate to some distant city, state, country, or island and make a lifelong commitment to serving the needs of the people there. He dared us to begin thinking of ourselves not as private citizens but as ambassadors of goodness and sanctity, to partner with our Creator in bringing heaven down to earth. He charged us with the tasks of igniting the native allegiance to higher purpose that simmers in the human heart, sharing responsibility for building a world of kindness, and ensuring the continuity of Jewish life everywhere.

Newly married, we packed our belongings, bid farewell to our families, and arrived at our new homes—some far, some near, wherever we were needed. Quickly acclimating to local culture, custom, and language, we pledged ourselves to the sacred mission of helping to meet the needs, whether social, spiritual, or economic, of our neighbors. Learning on the job, growing in our roles, we applied ourselves to cultivating and improving the quality of life, locally at first.

In St. Paul, Minnesota, I cofounded a school for young women of college age and beyond who had limited backgrounds in traditional Jewish studies. Eventually these educational endeavors extended beyond the confines of the school to far-flung corners of the world. I was reminded again and again that teachers often learn the most from their students, and that the greatest personal growth lies in sharing whatever knowledge we may have with others.

From my teachers I have learned the highest of values; from my students, the gritty realities of everyday life. Heaven and earth have thus combined to arrive at the conclusions that fill these pages. This book is, therefore, not a "self-help" offering, nor is it a "ten-step program to the good life." Here you will not be told what to do or not to do. Rather, this book seeks to empower you by clarifying the meaning and the significance of the words we use—to inspire you to live a more elegant life. It will bring you comfort in the realization that all that you have experienced, the agonies and the ecstasies, brought you to this moment. And in this moment, you can fulfill the mission with which your soul entered this world.

So come, let us reason together. Let us get to know our Creator and our rightful place in His vast eternal plan.

• • •

Among my students is one whose love of learning and generosity of spirit is an inspiration to everyone she meets: Rivka Goldstein. It was her initiative, devotion, and acumen in compiling the teachings you'll read here, based on more talks and lectures than any of us could count, that have resulted in this book. We all owe her a debt of gratitude.

Rabbi Manis Friedman

Introduction

This book began as a love letter to my beloved son, Yosef, an only child who was born as I was turning forty. As an older mother, I wanted to leave my child with the wisdom he would need to lead a fulfilling and purposeful life, a life of service and contribution. I wanted to give him a "life manual"—the one we wish we had received when life gets a little bumpy and we lament that "nobody taught me about this" or "I didn't learn these lessons in school." As you will see, my "letter" to my son turned into much more.

Creating a Life That Matters is inspired by and based entirely on the rare wisdom and vast experience of Rabbi Manis Friedman. A renowned author, teacher, and speaker, he has also counseled countless people for over fifty years on their journey toward self-discovery, better relationships, and a deeper connection with themselves and with God.

As one who was born Buddhist and raised Christian in a multicultural and religious state among Muslims, Hindus, and Eurasians, I found Rabbi Friedman's teachings to be a voice of reason and resonance. My own lifelong search for meaning brought me to Harvard, but it was not until I found Judaism that I knew I had found my true home.

As I gathered and then wove together the teachings in this book, and as I regularly met with Rabbi Friedman to discuss this life wisdom that is so crucial in today's demanding and often-confusing world, this work began to take on a life of its own. I came to realize that what I was creating was no longer just a legacy for my son but a practical guide for the spiritual path that could help people of all ages and traditions.

Rabbi Friedman's audience and readers include those of many cultures, nationalities, races, and spiritual traditions, and this book is no different. It speaks to all of us who grapple with the complexities and challenges of life today, whether we are facing loneliness or self-doubt, difficulties in relationships, marriage, or parenting, or ultimate matters of life and death. It is, in fact, an essential, lifelong resource that can be read and referred back to as the need arises—a road map, if you will, for navigating relationships with others, with our true self, and, above all, with our Creator as we seek to discover our specific and unique mission in life.

So often we go through life as though sleepwalking, reacting to what's happening around us based on our conditioning or the urgent demands of the day, and therefore we miss the preciousness and the purpose of life *in this moment.* This book is meant to awaken you. It offers solutions because it reveals the root cause of our struggles and gets to the heart of why we are really here.

Through the insights you'll find here, you will come to see that life can be free of anxiety, doubt, and depression. There is no need to go through life stumbling unnecessarily or silently suffering. We are not alone. The sages of old and their modern interpreters have given us the blueprint for creating a life that truly matters—and for living and loving with meaning and purpose. That is the message I want to share with my precious son, Yosef, and with you.

It is my heartfelt hope that this book will serve as a guide to illuminate your own quest to understand what life is all about and to live that life with greater clarity, peace, and happiness.

Rivka Goldstein

PART ONE

Get a Life

1

Living versus Existing

Existence is dead weight. You have to carry it.
Life is buoyant. It carries you.

When God created the world out of nothingness, the first thing He had to do was create *existence*—because nothing had ever existed before.

To exist is to occupy space. That's the scientific definition: everything in the universe exists because it takes up space, and if it does not take up space, it does not exist. For example, the chair you are sitting on, and the book you are reading, occupy space. There's no room in those exact spaces for anything else to exist.

Even the thoughts in our head take up space. When we are thinking, our minds are occupied, and another thought cannot fit in that same space. Emotion also takes up space; hence the expression "my heart is full." It implies that when you have an emotion, another emotion cannot enter that same place. Everything that exists occupies space—fire, water, stone, thoughts, feelings.

Another characteristic of existence is that it's conditional. Fine, so you exist; but in order to keep on existing you have to eat, drink, and breathe. You need a roof over your head, friends, security, a support system—the list goes on. As long as you fulfill these conditions, you can continue to take up space. Without them, maybe not, and certainly not for long. In other words, existence demands and depends on the use of resources.

God, therefore, gave to the world something more than mere existence, something that doesn't depend on outside conditions. He gave us *life*. Life is the effect something that exists has on its surroundings, the contribution it makes to the world. Fire and water both exist, but the contribution of fire is not the same as that of water. Fire gives light, warmth, and causes things to come apart. Water makes things grow, keeps things cool, and binds things together. Stones also contribute something that fire and water can't. They offer stability and safety.

Things get more complicated when we start to consider human beings. Like all creations, we exist, but our existence is not automatic. It's not even instinctive. We are consciously aware of *life*.

Every human being with even a smattering of self-awareness will at some point ask, "Why am I here?" We ask this question because existence alone does not justify itself. We have to justify our existence by contributing something. It cannot be that we are here simply to take up space, and then demand all sorts of things—"I need this, I want that, I deserve something more." That'd be embarrassing for any sensitive human being.

Taking up space means that *you* cannot come into *my* space. Cain and Abel were the only two brothers in the entire world, but the world wasn't big enough for the both of them. Pathetic. That's not a life.

Existence without life is burdensome and depressing. Not only do you have to eat just to exist, you have to eat the right kinds of food and the right amounts. You have to sleep in order to exist, and even that comes with many conditions. So the question we need to ask ourselves is not what the purpose of life is, but "What is the purpose of existence?" The answer is life! Life is the answer, not the question. And we ought not to confuse the two. There's a popular saying that goes, "Life stinks and then you die." What it should really say is, "Existence stinks." Life never stinks. Life only comes in one flavor, and that flavor is delicious. A moment of life is infinitely precious.

In short, existence means "Give me what I need!" Life means "Do you have any needs? How can I be of help to you?"

In the time of an epidemic, when everyone is getting sick, the doctor on duty does not allow himself to get sick. He doesn't eat, he doesn't sit, he doesn't even sleep. He works around the clock. He becomes practically superhuman. The reason is because his life and his contributions are urgently needed. What is needed of him and who needs him are so clear, so real, and so critical that he becomes fully alive, to the point that his existence simply takes care of itself. After the outbreak, however, when he is no longer needed, he then becomes susceptible like everyone else.

When you are alive, your existence is not heavy, because life is buoyant. It carries you. Existence is dead weight; you have to carry *it*. What is the solution? In a word: live! Put energy into living, not into existing. It has an astounding seesaw effect: when you put energy into living, you do not need to put as much energy into existing, but when you put too much energy into existing, you have no energy left for life.

Depression occurs when you add weight to your existence. You do so by worrying about this and crying over that, by fighting over this and sweating over that. When you give too much importance to your existence, you add weight to it. At some point your existence becomes so heavy that you can no longer carry it. That is when it comes crashing down on you like a ton of bricks. The next thing you know you can't get out of bed, you can't even make a phone call, and you've lost your ability to function. Your existence has completely taken over.

Some things are good for one's existence but not so good for one's life; some things are not so good for one's life but are good for one's existence. At times, conflict arises between the two. What should you do when living and existing come into conflict? Should you sacrifice existence or life? The answer, of course, is to humble your existence because it does not have an inherent value. Thus, when your spouse needs more space, give it away. If you think everything is about you, your existence is out of control.

This is also why when a person is down, we say find someone who has worse problems and help them instead. In other words, we should always sacrifice existence in favor of life. Look at a woman who is pregnant. Her existence is devastated—every inch of her space has been invaded—yet she is so alive!

Vulnerable, Invincible, or Both?

This, by the way, is the secret to Jewish survival. Against all odds and despite harsh persecution, the Jews are still here. Meanwhile, many powerful nations and civilizations, having amassed great wealth, built fortified cities, and formed huge armies for the sake of their own existence, have fallen. They do not exist today. Is this not a miracle?

Mark Twain asked the same question:

> *The Egyptian, the Babylonian and the Persian rose, filled the planet with sound and splendor, then faded to dream-stuff and passed away; the Greek and the Roman followed, and made a vast noise, and they are gone . . . The Jew saw them all, beat them all, and is now what he always was, exhibiting no decadence, no infirmities of age, no weakening of his parts, no slowing of his energies, no dulling of his alert and aggressive mind. All things are mortal but the Jew; all other forces pass, but he remains. What is the secret of his immortality?*

How is it that these bigger, stronger, wealthier civilizations are gone, while the Jews are still here? Before they entered the Promised Land of Israel, Moses gave a pep talk about what would lie ahead: you are going to come into the land, and you are going to get settled. As soon as you get comfortable, you will be thrown out. You will be scattered to the four corners of the earth and you will be reduced to a fraction of your number. You will be unwelcome guests in other people's countries. They will go after you, they will torture you, and they will kill you. You will suffer, you will be confused, and you will not know what tomorrow brings. It's easy to imagine the people asking Moses if there was a point to his making all these intimidating predictions. But Moses's real message was *forget about existence*. Be busy living instead. Live! Focus on life! If you stop worrying about your existence, your existence will simply take care of itself.

The Jewish people have barely managed to exist, and yet are so alive. In times when their existence was literally hanging by a thread, they produced the greatest scholars, teachers, writers, artists, scientists, books, social structures, schools, hospitals, some of the world's greatest charitable organizations, and even a few *tzaddikim*—perfectly righteous individuals.

Some people have very sad and painful existences, while others have it easy and comfortable. In either case, *life* is always good. Life cannot be ruined. Life means that whatever is going on and whatever your existence might be, you always have an opportunity to make a difference and a contribution.

God tells us, "Six days of the week you should work, but on the seventh day, on *Shabbos,* do no labor." What He means is, for six days do whatever you need to do to make your existence easier. If something is broken, fix it; if it's raw, cook it; if it is torn, sew it; if it's too cold, heat it up; if it's too hot, cool it down. But one day out of the week, stop, leave your existence alone, take a break, and turn your attention to *life*.

Even when Jews lived with dire poverty in the ghettos, when their existence was down to a hair's breadth, the minute *Shabbos* arrived, they had no problems. They were suddenly content with their existence, because they focused on life. So one day out of the week, appreciate your life. Whatever you have managed to put together before *Shabbos*, that is what you have. If you didn't buy something, if you didn't prepare something, so be it. Your existence is fine.

What, then, is the message of *Shabbos*? It's this: if you take your existence too seriously, work round the clock, and worry constantly, it will drain your life away and you are going to get depressed. Even people who are ostensibly successful to the point that existence stops being a challenge are left with the looming challenge of figuring out how to "get a life." This is commonly known as a midlife crisis.

Existence itself demands purpose; because the more comfortable your existence becomes, the more you need a life to justify it. This is why affluent and successful people, ironically, are often more likely to get depressed than those who have very little. Once your existence is all snug and comfy, you inevitably start wondering what life is all about. What's it all for? What's next? And if you don't ask yourself this, your children will.

Teenagers often think their parents have ruined their lives. This is impossible, of course, because teenagers don't yet have a life. They have an existence. And it's not even theirs. They are not paying rent, so the room that they call theirs is in fact one that their parents let them sleep in. Their things, they owe to their parents, so nothing actually belongs to a teenager. Instead of saying that their parents ruined their life, what they really should be saying is that their parents ruined their existence. In that, they are correct. Parents do ruin your existence. But not maliciously. They just can't help it.

Imagine a very important person who rules over an entire town. He's conducting a large public meeting, and he feels very powerful.

His existence is enormous. Then in walks his mother. He's not so impressive anymore, because he owes his existence to his mother.

This is why we are taught to honor our parents. It is one of the Ten Commandments. We fulfill this *mitzvah* not by showering them with gifts and cards on special occasions, but by lightening their load and easing their burden, by doing menial tasks for them. We carry their bags, run their errands, and bring food to their table. By giving up a little of our existence, we make their existence better.

When God said, "Honor your father and mother, and you will live," He meant that when you give up a little bit of your existence for someone else, what you have left is life. When you take a dollar bill, which is good for your existence, and you give it to someone who needs it more to help with his existence, now you have life!

We teach our children to be experts at existing, but we tell them so little about life. We show them how to cross the street, ride a bike, brush their teeth, avoid strangers, get good grades in order to get into a good college, get a good job, buy a new house, and have anything they want. It's all about existence. But when a child is hysterical about a lost toy or a paper cut, it's a good opportunity to teach them about the difference between living and existing. Seize the opportunity to teach them the importance of living, and how they can make meaningful contributions to the world.

When we say God is infinitely perfect, we are talking about His existence. He existed infinitely before we arrived and will continue to exist infinitely after we're not around anymore. His existence is enormous and occupies all of time and space. However, like a husband to a beloved wife, God came to us at Mount Sinai and said His perfect existence is not enough. Yes, His existence is perfect to the exclusion of all else, but His *own* existence is not satisfying. He wants to be with *us*, not just be Him alone. This is God's vulnerability.

Why do Jews say *l'chaim*, "to life," when they make a toast? When people consume alcohol and get drunk, their existence relaxes. Some say it's about overcoming our inhibitions, but it's really our existence easing up. When people get drunk, they ignore social etiquette and lose their sense of space. They no longer need space. Later, when they're sober, they once again respect the normal social cues and keep an acceptable distance from others.

At a wedding, if you are in a good mood and enjoying yourself, by all means have a few drinks. When you are excited about life, you want your existence to leave you alone so that you can celebrate life fully. Thus we say *l'chaim* because we are celebrating living over existing. This is why you should never drink when you're not excited about life. Because when you are down and out, all you have left is your existence. At that point you're better off not to relax, lest you be left with nothing.

If you want to be happy, don't look for gimmicks. Life is happy; existence is not. Do you want happiness? Live. You don't have to do anything to make yourself happy. Life itself is joyful; existence alone, even if it is solid and durable, is depressing.

This brings us to the heart of what makes the Jewish people unique: it's in the phrase *Am Yisrael Chai*, which means the People of Israel *live!* The Jews have lived and breathed this secret throughout our history. We choose life over existence, and because of that, the Jewish nation continues on.

In Jewish thinking, humility never brings about a depreciation of *life*. When the Torah tells us to be humble, what we're diminishing is our *existence*. We should never entertain the thought that life is meaningless, God forbid. But existence? What—you're proud that you take up space? You think you have a right to take up space and then demand all sorts of entitlements? Just so you can continue taking up space?

We have to get better at paying attention to things we don't need. It will help us get more in touch with life. That, by the way, is the definition of a *mitzvah.* A *mitzvah* is you responding to someone else's need—your Creator's need. *You* may not need it, and you may or may not want it. Someone else has a need for it. Can you be of help? When God asks you to honor your parents, are you available? Or are you too busy with your own needs?

Marriage is something that takes up so much space, it can ruin your existence. But it makes life worth living. Wedding vows should explicitly state: "Of all people in the world, and of all possibilities, I choose you to be the only one to ruin my existence. I do not want anybody else but you to ruin my existence." Otherwise, people get married, and a month later they start complaining that they feel cramped and need more space. "I love you" turns into "I love you, but I don't like you."

Are you suffering because he ruined your existence? Of course he did. That's what marriage does. What, then, would be the appropriate response? Very simple: "Go right ahead. Ruin my existence. Meanwhile I'll be busy living."

The reason we're having a hard time being happy is because we take existence too literally. You didn't get the job you applied for, so now life must be bad. You didn't get to marry the person you wanted to marry? *You* must be bad. Everyone is out to get you. Even God must hate you; otherwise why would He be picking on you?

Don't take existence too seriously. Existence comes and goes; it's good and bad, up and down, easy and hard. Take *living* seriously instead.

When we encounter problems, they are never meant to discourage us; they are simply a challenge. Yes, there are problems out there. This is a broken and unholy world. Our job is to fix it, and we can do it. Life is never bad or hard. Existence, on the other hand, can be downright difficult, even seemingly impossible. If we become victims of existence, then we are no longer the fixers but part of the problem.

Don't be surprised when you discover new problems in the world. We're here to make it better. This is a world in disrepair, with layers upon layers of unholy confusion and pain. But every layer presents us with new tasks. When obstacles arise, when something terrible happens in the realm of our existence, it should inspire us to dig deeper and come up with a solution. Problems are a challenge, not a tragedy. They're not working against us; they're inspiring us to rise to the occasion. Will you be part of the problem or the solution?

Choose life. Elevate life above the ugliness of existence. You can come alive, and instead of worrying about your own existence, concern yourself with others. You'll make a difference in the world.

2

Life after Death?

It's not a conundrum. It's an oxymoron.

A human being has a life, and an existence. When that existence ends, death occurs. It means the person does not take up space anymore. *Existence* does not need to eat, drink, or sleep. When a person's existence is over, his *life* no longer needs to share its energy or keep bouncing up and down on the teeter-totter of existing versus living. Now it's just pure life. The only difference is that it's no longer on the physical plane, because it no longer takes up space. (What a relief!)

Life has but one talent: it knows how to live. Life continues; it does not know how else to be. So that age-old question as to whether there is life after death is not some unknowable, unsolvable conundrum. It's not even a necessary question. It's an oxymoron. Living things live. Life cannot die.

Where is this life? In the world of Life.

The Itinerary of the Soul

When a person is born, the soul enters the body, and the body borrows life from the soul. The soul is a living entity. It always was alive and will always remain alive. The body, on the other hand, is not inherently a living thing. When the soul returns to being a soul among souls, the body dies while the soul continues to live.

Thus, when the time comes for the soul and the body to go their separate ways, the body returns to dust. "From dust you are made, and to dust you shall return."

What lives on after the body dies? Every aspect of our lives: emotions, memories, relationships, wisdom, knowledge, pleasures, and pains. They all live on, because they are all aspects of life; and life *lives.*

Hell—in Hebrew, *gehinom*—is neither a place nor a punishment, from the perspective of Jewish thought. The following story illustrates this.

An impoverished man, who was having a terrible time trying to eke out a living at home, set sail on a long journey to seek his fortune overseas. His ship was wrecked in a storm and washed up on an island. He awoke to find himself lying on a beach overflowing with diamonds. With great excitement, he gathered up as many diamonds as he could carry and rushed into town to trade them.

When he presented his newfound treasures to the townsmen, they all laughed at him. "Diamonds? They aren't worth anything here," they said. "They're all over the beach! Here, we trade in onions. Whatever we need, we take in barter for onions. That's what's rare and precious and valuable here." So he settled into his new life, became an onion grower, and over time became very wealthy from the onions he had amassed.

After many years he decided it was time to go home. He built a ship, loaded it with his vast fortune of onions, and set sail. By the time he docked at the harbor, the onions had already begun to spoil. While he was overjoyed to show his family how successful he had become, they took one look at his reeking cargo and gasped in disbelief. "What the hell have you brought home to us?"

When a soul leaves the world of souls and descends to the lower world, all it knows is the value of heavenly diamonds. But your body says, "What are you talking about? We don't deal with Godliness here. Here we deal with tomatoes, potatoes, and onions."

Over time the soul gets comfortable and accustomed to life on earth, and eventually begins to accumulate material things. That's fine while it lasts, but when the time comes for that same soul to leave its body and go back to being a soul among souls, it returns to heaven reeking of onions, and there's hell to pay. Hell is when a soul returns to the world of souls and does not "smell" like or resemble a soul. The fires of hell are not the burning flames that are often depicted by artists. These fires are shame—the only fire the soul can feel.

So hell is not a punishment, it's a consequence. It's the pain of adjustment, as it divests itself of the body. During life, the soul became very attached to its body; letting go of that relationship can be painful or, at the very least, a little awkward. Having grown accustomed to being a body, it doesn't remember how to be a soul.

But it's only an adjustment. The fires of shame, we are told, can only linger for a maximum of twelve months, after which they subside. These twelve months are a cleansing and refreshing process, wherein the soul peels itself away from the sights and smells of the physical world. Then it resumes its former status of a pure *neshama*, a soul among souls, and settles in *shamayim,* the supernal world. One might say getting to heaven can be hell.

Needless to say the story doesn't end here. But before we move on to the next leg of the trip, let's look more closely at the nature of this thing we call a soul.

The Godly Soul and the Human Soul

When God created the world, the world and everything in it had never existed before. There was no light until He said, "Let there be light." He said, "Let there be a firmament," and there was a firmament. The same with the sun, the moon, the stars, the waters—they were all new, unprecedented. A soul, however, has always existed, because it's a piece of God, Who has always existed. And just as God is alive, this little piece of God is alive. A little piece of Him is a little slice of Life.

As God is kind, the soul is capable of kindness. As God is all-knowing, the soul is capable of intelligence. Just as God can be strict and severe, so the soul has the capacity for justice, judgment, and even anger. It can understand, it can reason, it can come up with new ideas. It can also be stubborn, determined, and it can love or hate. And, as an extension of intellect and emotions, the soul has the ability to communicate. Mystically, we can break all this down into ten distinct soul powers—corresponding to the ten faculties with which God functions as the Creator.

At times, we find ourselves torn in two directions. That's because we actually have two souls: a Godly soul, with ten Godly functions, and a human soul, with ten human functions. A human soul is similar to its Godly counterpart except that it is created, finite—but in the image of the infinite Creator.

The mind of the Godly soul understands things from a Godly perspective; therefore Godliness makes sense. To the human soul, however, Godliness does not make sense, because it understands things from a human perspective. The key is for our Godly soul to teach our human soul to appreciate what is holy.

When He revealed himself at Mount Sinai, it was to tell us what He needs—not to tell us how to get to heaven. In fact, heaven isn't mentioned in the Torah, except in the very first line. The rest of the Torah is about earth. Because our mission is not to get to heaven but to bring Godliness down to earth. Every time we do a *mitzvah,* we are exposing our human soul to Godliness and holiness. By enabling the human soul to feel, appreciate, and participate in

Godliness, we elevate this physical, human blend of body and soul to Godliness. We've transformed a little piece of earth into heaven. It's called *tikkun olam*, repairing the world. For this purpose alone, to fulfill this mission, a soul is willing to spend 120 years here on earth in a limited, constricted, and burdensome body. Optimally, when the time comes for the soul to leave the body, it will return to heaven with no biological memories, almost as though it had never left; except for the fact that now it brings with it some of the human soul energy that has been elevated and become holy.

What Can We Expect from the Body?

Another story, also about vegetables. A princess married a peasant, and the couple went to live on the peasant's farm. The peasant was very committed and devoted to his beloved princess. After several weeks of marriage, the peasant noticed that his bride was sad. He didn't wish to question her, so from his peasant perspective, he assumed that what was making her sad was that the farm was not producing enough potatoes.

He worked harder and grew more potatoes. She did not become any happier. The peasant said to himself, "Silly me! She does not like potatoes! It's tomatoes that are lacking. She is sad because we do not have enough tomatoes!"

So he worked even harder and brought home more tomatoes. The princess remained depressed. Now desperate, he did everything he could to make things better. But she became sadder. Finally he confronted her. "What is wrong with you?" he said. "I have given you everything you could possibly want! How could you still be unhappy?"

"I was raised in a palace," she replied, "where the world's greatest and most talented artists, musicians, and philosophers would come to present their works. And in the royal garden, we had the most beautiful, exotic plants. It was a life of higher pleasures.

These are the things I miss; and when I see you trying to make me happy by giving me tomatoes and potatoes, it makes me even sadder, because I realize that you have no idea what it takes to make a princess happy."

This is the predicament of a Godly soul in a human body. The Godly soul is the princess; the body is a very devoted husband, but a peasant nonetheless. The body feels the sadness of the soul.

The body assumes that potatoes, tomatoes—physical things—will soothe the soul—more food, more money, more friends, a new house, beautiful clothing, a pleasant pastime. You try and try, but the soul cries, "You think *this* will make me happy?"

What's a king to do when his princess marries a peasant—a decent and talented guy in his own right, but clueless? Her father, the king, should send his daughter off with little mementos of the palace, some familiar royal regalia with which she can surround herself. Then, even on the farm, she'll still feel like a princess, and she'll turn the farm into a little replica of the grand palace from whence she came.

That is exactly what God does for us. He sends the Godly soul down to earth along with little specks of heaven—the Torah and the Commandments. Pack a suitcase before you go, He says. Fill it with Wisdom and Good Deeds, so that while living in the lower world you'll be able to connect with Me and with your original roots. Even down on the farm your soul will feel like a princess connected to her Father.

This is the mystery of the comings and goings of the soul. It justifies the risks of sending a delicate and sensitive princess into such a rough neighborhood. In the end the soul will have proven herself, and her positive influence will prevail. Both the body and the human soul will have been refined.

And together with other body/soul partnerships, this embodied Godliness has the power to literally transform the world. The

Baal Shem Tov, the first Chassidic master of modern times, tells us that when ten such Godly souls are gathered in one room even angels are afraid to enter.

Birth Trauma

The soul enters the body in increments. Forty days before conception, the soul is informed that it's going to be born. This helps us to at least get used to the idea. Then there's conception, the third month, the ninth month, and birth. All of these are stages of the soul's easing into the body as they become one. After birth, and for the first thirty days, the soul continues to adjust to its new environment. In fact the Godly soul doesn't fully settle in until a girl is twelve years old, or a boy is thirteen.

When the soul and the body merge, it has to be a gradual process, because it would be a shock to just throw them together. They're different; they vibrate on different frequencies. The same is true in reverse, by the way, on the way out. But that's not for now.

In the Torah an angel informs Sarah that she will give birth "this time next year." Why "next year"? It only takes nine months for a child to be born. But because the soul needs a period of adjustment, she is first given some time to prepare. She's by no means thrilled at the idea of leaving heaven. The prospect of being constricted within the limitations of a human body and sharing an entire lifetime with a human soul, with human demands, is unappealing, to say the least. But if God so desires, the soul gets ready.

The second step, of course, is conception. King David writes, "My mother and father have abandoned me, and God has gathered me in." David was not badmouthing his parents; he was simply marveling at the memory of having been conceived. What must that have been like? Imagine this tiny little being, all alone, about to make the biggest leap a soul can possibly make, from the sublime heavenly realm to this lowest of all worlds!

The Talmud explains it this way: the soul looks to the father; he is asleep. The soul looks to the mother; she too is asleep. Meanwhile the soul knows she's preparing for this traumatic, terrifying, life-altering moment, an expedition from heaven to earth. Birth itself, only a few inches from the womb to the world, is a walk in the park compared to this fearsome journey of the soul. Imagine this little being looking around for some reassurance, to see who's in charge. She receives neither comfort nor support from anyone. By the time conception occurs, her father and her mother have fallen asleep. But God neither slumbers nor sleeps. In this Psalm, King David is remembering having been comforted by the fact that God was right there with him, at the most frightening moment of his life.

In another Psalm, David writes, "Even when I go into the valley of the shadow of death, I am not afraid, for You are with me." What is this valley of the shadow of death? And why does he keep going there?

The Talmud explains that King David is describing every soul that has ever been born. Every soul goes through "the valley of the shadow of death"; it's the birth process. The valley is that blank space between life in the womb and life outside the womb. A touch of danger and death lurks there. Life in the womb is wonderful, akin to being in heaven. We're told that the soul is taught the entire Torah in there. Leaving the womb, however, is traumatic, so shocking that it erases one's memory of nine wonderful months of gestation. So David questions how he survived the ordeal of birth. The answer is that God Himself is present at every birth. It would have been absolutely unbearable had God not been there.

Every fetus that has ever been born in this world has had an encounter with God, as a guide through what seems like a near-death experience. In fact the same can be said of near-death experience itself, which is like a flashback, essentially reliving one's own birth back through that same valley of the shadow of death. What enables us to survive is our awareness of God's presence.

This is also where human faith in God comes from. We have no scientific evidence or rational argument to prove God's presence. We cannot see Him; we simply remember that He was there when we needed Him most, at conception and at birth. That's why every person who has had a near-death experience comes out of it with an awareness of God—because he or she was reliving and reexperiencing birth, remembering the encounter with God, recalling the trust and the comfort we received in God's presence. Contrary to conventional wisdom, *emunah,* faith, is rooted in experience.

Good Grief

As with birth, so it is when the soul leaves the body: it does not disconnect instantly, all at once. Moreover, it doesn't want to say goodbye, so it leaves the body in stages—hovering at first, feeling some separation anxiety. Before passing away there's a premonition, a sense that it's imminent. For some, it's very conscious, and for others, less so, but they all know. You can often see it from the person's behavior.

The Hebrew word for a funeral is *levaya,* meaning escorting. Our tradition has it that when someone close to us passes away, we escort the body to the cemetery. After the burial, we are obligated to go home for a mourning period of seven days, known as sitting *shiva,* during which friends and family come by to pay condolence calls.

Why sit for seven days? What is this arbitrary number? What if I'm not finished mourning after seven days? Or what if seven days is too long? Why is the Torah telling us how to mourn? Why not allow people to do what comes naturally?

These ritual observances are not so much about our own pain or sadness. Rather, they are offered in absolute consideration of the departed soul. *Shiva* is a continuation of the funeral. Once we've escorted the body to the body's resting place, we then sit *shiva* to escort the soul toward its heavenly destination. The Torah explains that it takes seven days for the soul to get over the shock of leaving its body; so we sit *shiva* to stay in touch, empathize, and accompany the soul on its journey.

The wrenching change after the soul leaves the body is at its most intense during the first three days, and over the next four days the pain diminishes. That's why in certain communities there's a custom not to pay a *shiva* call until the fourth day. After seven days, the mourners are obligated to get up and end the *shiva* period, since their having escorted the soul on the first leg of its journey is now complete.

At the end of thirty days we're encouraged to ease up in our grief even more, as by this time the soul has arrived at another milestone; and once again at the end of the year when it has fully adjusted and grown comfortable as a soul without a body. With the soul now at home in heaven, our sorrow has likely subsided as well. Twelve months is said to be the maximum amount of time the soul requires to have become accustomed to this disembodied state, freed of the memories and entanglements that may have persisted after its passing.

Some pure souls, we are told, are able to move on, to come unstuck from attachments to bodily pleasures acquired during its lifetime, after just a month or even a week. Still others are so unsullied, they return to their heavenly abode in a day, as if they had never left. It's for this reason that we customarily recite the *Kaddish* prayer for the deceased for eleven months, to facilitate the journey, yet not to imply that the soul requires the entire twelve months to be fully cleansed.

On each anniversary of a person's passing—the *Yahrzeit*—the soul advances further to a higher level of heaven, ascending again and again from year to year. We recite *Kaddish* to support these elevations. With the *Yizkor* memorial prayers that we say on festivals, as with *Kaddish*, we are actually making close contact with souls that are no longer among us, yet very much alive. It cannot be otherwise; because Life lives. Life cannot die. This living being with whom we are now sharing an unseen, intimate relationship is very real—more real than a body.

We often see Jewish people who do not regularly attend prayer services show up right on time for *Kaddish* and *Yizkor.* It's almost as though the departed souls will not let their living loved ones stay away. During the prayers of *Yizkor*, we are taught, these departed souls come to the synagogue, and in their mysterious presence our prayers comfort them and help ease their transition to progressively higher realms.

There's a common expression we tend to hear when people are trying to console a mourner—"He's in a better place now." This is really not a Jewish concept. There are things the soul cannot achieve in heaven. Without a body, living beyond this material world, one cannot perform physical acts of kindness and good deeds. The soul yearns to serve the Creator; it has no interest in retreating to a retirement home or being sent out to pasture, where it's "no longer needed." Certainly, the disembodied soul is able to experience divine love, to pray and study Torah, but without a physical body, it can't perform a physical deed. Most of all the soul misses the ability to give *tzedakah*. That's why we pledge during *Yizkor* to make charitable donations on the soul's behalf, which brings the soul so much *nachas*, immeasurable satisfaction.

The better we understand the journey of a departed soul, the more deeply we are able to empathize with its experience and grasp what it is the soul needs from us. When the soul is in great pain, we grieve intensely; as its transition draws toward its close, we grieve a little less. When it's completely settled in the supernal world, it behooves us to stop grieving. It's not a *mitzvah* to feel sorry for ourselves.

Nonetheless the soul does maintain some connection to its body, even after a thousand years. The essential soul never abandons its former body. Once established, that relationship does not end. That's why, for example, we visit the gravesites of our great-grandparents or pray at the resting places of righteous *tzaddikim* buried in Israel or elsewhere, to make real connections with them. And these earthly connections extend all the way to heaven.

The greatest pleasure of the soul in heaven lies in its complete and utter peacefulness. Therefore, the greatest *nachas* we can offer our departed loved ones is to foster peace among us, here on earth. We're important to the souls in heaven. Just as we need to know where we came from, they need to keep in touch with what they've left behind. They take an interest in our affairs, because we are their future.

If the soul were to feel that it is the cause of any conflicts between family or community members, such as a dispute over an inheritance or legacy, it would experience inexpressible pain. What's the point of being in heaven, if even there you can't have peace? The soul doesn't need our eulogies and exaggerated compliments; nor is it sensitive to insults. All the soul cares about is peace. So when we say, "Rest in peace," we had better mean it, stand by it, live it, and keep it real.

Back in the Saddle

Like most great stories, however, this odyssey of the soul doesn't end in heaven. We are taught that in the time of *Mashiach*, redemption from exile will culminate in the resurrection of the dead, *Techiyas Hameisim*. Since the soul needs no resurrection, it will merely return as is to its resurrected body. But the body will need some work. God Himself will reconstruct those deconstructed dry bones, permanently eradicating the element of death and granting eternal life.

The Talmud offers an insight as to how this works. There was a lame man and a blind man. One day they decided to steal fruit from an orchard, but there was a wall surrounding the orchard that made the theft difficult. So they came up with a plan: the blind man would lift the lame man up onto his shoulders, and the lame man would direct the blind man to where the fruits were. Together they were able to reach and steal some fruits.

When they were caught, the judge had to decide which one to punish—the lame man or the blind man? Neither thief could have committed the crime alone. It was a combined effort. Hence, he decided that the only appropriate way to punish them was to put the one man on the other's shoulders and punish them as a pair.

Similarly, but in the positive framework of the performance of a *mitzvah*, neither the body without a soul nor a soul without a body can get the good deed done. So God rewards us for the good we have done in the same form we were in when we did the *mitzvah*, with body and soul intact and undivided. The resurrection, therefore, makes perfect sense. Every soul that has been in a body and has fulfilled *mitzvahs* (and there is no soul that hasn't done a *mitzvah* here and there) will have to reunite with its body to receive its rewards.

Although the soul is initially hesitant to suffer the confinement and encumbrance of a human body, it knows its mission, and is humble enough to accept. We're here to fix the world—*tikkun olam*. It's the Creator's world; we are His agents and partners, and He has a plan. As a result of our efforts in serving God, we receive far more than merely the personal rewards of the *mitzvahs* we perform with body and soul. We bring Godliness into the world; and the world will be resurrected, as it were, by the revealed presence of God. *"Bayom hahu yihye Hashem echad."* The day will come when God will be reunited with His world, and His world will be one with Him. As the Jewish people, as a "light unto the nations," we have a mandate to share with the rest of the world this knowledge and this call to action, that can come only from the Torah.

3

The Real American Idol

False gods will always disappoint.

Whenever we read or hear about bygone generations and the idols they worshipped, we cannot help but ask ourselves, "Why are they so primitive and ignorant, bowing down to statues? How could anyone be so simpleminded as to worship the sun, the stars, and the planets, let alone turn to inanimate objects for reassurance about life?" It's laughable, ridiculous. And we secretly congratulate ourselves for being far more sophisticated and evolved. But are we? Is it possible that we too give away our power and worship worthless things, and allow these distractions to get the better of us?

In every generation there exist forms of idol worship. Some are obvious, others a little more subtle. A broad definition of idolatry is putting our trust in something that is neither trustworthy nor deserving of our faith. When this happens, we create a false god, which simply means treating something as though it were God, when in fact there can be no other god but God.

Any time we overvalue something unworthy and make it the sole focus of our lives, it's akin to idol worship. These things we worship may not necessarily have "divine" names, and we may not actually bow down to them. Yet if we put our trust and invest our lives in them, we don't differ all that much from the ancient idolaters we mock. There's no need to look very far; we too have made sacrifices to things that will inevitably disappoint us. We too have put our trust in objects, ideas, or ideologies that cannot see, cannot hear, and cannot help us in our times of need. Every culture has its own idols. Let's have a look at some of ours.

Worship of Love

The most prominent and popular contemporary idol, unquestionably, is love. Americans especially worship love. We've been indoctrinated with the idea that love is the solution to everything. "Love conquers all. Love never fails." In the name of love, we're willing to make all kinds of sacrifices; we're ready to give up just about anything, up to and including life itself. We deem love to be the highest form of life, when in truth, like all idols, it simply does not and cannot live up to the status and the importance we ascribe to it.

Take, for example, such anthemic proclamations as "Love is all you need" or "Love will keep us together." They're both faulty and inaccurate. If love were the glue that keeps all human relationships strong, then what happens when marriages fall apart? According to this theory, no couple would ever divorce, because just about every marriage in America is born of love. "Oh well, we fell out of love," one might say. Sorry, but that just proves that love is not enough. If it's that flimsy and unreliable, how foolish would we be to make major life decisions and base our lives on love? Any marriage that is founded on love alone rests on a shaky foundation. It is simply not solid enough to withstand the tests of time.

Everybody talks about love, everybody wants it, but nobody knows what it is. All we know is, love is supposed to be the answer to all our problems. Even if that were true, it would certainly be helpful first to gain a more realistic understanding of what love is and is not. Then perhaps we'd have a shot at evaluating the role of love in a given relationship.

Equally essential is to be able to distinguish between different kinds of love. There are so many different varieties that to lump them together and confuse their respective emotions, intentions, and experiences can be damaging. A mother's love is not the same as the love she has for her parents. The love you have for a child or grandchild is not the same love you have for your spouse. They don't compete; they reside in different sections of the heart, spin in different chakras, follow different pathways along the meridians of your body. We have the capacity, thank God, for a wide array of loves.

But love is not *important.*

Love is an emotional response to something or someone significant. It is not the beginning. It is not the end. Emotion itself does not make anyone or anything significant. No matter how much you love someone, that doesn't make him or her important.

The reverse is also true. People who are important in your life remain important whether or not you love them. In other words, your love is not what makes them important. Hence, if someone is important in your life, you ought to love them; if a relationship is significant, then love is appropriate. But if love becomes more important than the person you love, that love can destroy the relationship. The person you love should be more important than the love you desire.

Love is a gift. It's appropriate to give this gift when we're in a relationship with someone we value. If we deem a person important in our lives, then we ought to love that person proportionately, commensurate with the importance. The more important someone is, the more we should love him or her, and the more appropriate love is.

This brings us to the question of unconditional love—undoubtedly the most sought-after kind of love. Spouses will often go to great lengths to test whether their spouse's love is unconditional. Kids do it too. Love is never unconditional. Only a fact can be fixed and unchanging. *Unconditional* means you are important to me even when I'm not feeling the love; and you are mine, even if I hate you. You are precious, you are important. Our relationship has undeniable significance. Regardless of how much love I feel or don't feel, we are in this together.

It's also necessary that we distinguish between love and pleasure. We use the word *love* rather irresponsibly. A child says, "I love my mommy," and "I love Mickey Mouse," and "I love ice cream." Does that mean that the mother is only getting a third of the pie, and she has to share her child's love with Mickey Mouse and peanut-butter-chocolate-chunk? No. We need to come up with a different word. Love should be applied only in the case of someone who can love you back, but also may not. Imagine when your child finds out that the Mickey Mouse he's in love with is an imaginary character, incapable of feeling. It is going to be heartbreaking. The same is true with the ice cream: food cannot love you back. The word *love* should not apply to ice cream, as much as we do enjoy it. Pleasure is not the same as love. It's a language problem.

There's a certain danger to loving your children unconditionally. If you tell your children, "I love you no matter what you say or how you behave," what it sounds like to them is that they don't matter to you. What they do doesn't count. "I've decided to love you and there is nothing you can do about it. You can stand on your head. It's not going to help. I'm loving you." In other words, it doesn't matter whether they are naughty or nice. You're not responding to your children; to them this feels like a rejection. So what do the kids do? They behave badly. They're trying to force you to admit that you don't love them. Now it's gone too far.

This is a case where the word *love* is not helpful. To say that you still love your children when you hate them is confusing. Better to say, even when you detest your child, he or she is still precious to you. You may not be feeling very close to your child. In fact you don't want any more closeness at all at the moment. What you really want is a vacation from this kid. Nonetheless he remains precious to you, dear to you, no matter what. When you hate your child, you are still his parent, and he is still your child. That is unconditional.

How about when a wife asks her husband if he loves his mother more than her? These types of questions are ludicrous, because it is not a matter of more or less. It's a completely different emotion. The same is true when we speak of love of God; it's an emotion that calls for greater intimacy and unity. It's nothing like romantic love, yet both kinds of love can be understood as a quest for closeness. When God took us out of Egypt, He pursued us and proposed to us at Mount Sinai. Similarly, we pursue Him, as we depend on Him and seek to know Him better. In serving Him we hope to get closer. In the same vein we can pursue closeness with our family, tribe, nation, with all humankind. We are all connected. So pursue closeness; just be honest and discerning about it and don't make love into an idol.

Self-love is a completely different experience. Every heart is capable of love, as love is a component of the soul. We have love, but it is not meant for ourselves. Love is to give, not to keep. Self-love can be like a black hole—turning inward what should be radiating to others. Self-love will turn you into a dark star.

We all love ourselves on some level, though it's not really about getting closer. Can we get closer to ourselves? Imagine that you're accustomed to sleeping on a double bed. One day you go on a trip and find yourself sleeping on a single bed. How is it that you don't roll off the bed, thinking that it's a double? It is astounding how our brain adjusts; even while deep asleep we remain cognizant of the limit of the mattress and the need to not go over the edge. It's simple self-preservation, i.e., love.

There are those who claim they don't love themselves, or even that they hate themselves. It's quite a common assertion these days. To the biblical commandment *"v'ahavta l'reacha kamocha"*—love your fellow as you love yourself—they respond, "I don't even love myself, so how am I supposed to love you?" But it's a poor excuse, a fallacy, because loving oneself is not the pursuit of closeness, but a sense of preciousness. Because you are precious to yourself, you are going to be careful not to hurt yourself. Even when you hate yourself—sometimes with good reason—you are still precious to yourself. You're still going to wake up at the edge of the bed, not on the floor. In fact the hatred *comes from* self-love. You care enough to hate. Likewise, the Torah tells us to love others the same *way* we love ourselves—not to the same degree.

The same is true of God's relationship with us. When the Torah says God loves us, it can hardly be characterized as romantic love. In fact there are times in the Torah when we are told that God is disgusted with us. He is fed up. He wants to quit. Still He tells us, "You are my children, so what am I going to do? I'm stuck with you. You are precious to me. You are mine. But do I love you? Not right now. You belong to me; and I belong to you, even when I hate you." Now *that* is unconditional.

Emotional love cannot be unconditional. If it were it would no longer be emotion. That a child can push your buttons and get you angry is evidence of your love, but it's emotional, reactive. The same is true when the child gives you *nachas*, pride and satisfaction—also emotion. There are feelings, and there are facts. The preciousness of our children to us and our preciousness to God are factual.

It is not correct to say that love is important, or is all we need, or makes the world go 'round. Rather, love is *appropriate*. You love your husband or wife because he or she is important. You love your fellow humans because they are important. You love God because God is important. But not because *love* is important. Allow love to be what it is; we should certainly not expect love to create or repair our relationships. The sentiment "God is love" suggests that love is God. To worship Him for the love is to worship the love. That is an idol.

Worship of Self

The worship of self is a particularly insidious form of idolatry, more destructive even than the black hole of love turned inward toward oneself, as we discussed above. Self-worship is widely promoted as something positive—not only by the media, but by the experts and authorities in many fields who make a lofty self-image the be all and end all of well-being. The message they put forward is that in order to be healthy, you've got to put yourself first. Is that really true?

There are positive and negative sides of the self. There's a side that is dignified, inspiring, and challenging. You are a human being, which is high praise indeed, a compliment to be taken seriously, and it carries with it certain responsibilities. One of the first is to protect the dignity of the human condition—not to do things that are distasteful or embarrassing to oneself. The Torah gives us actual commandments that prohibit the degradation of self. That's the positive self, the self that makes us moral, that demands better and higher achievement, fulfillment, and purpose.

The self that is being promoted in the media is our weaker self. It tells us to indulge our desires, to surrender to our thirst. But we're not supposed to obey our thirst; our thirst should obey us. *We* decide when we drink, what we drink, and where we drink. We are not our thirst, and we certainly don't worship our thirst. To do so not only violates divine law, it goes against the grain of what it means to be human. It diminishes and degrades us.

It makes no sense for you, as the highest of God's creations, to reduce yourself to a miserable dependency on something lower than yourself. To focus on and pursue the demands of the lower self is idol worship—it's not only an affront to God, it violates the dignity of a human being. If on the other hand we're focused on the noble self, a self that elevates, it is a holy and Godly thing.

Take, for example, the exhausted parent. If a mother needs to rest, then she must rest. But not, as suggested by the experts, because her needs come first. Her children need a strong and healthy mother; her sacred role and responsibility as a mother is why she must take good care of herself. She needs to be a healthy mother first.

Let's step back and ask a more fundamental question. Is worship a good or a bad thing? What is the point of worship altogether? And what is so bad about idol worship anyway? Why is there this assumption that if you worship an idol it's the worst thing in the world, but if you worship God it's the best thing in the world?

In the macrocosmic view of Creation, the human stands right in the middle between huge and microscopic. The universe is vast and infinite; the subatomic particles of which we're made are minuscule, infinitesimal. We're either tiny in relation to the whole, or colossal compared to the parts. And we're agents of free will. We each have our own intelligence, and we make our own choices—when to expand, when to contract. A human being is always in flux, either rising or falling, growing or decomposing. But he is not static. To remain in the middle is not a goal.

So is it okay to worship God? If so, what happens to our freedom of choice, our individuality? Why is God allowed to dictate our behavior, sometimes down to the petty details? For that matter why is *anyone* allowed to dictate our behavior—a parent, teacher, mentor, coach, or sergeant in the Army? When is it good, and when is it bad? What's the rule of thumb? Answer: what makes you subhuman is bad; what makes you a healthy human is okay; what makes you more than human is awesome.

It's very simple. If it elevates you, it's wonderful. If it disgraces you, it's wrong.

Worship is a very powerful tool. You are what you worship. If you worship the right thing it dramatically uplifts you, and if you worship the wrong thing it drastically degrades you. The greatest, most noble achievement of a human being comes through worship of God, the holiest being. By the same token the vilest form of self-abuse is idolatry. When we submit our will, intelligence, and choices to the dictates of a statue, person, or thing, we demean ourselves, becoming more like the things we are worshipping.

When we worship something, we take on certain qualities and characteristics of that which we worship. By worshipping God, we become Godly. By worshipping something beneath us we become degraded. When a person is pulled toward heathenism, for example, he starts to become heathen-like. At first it's only to the degree that his mind can be convinced. When he begins to worship it, however, he also surrenders his soul. Worship is immersive. A person becomes absorbed in the object of worship, far more than in the subjects he merely studies, thinks about, or speaks about. When you worship something, you're dissolving into it. You literally become it.

Hence, even more than we ought to avoid thinking, saying, or even eating the wrong thing, we have to be careful not to worship the wrong thing. Doing so is a total surrender to something unworthy and beneath us. Conversely, when we worship God, it ennobles and elevates us to something more than human.

Worshipping God is not a denial of self, it's a transcendence of self. God in turn strengthens and reinforces our ability to be like Him. Unlike the worship of unGodly things, this type of surrender is neither senseless nor suicidal.

The same is true with marriage. The mutual surrender of husband to wife and wife to husband does not diminish them, it elevates them. Surrendering means submitting to the bidding of someone other than yourself. If the other is more important than you in your eyes, you are doing exactly what a human being is meant to do. When people put their trust in another human being, it's empowering to both.

Incidentally, if idolatry is as ridiculous as we think it is, it shouldn't be a sin. What's the harm in worshipping a statue? Fine, you're making a fool of yourself, but so what? The answer is that the act of worship is in itself so powerful, we empower whatever we worship, however unworthy. If we feed evil, we become its agent. We give it power.

When we appoint people to positions of leadership, for instance, their talents expand. The trust and faith placed in them charges and changes them, rendering them more capable and taking them to greater heights than they would likely have achieved on their own. Whereas if we worship something that is beneath us, we are surrendering to something less worthy than us. This adds power to that which is unholy and which will ultimately destroy us.

Imagine putting trust in someone utterly immoral. Hitler, for example, became a powerful force due to the power that the masses accorded him. On his own he was merely a dropout, a loser. The people's surrender of their energies to him turned him into a monstrously effective agent of evil.

That's why putting our faith in and worshipping anything other than God is considered a violation of God's laws—it empowers and strengthens that which shouldn't be strengthened.

Which brings us back to self-worship. The more we feed our weaker or lower self, the more we empower it to take over our lives. We then cease to be "the master of my fate . . . the captain of my soul." Like Dr. Frankenstein who created a monster he could not control, we are now a victim of the self.

We see this in a person who habitually rejects advice, rules, or moral teachings. He doesn't have to listen to his parents; they're not the boss of him. Then he goes to school, and neither the teacher nor the principal can tell him what to do. Next, his friends, family, mentors, and counselors can no longer advise him. "Gotta be me. Gotta do it my way." Some might see this as legitimate. Why not? What could possibly go wrong? Is it not healthy to be independent, free of the dictates of others, more yourself? But before long your self becomes a demon that consumes you. You can't even tell *yourself* what to do. This runaway self of yours is now totally out of control. "Talking to myself is like talking to the wall."

Ever hear people talk about their New Year's resolutions? "I know, I should give up this bad habit. But I just can't help myself." Because the self, having been indulged to the point of being worshipped, has become so emboldened, it's now stronger than you. The more you feed it, pumping it full of energy and life, the more unreasonable and demanding it becomes. The self can be the most powerful and evil of all false gods. It takes itself very seriously.

By worshipping God, on the other hand, you're doing exactly the opposite. What you are doing is empowering your noble, Godly self to become more Godlike—less about yourself.

Becoming more like God does not make the self important. You feed the poor because the poor are important, not because you are important. You're a teacher of children because the children and the knowledge are important. It's a virtue to cure the sick because they are important. You have been given the privilege of helping them. If you can do that for them, you can become almost as important as they are. Being like God is important; but beware of the self that can turn it all upside down.

When God told Moses to pass his leadership on to Joshua, He explained that to be a leader is to be slave to the people, and therefore noble. Since the people are important, if you have the opportunity to serve them you borrow some of their importance as well.

There's this little cartoon that depicts two women walking side by side. One says to the other, "Between gym, Pilates, yoga, and meditation, I have no time for myself."

Which self is she talking about? There's a difference between improvement *of* self and improvement *on* self. Improvement on self means elevating yourself to become something greater, by deferring to something higher. Improvement of self means the opposite—you're indulging what may be your unhealthy, unworthy, less-than-dignified self. You may be worshipping something lower than you, even if it's ostensibly in the interest of health.

You do not improve yourself by becoming more of yourself. That's not an improvement. Is the idea of being the best you can be self-improvement, or is it just being self-absorbed? Self-improvement should mean that you can become something other than yourself, rather than more of yourself. This is achieved primarily through worshipping something greater than you. Where your heart lies is where you are transported.

To worship means to yield, to surrender, to melt into and become one with the object of worship. We're not always conscious of what we yearn for, but everybody yearns for something. If you're yearning for something greater than yourself, that is self-improvement, an elevation of self. If you yearn for something less noble or less important, then you're worshipping the unhealthy self. You're empowering the little monster that will become uncontrollable, not to mention headed in the wrong direction.

Self-knowledge is not self-worship. There is virtue in knowing. If you know yourself, then you know where you need to be. Self-knowledge is an indispensable tool for self-improvement. People who don't know themselves usually destroy themselves, with perhaps the best of intentions, in their attempt to make things better.

If you don't know who you are and you don't know where you are, you don't know whether you're going up or down the ladder.

An example: God had to locate and identify the Jewish people before assigning them the task of becoming a nation of priests, responsible for sharing with the world the knowledge He gives. We need to know what God's expectations are, which is another way of saying knowing who we are. Being chosen for any task comes with responsibilities. That's not arrogance—it's a tool for self-improvement. Without it, you'll almost always end up improving your self, at the expense of self-improvement. But if you don't know what God expects of you and what your mission is, you could spend your entire life working at things not meant for you.

Worship of Entitlement

It seems as though nearly every product all over the world today is being advertised on the basis of the assumption that you deserve it. You deserve to have a good night's sleep. You deserve to have beautiful hair and skin. It begs the question: if I truly deserve this, why do I have to pay for it?

Imagine how often people are being bombarded with this dreadful idea. Imagine children subscribing to this corrupt message of "I deserve it." People might grow up thinking there's no justice in this world, especially when they pay for a product and it doesn't satisfy the desire. The marketers know how distorted and evil these messages are, but it doesn't matter. It sells, and it's profitable.

This *entitlement* idol is an especially self-destructive strain of the self-worship syndrome. It may very well be based on a theological fallacy. Since God created me, you tell yourself, I must be really important. Obviously I deserve to exist. In other words, whatever it is we are given must be because we are worthy and deserving. So if God gives us life, we must deserve life. If God loves us, we must deserve that love. Seductive, but misleading. What might be the nonidolatrous version of this story?

In the Book of Psalms, idols are described as having eyes that do not see, noses that do not breathe, mouths that do not speak, legs that do not walk, and so on. People tend to think the author, King David, is describing manmade statues. In actuality he is referring to the human being. A statue doesn't have eyes, so it would be false to say it has eyes but cannot see. It's just a chunk of marble or whatever. It doesn't have legs, so you can't judge it for having legs that don't move. What King David is describing is the ultimate idol: the human being himself. We have eyes, yet we don't really see the truth.

When a person's definitive statement is "I don't want" this, that, or the other thing, that's idolatry. It's like saying, "If I don't like something, it's not valid. If I want something, I must have it. I'm entitled." One's first thought is of oneself. When that first thought goes unchallenged, when this absolute focus on the self remains the most important and the only real thing to a person, that's the origin of idolatry. It's what God had in mind when He said, "I am God, your God. You shall have no other Gods."

This type of person is basically saying that God's existence depends on my approval. If I don't believe in Him, He may as well not exist; if I don't understand Him, then He must not be real. Only if and when I am convinced is there a God. It's tantamount to saying, "I am the Godmaker. I decide who and what God is. Not only am I God, I am the God of Gods."

Having eyes is not enough. The virtue of having eyes is so you can see what's real. Likewise, the ability to walk is a blessing only if you have some place to go. If nothing is real, what do you need eyes or legs for? For that matter, why do you need a mind? You have an opinion, but you're not thinking.

Plainly, the first idol we have to smash is the idol we're born with: "I know, I think, I want." It's probably the most difficult idol to get rid of, because it comes so early in life. It's our default mode; we may never even be aware of it.

So when we tell the kids they can't have somebody else's toy, or they have to wait their turn, we are chipping away at that idol of self. We're teaching them that their needs, their demands, and their opinions are not the ultimate reality. We help them open their eyes and ears so they can see and hear what life really is.

That God created you doesn't mean you deserved to be created. How could you deserve anything before you even exist? That God gives you life doesn't mean you deserve to be alive.

It may be plausible to say that God created us in anticipation of our eventual greatness. Since He is all-knowing and not bound by time, He can see our greatness before we achieve it. It's in the same vein as the way we're told God inscribes us in the Book of Life on Rosh Hashanah, the Jewish New Year, for the coming year, based on the knowledge that we're going to be doing great things this year. It's like getting paid in advance. But while this can be true regarding the details of our life, it doesn't apply to our *existence*.

What shall we make of the fact that God creates us? What sort of significance does that impart to the created me?

We're told many times throughout the Torah how important it is—how *divine* it is—to do a *mitzvah*. His commandments are His gifts to us. And of all the *mitzvahs*, God says, "I have a gift in my treasure house, and its name is *Shabbat*. I am giving you my most precious gift."

The more precious the gift is to the giver, the more precious the receiver must be to Him. What God is actually suggesting is that we are more important than the *mitzvah* itself. That's why He's giving it to us. "If You are willing to part with this most precious gift and give it to me, then I must be more precious than Your gift."

If God gives you existence and life and health, it's not because you are entitled, but because He needs you. God's gift of the Torah to you is the ultimate compliment. You must be infinitely precious to Him.

Worship of Success

Here's another modern-day idol we'd be wise to beware of worshipping. As with all false gods, undue devotion to success can only lead to disappointment.

One day at Oxford University I saw a bulletin board announcing a long list of distinguished speakers scheduled to lecture at this revered institution. Among the impressive names on the list was that of a famous boxer. A student next to me was scanning the same bulletin board, and I casually remarked to him that I thought it somewhat incongruent to find this boxer listed among philosophers and scholars. The student replied, with great candor and sincerity, "We admire anyone who excels at anything he does. If he is the best boxer in the world, then we want to hear from him."

The boxer happened to be Mike Tyson, a former world heavyweight champion who was known, among other examples of questionable character, to have been disqualified from one of his last fights for biting off part of an opponent's ear.

What the student was saying—and what our society basically subscribes to—is that success is its own justification. If you are extraordinary at something, no matter what it is, you are worthy of admiration. By that logic, we ought to venerate the Unabomber. And someone who manages to steal fifty billion dollars should be the hero of the century. How about the prominent politician or the movie mogul whose résumé includes assaults on multiple women? All these people are skilled and excel at what they do. The only thing that diminishes them in the public eye is the fact they got caught.

Success doesn't guarantee or demonstrate virtue. It proves nothing. It is fleeting and unreliable, it comes and it goes, and it's neither as noble nor as powerful as we make it out to be. It's certainly not a definitive attribute of divinity, as we deceive ourselves into believing when we idolize and revere the successful, in whatever field. As with all idols, our admiration will end in disenchantment.

It's sad that we tell our children they should be the very best at whatever they do, and only rarely teach them *what* they ought to pursue. Where should they place their energies? Toward that which is good, proper, decent, moral, and virtuous.

In America we live in a "free country." People decide for themselves what values to live by. Yet everyone seems to agree that the cardinal principle is to be better than everybody else—in your class, in your business, in any and every worldly pursuit. Such recognition is what constitutes success. Only then will you have "made it." We dare not be different, as long as we're better.

But the opposite is true. To know and do what is just, moral, and virtuous is far more important than being successful. How good you are at what you do is inconsequential unless you are doing the right thing, or trying sincerely to do the right thing. That is as good as it gets. Then sure, be the best you can be at what you do; but being more successful than the other guy without regard for values has no value whatsoever. The emphasis ought to be on doing what is right. That's the true measure of success.

Worship of Money

A story is told about a fabulously wealthy man whose vast fortune included factories, warehouses, and ships carrying a wide variety of goods all over the world. One day, as he was walking down the street, for no apparent reason he began thinking, *I know God runs the world. Surely He can do anything He wants. But there's no conceivable way I could ever lose all my wealth. My ships alone fill the seven seas. If I* were *somehow to become poor, it would certainly take a lot of doing, and a very long time.*

At the very moment he was thinking this, he was attacked by highwaymen, abducted, held at the point of a sword, and forced to sign over all his wealth or be killed. The man did as he was told. In a single instant, all of his wealth had disappeared.

Now suddenly impoverished, the man was humbled, crestfallen—but his strength of character was such that he could not let this tragedy take away his hope, or even his sense of humor. *Well, that was exciting,* he thought. *It seems God can make everything disappear in a flash, but even He can't make me wealthy in a flash. I guess now it's going to take the rest of my life to restore my portfolio.*

Just then, the sheriff appeared, dragging the thieves in handcuffs. "These men are known, wanted criminals, and we can see from the documents in their hands what they have done." The highwaymen signed a paper nullifying the first deed. And just like that, the man went back to being as wealthy as he had been.

Wealth comes and goes. There's absolutely nothing a person can do about that. Putting one's trust in money is only going to lead to disappointment. Some people think they can outsmart the system by investing heavily in real estate, rather than cash or equities or volatile commodities. But there are no guarantees. As we've recently seen, even the real estate market is not as real as it seems. It can still get us into a lot of trouble. The key is never to place our trust in possessions, not even those that appear to be permanently stable.

There's a Yiddish expression that goes "Money is blind; that's why it keeps ending up in the wrong pockets." The implication is that money doesn't watch where it's going and therefore often falls into the hands of the wrong people. It's cute, but inaccurate, because money has no eyes to be blinded. Nor does money possess will or intelligence. Therefore, to place one's trust in money is to worship a false god. More than not trusting in wealth we should not confuse being wealthy with having a life.

There's a reason the United States Department of the Treasury inscribes and engraves the words *"In God We Trust"* on its currency.

Many of the original pilgrims and refugees who fled Europe for America did so not only to escape religious persecution, but also in repudiation of the *values* that had prevailed in the nations from whence they came. These monarchies and fiefdoms and the landed aristocrats who ruled them valued *possessions* above all else. It was all about money and the military might required to keep it—and it did them no good. Our Founding Fathers left all that behind and came to the New World in search of a new life, to establish a nation that would not make the same mistake. They would no longer live for their possessions.

America turned out to be a very hospitable country to the millions upon millions of immigrants who eventually arrived. There was no tzar to confiscate your wealth, no emperor to behead you and take what you had, no king to claim the authority and the right to seize everything you thought you owned. "All men," said the founders, in expressing their new and historically unprecedented core values, "are created equal." And more to the point, all men are endowed *by their Creator* with the right to rise above the injustices of the past and pursue a higher ideal. We invoke God on our dollars to remind us that to revert to worshipping money rather than God would be a major mistake, and a very bad trade-off. We call it making a "living," but it's merely making "existing" more comfortable. You still need to get a life.

Another reason we can say worshipping money is like serving an idol is that you are worshipping the works of your hands. Your money, like the idol, is actually weaker than you are. You made it, it didn't make you. It's therefore inferior to you. It would be senseless to worship the work of your own hands, to put your trust in something that has less power and is less real than you.

A person whose leg is injured and can't walk puts his trust in a crutch, because the crutch is stronger than his leg. His leg can't hold him up, but the crutch can, which is why the crutch is not made of Silly Putty. The support has to be stronger than the infirmity. The money you make may seem to support you, but in reality money doesn't give you power; you are the one who gives power to your money. We've learned this the hard way: it is the values, goals, decisions, and even the moods of the people that determine how worthwhile or how useful their dollars are going to be.

To put your trust in something means you anchor your existence to that thing or that thought. By putting the words *"In God We Trust"* on all currency, we are making a strong statement, denying a false god, affirming the reality of where our security truly lies and can never be lost or taken away. Even skeptics and atheists who claim not to believe in God can often be heard to say, when things are going badly, that from this point on it can only get better. On what basis do they say this? Where's that confidence coming from? It's not because they think that if all else fails, at least they'll have their money. What they're essentially saying is that whoever created this world won't let it be so easily destroyed.

"In God We Trust" doesn't mean I think God is going to make me rich or help my team win. Belief in God means that morality, right and wrong, good and bad, are absolute imperatives, because God takes them seriously. Because they are important to Him. It means I know He created the world on purpose, that life is real, and valuable—because God says so. That's trust in God—not in His existence, but in His values.

We often see people in ads and commercials vacationing at beach resorts, sipping cold drinks on chaise lounges by the pool, working on their tans. This, we are told, is really living. It doesn't get any better. If that's the message our children grow up with, we have misled and handicapped them. By the time they realize that this "good life" is no life at all, they will have become completely disillusioned, if not suicidal. Such idolatrous dependence on money and the material comforts it can buy is demeaning to our essential humanity, not to mention our sense of morality. To live is to fulfill a purpose, to play a part in the vast eternal plan.

The sages say, "Who is rich? He who is content with his lot." This doesn't mean that the rich person is content with the money; it means he is content with his life—his wife, his children, his community, his rabbi. He uses his wealth to improve his *life,* rather than his *existence.*

Worship of Celebrity...and the Art of Real Leadership

The pursuit of fame has become epidemic. It seems everybody wants to be famous, even if just for the proverbial fifteen minutes. This is why social media has become the focus for so many young people (and the not-so-young as well); they're hungry for the approval and applause of the masses. The desire for recognition and popularity drives them to pursue a lifestyle so artificial, they risk forfeiting life itself.

Most people recognize that the lifestyle Hollywood promotes is not reality. We are well aware of the many innocent children and teenagers who were seduced and deceived by fame and robbed of an otherwise good and noble life. Sadly, it is not uncommon for adults to fall into the same trap. In their pursuit of fame, they readily alter their faces, bodies, values, families, and ultimately their very lives.

To pursue fame is to chase after a false god and deny life itself. When we turn to an idol for energy and vitality (which it can never give us), it will in turn destroy us.

While there have always been powerful leaders, public personalities, or role models of questionable merit, celebrities are a newer invention. Among the myriad idols Americans engage with, the worship of celebrity is one of the strongest and most widespread.

Celebrities differ from true leaders in a number of ways. The first is that celebrities have at best a love-hate relationship with their devotees, while genuine leaders are concerned about and committed to the well-being of their followers. Though many celebrities are thrilled about the attention and livelihood their fans afford them, they are often confused by it, and secretly despise their idolizing fans.

A renowned celebrity once confessed to me that when he performs in a stadium for thirty thousand people, he doesn't understand the people sitting in the upper decks. What are they really seeing? He realizes the meaninglessness of this experience for both himself and the fan.

We sometimes expect celebrities to be leaders and role models, but they are unable to live up to such lofty standards. To be a role model, one needs an extraordinarily high set of personal values, larger than oneself, so that they can influence and rub off on others. Most celebrities cannot claim this kind of virtue.

What should we be looking for in a leader? One of the characteristics of a true leader is his or her ability to move people to a better place—however that may be defined. Unlike a celebrity, they're interested in results, not in fame. They are there to lead and make a positive impact.

One of the earliest examples we have is Moses. To this day, Moses is our teacher because his teachings are still vital and relevant to us, generations later. By his example we see clearly that a true leader has an important message.

There have been leaders who were good for a generation or two, until their teachings became irrelevant. Not that there's anything wrong with that, but it means he or she was a short-term leader. A great leader will have a message that is long-lasting, one that remains pertinent and embraces the changes that take place from generation to generation.

No one is born a leader of multitudes. One develops gradually. First, you master yourself. You marry, you start a family; now you are the leader of a small, intimate group. Then a broader range of people notices what guidance you have to offer, and they seek your counsel. Next, your sphere of influence extends to a community, and from there you become responsible for a city, a state, a country, and then for the whole world.

Another sign of a true leader is the ability to move on to greater responsibilities without abandoning the previous ones—adding to, rather than forsaking prior obligations and accountability. A man who runs a country but has forgotten his responsibility to his family, or even to himself, will never be the greatest of leaders. He is simply not equipped.

Leadership means having something to offer to all the people in your life. If you have to disregard or compromise any of your obligations in favor of what you see as the more commanding role, then you're not made for that job. The celebrity who loses control in his personal or family life while striving for fame and fortune in the world at large is not a genuine leader and is unfit to be a role model.

A genuine leader, or even a good teacher, is one who *empowers* his or her students and followers—not one who allows them to become dependent, surrender their decision-making powers, or abdicate their responsibilities. A true leader fosters independence while strengthening the quality of his bonds with those he guides, helping people with their struggles in order that they will then carry their own burdens. In other words, a genuine leader produces junior leaders, not just followers.

A woman once confided in me that she had given up on having children. The infertility experts had told her that it was impossible. I asked why she went to an infertility expert, and suggested she go instead to a fertility expert. An infertility expert knows people who can't have children; go to somebody who knows those who can. A true leader always looks for the possible rather than the impossible.

Another quality of true leaders is that they don't get burnt-out; their purpose gives them energy. Those born to lead don't get tired, which is why people consult and confide in them. If you are born to do something, it means you have a talent for it, and it energizes you. Whereas when you're doing something that goes against your nature, you're easily exhausted. It wears you down because there's friction and resistance.

Someone once asked the then-aged Lubavitcher Rebbe, a world-renowned Jewish leader, how he could stand from morning to night giving out blessings and charity to people he had never met without getting tired. He answered that when you're counting your treasures, you never get tired. If you see your work as just a job or a burden, it will exhaust you, but if you see it as a treasure, something you were born to do, it gives you life.

A true leader is also one who is able to awaken and inspire others to turn around and make a difference among their peers, because the message is vital, relevant, useful, and meets its target. For example, if you're studying a subject and master it, but aren't able to help a fellow student, then your knowledge is impotent and ultimately futile.

The Rebbe put it in simple words: "If you learn an *alef*, teach an *alef*," meaning teach what you know, no matter how small your knowledge may be thus far. When you've learned something valid, then of course you are capable of sharing it. If you are unable to put it into your own words, then what you were taught was too vague or distant, or you have failed to internalize it.

Unlike real leadership, the danger of celebrityhood is that it is destructive to life—both to the star and the fans. Distorted values lull us into the illusion that we have direction; this in turn distracts and prevents us from seeking real teachers and role models. As a result, now, after a few generations of this brand of idolatry, we have a nation without real leaders. Celebrities have replaced them.

Genuine leaders are teachers, not dictators or manipulators who impose themselves on others. The only way true leaders develop is when others seek their teachings. A society that ceases to search for proper role models will have none. When we idolize celebrities, we lose the ability to recognize what true leadership looks like. That's why we don't know what to look for when we elect our political leaders; we are accustomed to seeing and judging only superficially. Celebrities are becoming political leaders, and political leaders are becoming celebrities. The distinctions between them are slowly disappearing. When popularity becomes entangled with power, those who should actually be leading us remain unknown and unsung.

Celebrityhood in our society is a major cause of confusion, and therefore of unhappiness. We make an idol out of a man, put him on a pedestal as the epitome of the good life; then he turns out to be a disaster. If the most popular, glamorous, famous, and richest of people can't seem to find satisfaction in life despite all their resources and opportunities, what chance do we have?

And still we find ourselves looking up to celebrities and admiring their empty, artificial lifestyles. One needn't look too far to see how the falsehood of fame can lead to such tragedies as adultery, drug overdose, even suicide. We have to be very careful as to where and in whom we place our admiration. A true leader is a person with a perspective the average person has yet to think of—ideas that lift the human spirit and move others to become better versions of themselves.

During the counterculture movement in America in the 1960s, people were rejecting mainstream values in favor of the unconventional. Religious leaders were concerned about the collapse of morality; the Rebbe, on the other hand, saw the rebellion as a sincere search for meaning, and the nonconformism as the rejection of a superficial world. He viewed the world as God's garden, and the hippies as its gardeners. The Rebbe taught us how to channel and transform this perplexing epoch into a powerful force for good.

The people we admire should be those whose lives are consistent with their philosophies. Aristotle wrote a famous essay condemning what he considered the evils of homosexuality. Yet he led the exact same lifestyle he had condemned. How did he reconcile the hypocrisy? "Aristotle the philosopher," he answered, "is not Aristotle the man." A true leader's lifestyle should match his own values.

There are great public figures whose talents we admire, but whose reputations leave much to be desired. We ought not emulate them, and certainly not hold them up as role models for our children, no matter how brilliant, talented, or accomplished they are. If we are to provide our children with a vision of what they can be, we need to show them moral, wholesome, and upright examples. A confusing message is best not delivered at all. It would be ludicrous to tell a child, "Be a writer like Tolstoy, but not the kind of husband he was." It doesn't work.

Another characteristic of great leaders is that they have their own personal role models. Every great mentor, teacher, or leader is also student or follower of some sort. Before we choose a mentor, it is important to know who the mentor's mentor is. A person who answers to no one is dangerous, possibly even a potential dictator. It's a warning sign.

Yet another vital feature that distinguishes leadership from celebrity has to do with the person's relationship with God. Our sages tell us that God humbles men not by humiliating them or bringing them down, but simply by virtue of the fact that *their* greatness has its source in His divinity. The more deeply they appreciate His greatness, the greater *and* more humble they become. Humility is not a denial of one's talents. Great leaders know their gifts, but do not claim credit for them; Moses himself was the humblest of all men. He knew that he would never have amounted to anything if not for the unique opportunities and the prophetic wisdom he received from beyond himself, granted from above. His greatness was part and parcel of his humility.

Like Moses, humble people know their strengths and are therefore able to carry the mantle of leadership naturally and transparently. You can see where they're coming from, what their values are, and how they formed them. As a result they don't hesitate to act. They're not in competition with anyone. They don't draw attention to themselves. Nor do they fear losing their followers. As messengers of God, they may well display Godlike qualities, but they do not claim their message as their own.

The celebrity, on the other hand, is obsessed with the attention of the fans, with the need to stand out in a crowd. When the message sounds like it's the messenger's own invention, it's questionable at best. It will always fall short of having that unmistakable ring of everlasting truth.

People are forever astounded by the Lubavitcher Rebbe's vast span of knowledge and authority on just about any and every topic. Moreover, his teachings continue to be relevant beyond his own generation, not least because they are clearly not his alone—they are faithfully rooted in the unwavering wisdom of generations past, sourced in Torah. It's for that reason that he had the unparalleled ability to dispense pinpoint-accurate advice to individuals and large organizations alike, with both insight and foresight.

Fame and celebrity are akin to the idols that left the ancient idol worshippers high and dry. Competition is so embedded in their existence, they compete with life itself. Life is far too valuable, precious, and holy to be wasted on the ruinous pursuit of renown.

4

Is Religion Necessary?

Religion is about what I want from God.
Judaism is about what God wants of me.

Karl Marx's much-impugned expression that "religion is the opium of the masses" is not so much controversial as it is foolish. He overestimates religion and underestimates people. Sensible people don't put their trust in things that are weaker than they are. In any event, the smart money is on putting your faith not in religion, but in God.

In the classical Hebrew language there was no word for religion. To treat Judaism as a religion is a big mistake. We were never meant to have a religion. If you were to ask a newcomer to the study and practice of Torah Judaism, "What were you before you became observant?" chances are the response would be "Jewish." If you ask, "What are you now?" the answer will still be "Jewish."

You'd probably hear slightly different (though similar) responses when asking the same of non-Jews. "What were you before you got interested in religion?" Unless they had been raised from a young age in a very devout family, they'd likely say, "nothing." The obvious implication is that you can be a human being without a religion. Clearly, in either case, the whole emphasis on religiosity is a misconception. Religion per se is beside the point.

The difference between religion and Judaism—putting aside all the philosophy and theological fancy talk—is that religion says, "I need something from God. What can I do to appeal to Him so that I'll get what I need?" Judaism, on the other hand, asks, "What does God need from me?"

Religion demands a certain lifestyle, and presumably guarantees certain rewards. If I behave in such and such a way, God will give me all the things I need and want—if not in this world, then after I die. In Judaism the opposite is the case. We're not asking God to do anything for us, nor to assure us we'll get a good seat in heaven when we die. We are simply here to serve God. It's about a relationship, not a transaction. If religion's slogans are "God is good," "God is powerful," "God is love," or "God is salvation," the Jewish slogan is simply, "This is my God."

Judaism is not about going to heaven. It is about bringing heaven down to earth. If you can say to God, "I don't want anything from You. I just want *You,* and to do for You what You need from me," you're well on your way toward having brought heaven down to earth.

Conversely, if all your contemplation, supplications, and good deeds are for your own benefit—*Look at me! I'm so good, I'm so spiritual*—then you are practicing a religion, not fulfilling the purpose for which you are created.

We're often told that God is perfect, and that He therefore can't possibly need anything. But here's the problem with that: why, then, would He create the world? Clearly, God is not frivolous. If He created the world, it's because He was after something. And it certainly wasn't religion. He doesn't need religion, and neither do we.

Here's the story in a nutshell. God, who is indeed perfect, existed all by Himself. In fact there was nothing else *but* Him. His existence was colossal, endless, and eternal. But for that very reason He wasn't content. One day, God said to Himself (I'm paraphrasing here), "Existing is simply not enough. I have to get a life!" So God created the world and thus began the saga of the most impossible story ever told. Having initiated a split between the holy and the unholy, the Godly and the unGodly, He made of His original singularity a reality that was suddenly lacking in oneness. "Not good," He said, "not yet. I want everything together in holiness, including these new things that are far from holy."

Everything God created, even the most unholy, He created in order that it too can become part of the oneness. What's the most unholy thing in the world? No, it's not a pig. The most unholy thing in the world is freedom of choice. A pig doesn't have freedom of choice. It didn't choose to be a pig. Freedom of choice means you know you shouldn't do something, but you do it anyway. There is nothing lower in Creation.

It is God's intention that all unholiness—be it a thing, a place, a situation, or a condition we call sin—be elevated to become part of holiness and oneness. How do we do that?

The first step is through recognizing that God created it all. As it happened, He recruited the Jewish people to help Him with this project. "The world is unholy," He explained. "Can you make it holy for Me? I want everything together in holiness, and the only way to do that is by giving you freedom of choice. Even the mere awareness that freedom of choice is a gift from above already makes it holier. If I take away your freedom of choice, then I'm not allowing the unholy to become holy; I'm just denying its existence."

This is the key: God created the world without our asking Him to. He created the world because He was not content with being perfect. God has a very definite plan for how the world should be; yet He gives us the option of refusing to collaborate.

How is all this going to end? If you can ask—and begin trying to answer—that question, you're on the right track.

And you're on the road to a healthy view of what Judaism and the Torah are all about.

God gathered us at Mount Sinai to tell us exactly what He needs from us. He wasn't going to keep it a secret. It was then that God gave the Jewish people the responsibility not only to be true to our relationship, but to demonstrate to the rest of the world what a relationship with Him is all about. The only goal is to eventually serve God together as one. If only we could stop being "religious."

If you think you're better off by being religious, you are mistaken. Any nonreligious person understands this. "I'm just as Jewish as you are," he'll tell you, "even if I am not observant." Exactly! Still, people who are religious often think and feel otherwise. They focus on the differences. They think you are only as Jewish as you are pious and scrupulously observant. The truth is, a Jew is a Jew simply because of his or her *neshama* or soul. The soul is a little piece of God, and that's an irreversible fact.

Have you ever considered that when God gave the Torah to us at Mount Sinai, there was not a single Orthodox Jew? So how did some Jews become Orthodox? It's practically blasphemous to characterize people as *Orthodox* or *religious,* because such labels imply that simply being a Jew is not enough.

This erroneous notion has caused all sorts of problems and disunity among religious and nonreligious people everywhere. In Israel in particular, the polarization can be so intense that it's frightening. If people in Israel would stop being *Haredi* or *Hiloni*, religious or secular, and just go back to being Jewish, we would have a much better, healthier society.

It's actually comical when people call themselves secular. If you're Jewish, you're not secular. That'd be like saying, "I'm a non-Jewish Jew," which is just about as absurd as saying, "I'm a religious Jew." If you were already Jewish, why did you have to become "religious"? Being Jewish is enough. You don't need to embellish it. This is a gulf we need to bridge.

The Torah offers a thoroughgoing account of the nature of the Jewish people and what God expects from them. Does a Jew living Jewishly mean being *religious*, or is it just being authentic? When a Jew decides to become Torah observant, he or she is not practicing a religion, just being Jewish. Observance is just about being true to one's nature.

A Jew who keeps the Ten Commandments is Jewish. If you keep all 613 *mitzvahs*, you're still Jewish; if you keep none, you are still a Jew. You can't become more Jewish, just like you can't become less Jewish. Thus, if your friend says, "Oh, you've gone kosher now? When did you become so religious?" you can answer, "I haven't gone anywhere. I'm just being Jewish—you know, true to myself."

Being religious can also be problematic when it comes to our relationships. There was a young man who decided to become Orthodox. One Friday night he realized he had forgotten to call his friend before *Shabbos*, so he asked his mother to call on his behalf. His mother, who was a nonobservant Jew, was indignant. "My son is asking me to make a call for him when he can't? I'm the one who made him Jewish!" The problem here is exactly that he became *religious*. So he thought that since his mother is not religious, she could break *Shabbos*. What he should have done was to honor his mother and leave religion to others.

At the outset of our relationship with God, He took the initiative and came looking for us. He chose Abraham, took him from his birthplace, brought him to the land of Israel, and then said, "Have I got a plan for you!" As in a marriage, He proposed to us.

In giving the Torah to us at Sinai, God was petitioning us. We did not petition Him. We didn't go to Him with 613 demands; He came to us. If in a situation like that you reply, "Okay, sure! If that's what you need from me, I'll do my best," does that make you religious? Or just a decent human being?

If our goal is to be spiritual, or personally holy, that has nothing to do with fulfilling God's purpose. We're just gratifying our own egos. We've become religious, and we're missing the whole point of our existence *and* our lives. If, however, we can say, "It doesn't matter to me how holy, spiritual, or religious I become. I'm not trying to become a righteous *tzaddik*. I just want to do for God what He wants from me!" *That* is bringing heaven down to earth.

The Talmud brings up a very telling question. In observing the *mitzvahs*, should we be responding to the commandments, or should we respond to the Commander? There are two ways of looking at it. One tells us to respond to the *mitzvah*. If it's a positive *mitzvah*, we should say yes, I will; if it's a negative *mitzvah*, a prohibition, we should say no, I won't. From the other point of view we're told to respond to *God*, no matter what type of *mitzvah* it is. If He says to do a *mitzvah*, we say yes; if He says don't do an *aveira*, a sin, we also say yes. The emphasis here is not on the specific nature of the commandment. It's on our relationship. And the key to a good relationship with God is to say, "You are our God. Whatever YOU want. It is all about YOU."

If I ask you to do me a favor and you respond, "What? Why would you want such a thing?" you're responding to the favor and not to me. But if you say, "For you? Yes, of course! Whatever it is, I'll do it!" then you're responding to me. A good relationship means being able to say, "I'm here for you. What do you want? Even if I think it's off the wall, that doesn't concern me, I am here for YOU." In the same vein, if God needs you to do something, you do it. Not because you agree that it's a good idea, but because you can't say no to God. That's why just about every blessing we make begins with "*Baruch atah*—blessed are YOU." It is all about YOU. Your train of thought goes something like this:

If You (God) need me to put on *tefillin* every day, then I'll do it. I don't understand why You would possibly need such a thing, but for You, I'll do it. Do You want me to keep kosher and *Shabbos*? That doesn't do anything for me; I really don't need it. But I didn't create the world. I didn't write the Ten Commandments. It is YOUR *Shabbos*, YOUR world. If You want me to keep it with You on Your terms, then sure, I'll be happy to.

Think about your parents. Are they weird? All parents are a little odd in their kids' eyes. How then should we introduce our parents to our friends? "This is my mother. She's a little weird, but she's my mom. Her weird is my weird, so she's my weird mom." Or your husband. "I am not ashamed to introduce you to my husband. You'll soon find out he's weird, but he is my weird."

The same is true with *my* God. A young married woman once got into an argument with her mother because she had decided to cover her hair, in accordance with Jewish Law. Mom was appalled. Instead of fighting over it, she could have simply said, "Yes, Mom, you're right. Covering my hair is weird. God is weird! But He's my God." For some of the things we are commanded to do, there is no explanation. Still, we respond to the Commander, not the commandment itself. We never know what to expect from God. There's certainly never any need to apologize for Him.

So how does God want to be served? By covering hair? That's weird! By putting on *tefillin*? That's *way* weird. But if that's what He wants, fine; He is *my* God. And what if I don't do all the things He wants? He is still my God. That's called a relationship, not a religion. We have to get past religion.

Hence, the next time someone says, "Oh, you keep *Shabbat*? You must be really into it!" The answer is, "No, we are not into *it*. We are into Him. He is my God." Otherwise the issues that sometimes crop up around the observance of the details can become competitive, even nasty. For example, it's dreadful how people judge one another on the use of an *eruv*, a *Shabbat* enclosure that enables those who observe *Shabbat* to carry objects in the public domain.

Incidentally, if you start to become observant, don't let that make you forget how to laugh. That'd be a tipoff that you're becoming "religious." God forbid.

Whose World Is It Anyway?

What if we could teach the rest of the world to listen to God, hear what He is saying, and stop being so religious? It could change the world! As we've seen throughout history, when people get "religious" they start killing those who don't agree with them. Why not let God speak for Himself? Whatever He needs from us, that's what we're here for. None of us needs a religion, regardless of who we are or what language we speak. We just need Him.

At Mount Sinai, when God said, "Here, take this Torah, it comes with all these *mitzvahs*, we didn't ask how many. We didn't bargain or negotiate, as in, "If I do this *mitzvah*, what's in it for me?" We simply said, "Your Torah? Absolutely! We want it because it's about You. Just keep talking to us!" Some people may say 613 commandments is a bit much. Isn't that overreaching? If you think about it, however, how many things is a wife or a mother expected to do for her family? Would you call someone who cooks, cleans, and cares for everyone in the home a religious fanatic? Nope, it's just what people do for their families. Nobody is keeping score.

So for the Jewish people, a genuinely healthy attitude toward religiosity might sound something like, "I don't want to keep kosher, or become *shomer Shabbos* (as if it were a profession), and I certainly don't want to have to be careful not to touch nonfamily members of the opposite sex, according to the laws of modesty (*shomer negiah*). But I'm into God. So whatever He wants, I'm fine with it, as bizarre as it may be. It's just me and my God."

Too much of this family we call humanity has gotten hung up on being served. You're here to serve, not to be served. When you get into the habit of doing things for others, you become a *mensch*. That's called having a purpose in life.

Serving God is also good practice for marriage. Back when people were more focused on God, they had better marriages—the two go hand in hand. Relationships today tend to be extremely selfish; suddenly one spouse has different needs or desires or opinions than the other, and it's over. Marriage doesn't demand having everything in common or living a life of easygoing affinity. It means as long as we are together and here for each other, everything else is negotiable. We can't be wholehearted with our families, communities, or anyone else if we're just here for ourselves.

Our sages, wise and practical as always, said, "Do not serve God for the sake of receiving a reward. Serve Him without regard for rewards." Really? Why? What's my motivation?

It's because God comes and says, "I created the whole universe to have a relationship with you." Knowing that He needs us is reason enough. Serving God ennobles us, renders us significant.

We have many needs that aren't really needs: eating, drinking, sleeping . . . a pain in the neck! I didn't ask for these things; I need all this toil and trouble like a hole in the head. But the point of life is not to get everything we need with as little pain as possible. We're here to help God actualize His vast eternal plan. For this we need to let go of being religious and fulfill the purpose for which we were created: to serve God, by doing something aligned with divine intent. To become more than a mere human being driven by self-serving needs.

The Jewish people have striven to live by this prescription for thousands of years. But it's a principle we are mandated no less to share with the world: quit trying to get something from God and start serving Him! It's His world. He created it, and it's about Him—His plan, His purpose, His vision. If you want to be a part of it, then do so. If not, well, that's why you're granted freedom of choice.

If everybody thought this way, would there be war? Would religions around the world be killing one another if we were all busy seeking ways to serve God, rather than waiting for Him to mobilize all His powers and people and precepts and promises in service of us?

5

The Human Psyche versus Modern Psychology

Trying to identify your needs will only get you more depressed. Seek instead to discover the part of you that is free from needs.

Human beings, by nature, exhibit stubborn tendencies toward self-sabotage, toxic dependencies on people or things, and long laundry lists of needs. These needs do not, however, define us. Clinical psychology today strives to provide therapeutic methods for confronting and resolving inner conflict and outer dysfunction. Regardless of how often it succeeds, it does not offer a clear definition of health, and generally fails to present a model for life. As a science, and—more to the point—as a perspective on what it means to be a human being, it is imperfect at best. Let's not get into what it can be at its worst.

Sigmund Freud, one of the fathers of modern psychology, was a doctor, not a philosopher. He was trained to see illness and disorder and to search for a cure. His foundational theories were focused on identifying and addressing disease. Are his methods applicable to healthy, normal lives?

Imagine a detective who spends his days looking for fingerprints, crimes, and perpetrators. He comes home and discovers that his wife is upset, agitated, inconsolable. "Ah," he explains, "you're angry because of childhood issues with your parents." Really? What she needs is empathy, not analysis. Don't come home from work and start looking for fingerprints. Similarly, a psychologist needs to know when to keep his powers of interpretation at bay. If a professional observer keeps looking for pathology, he'll probably find it. He might even invent it and make things worse.

From a Torah perspective, morality is a key component of healthy human character. It can provide correct and beneficial guidelines that extend beyond the definitions offered by psychology. But psychology has pigeonholed morality as a purely religious concept that has no relevance to science. And now we're paying the price for having pitted science against religion.

The Torah differentiates between healthy animal behavior and healthy human behavior. There are times and places in our lives where our animalistic aspects are more or less normal. But human behavior needs to be consistent with healthy human nature, at the very least. Someone who doesn't know right from wrong, or yes from no, is not a fully developed human being. The same applies to children, obviously—they're always testing the limits. The ability to recognize boundaries and delay gratification is a very apt definition of a grown-up, healthy human. A child who doesn't outgrow the selfishness of the natural, animal-like soul is stunted. If children grow up being cruel and ignoring the pain of others, they're not full-grown human beings.

What Meaning Means

One of the best-known clinical diagnoses in the practice of psychology today is called narcissistic personality disorder, defined by a specific set of symptoms and behaviors. In a less medical, more casual use of the word *narcissism*, it's about seeing everything and interacting with everyone from a self-centered point of view. We don't have to look too far in our contemporary culture to see how selfishness and self-absorption have become dominant in the human experience. It's a trend that has even made its way into psychological schools of thought. Beginning with Freud, the assumption has been that if you are unhappy or suffering, it's because you have a deep, desperate, unfulfilled need. Freud said the need was for pleasure. Alfred Adler said it was for power. Others emphasized the need for a sense of security or for meaning (which of course means different things to different people). These were true geniuses, pioneers in an entirely new field of study.

Their solution? In simple terms, discover what the repressed or otherwise unmet need is and find a way for the person to fill the need. In whatever way I define my needs, these various theories are based on the notion that fulfilling my needs will relieve my pain. Neediness is a taxing endeavor, driven by the constant, demanding tasks of fulfilling the physical needs of our bodily soul, our *nefesh habehamis*. The survival instinct can be a nuisance.

From a Torah point of view, there's more to this story than what psychologists understand. Both perspectives agree that the human heart is comprised of conscious, subconscious, and unconscious needs. Torah, however, and Chassidus in particular, address an aspect of the soul that is not lower than, but actually higher than consciousness. If we go deep enough, what we will discover is an inner reality where we can experience a freedom from all needs. And if, after searching your soul, you are still feeling needy, you have not gone deep enough. You haven't yet reached that innermost core where there is absolutely no need.

Not even the need to exist.

This can feel risky or dangerous. We're afraid that if we discover that in reality we have no needs of our own, we might just lose the desire to live altogether. That's why it scares us when a child says, "I didn't ask to be born." If we allow ourselves, we might come to the same conclusion as the child.

Dr. Viktor Frankl, an extraordinary Viennese neurologist and psychiatrist who was himself a survivor of the concentration camps, went beyond Freud's and Adler's emphasis on the neediness of the human condition. He developed a new school of thought based on his firsthand observation that most of those who survived the concentration camps were not necessarily those with a fierce desire to survive. Survival is about maintaining *existence*; those who *lived* were those who found *meaning* in life, in the face of suffering. Incredibly, they were able to make peace with the painful reality that at any moment of every day they might die. How does a person in such a terrifying situation arrive at a point where the threat of death is no longer intimidating or paralyzing? By focusing on the realization that at every moment, even if it may be one's last, there's a choice: to do something that has meaning and goodness.

The sages of the Talmud tell us that the ultimate meaning of life is that we exist to serve. But that's a paraphrase; the actual language is not quite so straightforward: "I was *not* created," cries the soul, "*except* to serve my Creator." Why the inverted, negative phrasing? Why not say it simply?

Chassidus explains that the somewhat awkward way the verse is written is to remind us of something that may have once dawned on us, but lurks somewhere beneath our conscious awareness. Like that rebellious child who complains, "I didn't ask to be born," we know, perhaps intuitively, that as far as we're concerned, for our own sake, we had no need to be created. To *not* be created was in fact our default reality. Moreover, had we not been created, there'd be no suffering and nothing to complain about.

So why am I here? Not for the sake of my own needs, but because I am needed.

This is the ultimate truth of the human psyche: we were created as unique individuals, each for a specific reason. The creative spark that defines our lives used to be called *Elokus* or Godliness. But in reality it's not as mystical or otherworldly as these words imply. It's a fact of human life. And it's capable of liberating humanity from our neuroses and psychological suffering.

The needs we think we have are part of a package deal that comes with having been created. Therefore they're *God's* needs. We didn't ask for them—why would we? We'd prefer to be free and unburdened by these needs.

God's needs are the reason not only for our existence but for the purpose of our lives. He needs us to eat and sleep in order to live, and to live in order to fulfill the purpose for which He created us. My eating is His need; my sleeping is His need. Life means service, and we live to serve. You might argue that these needs *distract* you from serving. "I wish I could help You," you say, "but I've got my own problems. When I'm done with them, maybe I'll be able to help You." However if you can reach deep into that place in your core that is free of all needs, then nothing will stand in the way of serving your purpose. You just need to know what your purpose is.

Imagine you're shown a sink full of dirty dishes and you're told it's your job to wash them. No worries, you'll be paid. Knowing that it's your mission you'd readily get it done. But if you come upon those same dirty dishes and have no clue you're the one assigned to wash them, it's just a mess, and depressing. When you know Who needs you and what He needs you for, you'll happily take care of all the ugliness in the world, because you know it's your job.

Here's a true story. There was a fourteen-year-old boy in Minnesota who tried to commit suicide together with his friend. They did not succeed, thank God, and were placed in different psychiatric hospitals for evaluation. One of the boys ended up in a place where criminals were held to determine whether they were insane; most were seriously dangerous adults. This ward was run more like a prison than a hospital, surrounded by double-barred windows, metal detectors, and doors along the corridors that lock before the next door opens. Even the nurses carried clubs, tasers, and handcuffs.

The only outsiders allowed into this ward were clergy, so the boy's mother could not visit him. She was desperate when she phoned me. Though we didn't know each other and had never met, she asked if I would visit her son, since she had heard I'd been up there a few times before. I knew what a dangerous and frightening place it was. A fourteen-year-old kid with these psychopaths? Horrifying. I agreed to visit him.

When I arrived I found him lying in bed, apparently calm and relaxed despite all the screaming and chaos just outside his room. I said, "Hi! How are you doing? Your mother asked me to come see you." He didn't even look up from his comic book. "She's really worried about you," I said. "What should I tell her?" Not a word, as he continued reading. "Are you okay? Do you need anything?" He was not interested. I tried and tried, but the kid still didn't bother to look up, just shrugged me off.

Finally the boy said, "Why don't you just go home? The chaplain has already been here."

"Really?" I replied. I was very curious. "What did the chaplain say?"

"Something stupid."

"What did he say that was so stupid?"

"He said I shouldn't kill myself because God loves me."

"And that's stupid?" I asked.

"Yeah," he said.

"Actually I agree with you. I can't imagine God would love such an obnoxious brat."

He looked up. "Yeah? What's your point?"

"Obviously God created you because He needs you," I said. "You're a piece in His puzzle, and without you the puzzle is not complete. He stayed with you because He needs something from you. But personally I don't think He likes you very much. What is there to like?"

He answered my question with another question. "What if I don't want to do what God wants from me?" he asked.

"Well, that's called freedom of choice. You can either do it or not. But God still needs you."

Truth is, this boy was delivering a message that we can't afford to ignore. He came from a good, stable, comfortable family, did not have a miserable or difficult life at all. Why then did he try to kill himself? How could he lie there reading a comic book right after the incident, as if nothing had happened?

He and his friend were making a statement, loudly announcing to the world that they were not necessary, that it didn't matter whether they were here or not. The boy was essentially saying that his fourteen years of existence was enough. *I tried it. School's boring. Life is meaningless. So I'll try something else—I'll kill myself. What's the difference—God loves me? He doesn't even need me.*

Love makes no sense when directed toward someone who feels worthless. *What good is love if I'm not necessary?* He was absolutely right. To tell this boy God loves him *was* stupid.

A human being needs to be *needed* more than to be loved. When we know we're necessary, our existence is justified. Then, if somebody loves you, it makes existing more pleasant, but only if you're necessary. So what was stupid about what the chaplain said was that he was actually affirming, "Yes you are unnecessary. But hang around, because God loves you."

Imagine a parent saying to a child, "You're not really necessary, we don't need you, but you're so adorable we love you." That's like a pet: something you don't need, but it's cute, so you keep it. What human being could handle being treated like a pet? It's denigrating. "Excuse me, I'm not your pet. If you need me, I have a life. Otherwise you can keep your love."

In the past, who would ever reject love? It used to be that people would hear the message "God loves you" and think, *Wow, that's it—I'm converting!* There was a different perspective back then, born of *necessity.* People had children because they needed them to plow the fields or pick cotton or whatever else was required for the family. Everyone was necessary. Then, if someone were to come along and say, "You're not only necessary, you're also loved," so much the better. But that's like the icing on the cake.

Today there's a new phenomenon. For this boy, and unfortunately many others like him, that "God loves you" message is stupid. If there's no cake, who needs icing?

Ulterior Motives Are Overrated

Knowing that we exist not for our own needs, but to fulfill God's needs, is liberating; it's a sigh of relief. The soul's definitive pronouncement that *I was not created except to serve my Creator* essentially means "I don't need to be here for my own sake, thanks anyway. If that's what it's about, please don't bother. I didn't ask to be born, and I'm not a problem to be fixed. Don't worry. I'll be fine."

From the perspective of psychotherapy or psychiatry, such a monologue would more than likely be taken as a sign of depression. That's because, again, most contemporary schools of psychology are focused on people's needs: there's something you're desperately lacking, you're miserable, you need therapy. But if we can be comfortable with the realization that we didn't ask to be born, the fact that we *were* born can only mean that a greater power compelled us into existence. And that we're here for a purpose. In other words, we were essential even before we had family and friends; we are essential to God. The more clearly we see that, the more empowered and positive our lives. The most effective cure for anxiety or sadness (or better, the ideal *preventive* medicine) is not self-esteem, nor a positive self-image, nor even love—self-love or otherwise. It's the realization that we have no needs.

Deep down inside, that's what children are saying when they say, "Leave me alone." They don't really want to be left alone; they want us to stop making it about them. "Leave *me* out of it."

They're very smart.

Which brings us back to narcissism. Virtually the entire advertising industry is based on the premise that if we deserve something—and we do!—then we should get it. The industry is trying to convince us that life revolves around us. Which of course is not so; and to imagine it is so lies at the heart of narcissism.

People question whether there actually is such a thing as altruism. Can you really do something for someone else with no personal agenda? The answer is yes, and it's the key to true freedom. The prevailing culture is drowning in narcissism. Altruism is the antidote. God grants you the capacity to enjoy or appreciate love in order that you'll be able to understand how other people feel when you love them. As soon as you start thinking that love, life, and success are for your own sake, you've lost your way.

Psychologists often interpret repressed feelings or other issues as stemming from taking care of others too much, while ignoring one's own needs. We'll understand ourselves, they assert, when we take better care of ourselves. The Torah tells us otherwise: it is in caring for others, in serving God Who presents us with the opportunities to serve others, that we discover who we truly are.

The point is that we are each necessary and real. What makes me necessary and real? The fact that I didn't ask to be here makes me more real than I would have been had I asked. I am bigger than my needs because I don't have any needs; they're not mine.

Don't burden me with the challenges of life just so I can overcome them. The reason I exist is God's need, not mine. The only thing I need is to know why God needs me, the purpose for which He created me. That's the whole reason I am here.

Spend your life trying to fix your own needs and you'll be miserable. Do your best to do what you're needed for, and you're free. To be selfless means you need nothing; needing nothing, you are free to change the world. Serving God is our only refuge from the scourge of narcissism. It's the truest freedom.

To serve God is to experience the joy of needing nothing, yet being needed. If I were to convince myself that my needs were real and pressing, it would take the joy away. Give me my job in life, and I'll free myself from myself, and be happy. If I could but get to the part of me that truly has no needs, I'd live in bliss. What would my life be about? Service. People who serve people are the happiest people in the world.

The future of psychology depends on recognizing that we humans are not merely the sum of our deep, self-serving needs; rather, we are needed to fulfill God's vast eternal plan. Chassidus, the philosophy that grasps the human condition as no other philosophy can, explains that while human beings can be the most vile creatures in the world, we are imbued with all that nastiness precisely because it's our mission to clean it up.

So there's nothing to be upset about. Get to work, and we'll have a better world. Just being on the job will itself prepare us and lead us to the coming of *Mashiach*, redemption, at long last; the era of ultimate peace on earth.

But we're getting ahead of ourselves.

6

The Good, the Bad, and the Inexplicable

We're looking for more than just answers. We are asking for justice.

When we begin a question with "Why?" we're actually expressing some sort of pain or discomfort. We're essentially saying that we cannot accept at face value what's happening, and that we're not satisfied with whatever reasons may have been put forth until now. So the question, "Why do bad things happen to good people?" is not exactly meant to be a question. It's an objection.

Everyone is bothered when something bad happens to good people. Equally troublesome if not more so is when good things happen to bad people. Now we're really disturbed. Where is the justice? We're not necessarily looking for an answer or further information or an education. We're certainly not asking for a lecture on the benefits of suffering. We are demanding justice.

Let's examine what we mean by bad. It's a tiny little word that we are all familiar with, but what is its precise meaning?

Is death bad? On some cosmic level, probably—because we're all looking forward to a time when death will be removed from the earth—which will undoubtedly be good. On a more human level, however, death is tragic, but not necessarily bad. A man is 110 years old and passes away peacefully and comfortably in his home, surrounded by his family. We're not happy about it, but no one gets morally outraged. What we do get seriously upset about is what we call wrongful death. When a young person dies, we are bitter and angry. Why? Because we deem that it shouldn't have happened. The same is true with all pain and suffering. Major surgery is painful and dangerous. Is it bad? No, unless it had been scheduled to be performed on the guy in the other bed, and they performed it on you by mistake. Then, it's bad. It should not have happened.

In other words, the word *bad*, if you are using it correctly, describes something that happened that shouldn't have happened. If it shouldn't have happened, then it's bad, because of the injustice; but if it should have happened, well, then, it may be painful, tragic, frightening—but you can't call it bad, because there is no injustice. If we can understand what's going on, we feel much better. We can handle it. So by definition, death is not bad, pain is not bad, loss is not bad. It's only the thought *it shouldn't have happened* that makes it bad. But who really knows what should or shouldn't happen? Who is a true judge?

Take labor pain, for instance. A woman would hardly survive this kind of pain if she didn't know what it was all about. Knowing makes a huge difference. In fact just knowing that everything that happens, happens for a reason, helps a great deal even if we don't know the reason. The one thing we really can't stand is the thought that something is happening without rhyme or reason. This meaninglessness is totally unacceptable to the human spirit.

Viktor Frankl wrote in his book *Man's Search for Meaning* that while in the concentration camps he realized that the people who survived were those who saw some purpose to what was going on. Those who did not survive were the ones who thought the world had gone insane. The belief that everything happens by divine plan is literally lifesaving.

A few years ago my daughter was running a summer camp. One of the campers fell and broke his leg; his father wanted to sue the camp for negligence. A couple of months after camp was over he called to apologize. "I'm sorry I was such a pain in the neck," he said. "My kid was in a cast with his broken leg, and finally the day came when I had to take him to the hospital to have the cast removed. Unfortunately, or so I thought, I missed a day of work. That day was September 11. I work at the World Trade Center."

What do we know about what should or shouldn't happen?

The reason we cannot handle pointless pain or suffering is because we assume that life has a purpose, and the world is not an untamed jungle. When the world suddenly looks like a jungle, when we're convinced something happened that should not have happened, then things are out of control. That's bad. Where is the justice? Can we know what should have happened?

Our sages, on the other hand, never asked, "Why do bad things happen to good people?" because they knew that nothing bad ever happens. Here is another problem with the word *bad*. The definition of bad is that which should not happen. But if it happened, then how did it? Nothing happens unless there's a reason for it. If God is making it happen, it's for a reason. To suggest that it happened for no reason is akin to saying there's some other force besides God (the devil?)—some alternate God, a bad God, who is up to no good. This is not possible. There is no mover and shaker other than God. This is why nothing bad has ever happened or could ever happen. Nothing moves unless there's a Mover. Nothing happens unless there's a Creator, and nothing happens unless His plan calls for it. Thus, bad things never happen. Not to good people, not to bad people, not to animals, not even to a bug. Unless you have more than one God, no bad things can happen.

As painful and difficult as life may have been for the sages, they never defined their pain as bad. They thought of it as suffering, and suffering by definition is not necessarily bad. Still, suffering is suffering, so the question the sages posed was, "Why do the righteous suffer?" If we know nothing bad is happening, then what are we complaining about?

The answer is that anyone with a drop of decency will complain about injustice. Even young children are fond of saying, "It's not fair!" Every child has a sense of justice. You don't need to be particularly sensitive to object to injustice. Everyone objects.

Does knowing that it's meant to be make it acceptable to see someone suffering? Take for example a woman in labor pain for hours on end. Sure, we know something good is happening. But should we be comfortable with it? Of course not. We are never to be so insensitive as to sit and listen to someone's agony and not be bothered.

Bad things don't happen—not to good people, not to bad people—because if it isn't meant to be, then it cannot be.

God came to Abraham and said, "The people of Sodom are exceedingly evil. I am going to destroy the city of Sodom, where they are deserving of annihilation." Abraham could have said, "Go for it." After all, these people were guilty, beyond redemption. Yet the thought of so many people dying disturbed him so much, he argued and bargained with God again and again on their behalf. Similarly, when Moses delivered God's message to Pharaoh saying, "Let My people go," the persecution of the Jews grew exponentially worse. Moses went back to God and complained. "Why did you make it worse for Your people?" He knew the suffering would eventually end, that liberation was at hand. Therefore there was no injustice to complain about. But his fellow Jews were suffering;

and when there's pain, you complain. We're not supposed to be complacent or comfortable with human suffering, even when we know there's been no mistake.

While the moral position is to object to the suffering of others, it would be beneath our dignity to complain about our own pain. The same Abraham who demanded justice for the Sodomites did not protest when tested with the sacrifice of his own son, Isaac. He didn't cry out, "What?! You want me to offer up my son? He is my future, he is my everything!" There is nothing virtuous in failing to complain about another's trials and tribulations; but like Abraham, we may be prepared to suffer silently and graciously in the face of our own challenges. It's a sign of wisdom, of maturity.

Interestingly, the question "Why?" is coming from a place of belief, not from a lack of faith. To believe that good people are supposed to be rewarded and bad people are supposed to suffer consequences, you have to believe in God, the ultimate Judge. If not, you won't have that question in the first place. If you are looking only through the lens of evolution, when people are dying, it's just natural selection, weeding out the weak, however horrific. *Why* is an expression of faith in God.

A story is told of a wealthy Chassid three generations ago in Russia, who poured out his heart to his Rebbe about how he had lost his fortune and was now living in dire poverty. Another Chassid, also a wealthy man, approached as they were speaking. "God knows what he's doing," he assured his friend. "It will all turn out fine."

Before long the second man also lost his fortune. He came to the Rebbe bemoaning his fate. "When the other fellow lost his fortune you told him God knows what He's doing," the Rebbe reminded him. "Though you're a man of great faith, that was the wrong response to a friend in need of comfort. Now that you know how it feels, you're not so quick to justify an unfathomable act of God."

We tend to think of God as superhuman and invulnerable, and therefore He cannot possibly experience suffering. This is presumptuous, to say the least. As we have discussed, the capacity for feeling the pain of others is a moral virtue, certainly not a weakness. If so, then how could it be that God lacks this virtue? If we think God is indifferent to human suffering, we have diminished Him. Do we think ourselves more moral or more compassionate than God?

In Exodus, when the Egyptians were drowning in the sea as the Israelites fled to freedom on the opposite shore, the angels wanted to sing songs of victory. God was pained: "How could you sing at a time like this? People, my creations, are drowning!"

God not only feels our pain, He has our back.

Of Exile and Opportunities

During the time of the Roman conquest of Jerusalem, there lived a man named Onkelos—a Roman convert to Judaism. So holy was Onkelos, he penned an Aramaic translation of the Torah that until today is printed in virtually every edition of the Bible, alongside the Hebrew text. It became an essential and indispensable aid to biblical scholarship; even Rashi, the preeminent Torah commentator, would consult Onkelos's authoritative Aramaic rendering when he was uncertain as to the precise meaning of a word.

Under Roman rule, Jews were not allowed to practice Judaism, and it was against the law to convert. So the emperor sent soldiers to arrest Onkelos. As they were leading him out the door, Onkelos reached up and kissed the *mezuzah*, the holy parchment by the door. The soldiers asked what that was about. "*You*," said Onkelos, "have to stand guard at the door of the palace to protect your king. *Our* King stands at our door to protect us. That is what the *mezuzah* represents." Upon hearing this, all the soldiers renounced the Roman gods and converted to Judaism. The emperor promptly sent another team of soldiers to arrest Onkelos, and the same thing happened; he kissed the *mezuzah*, they asked why, Onkelos explained, and they converted.

What exactly happened there? The soldiers heard something nice and they converted? No, that would have been merely frivolous. Standing guard at the door of the palace was not just ceremonial, as it is in the United Kingdom today; there was an actual clear and present danger that the emperor would be assassinated. The role of the guard was to absorb an initial attack, to risk his life and take a bullet for the king. These fearless soldiers were flabbergasted by what they heard from Onkelos. They had never heard of a God Who would take a bullet for you. The idea that God cares enough to put you before Himself (however simplistic their understanding may have been) turned the soldiers completely around.

But if God is infinitely more compassionate than we are, if it bothers Him even when bad people are dying, like the drowning Egyptians, why would He allow such a thing to happen at all? Moreover, why would God inflict so much pain on *Himself*? And how in modern times, for that matter, could God allow the Holocaust? A cosmic question. Obviously we can't get into God's mind and explain what He is seeing or planning. If we were to try to answer this question we'd make fools of ourselves. What could possibly justify the enormity of such inconceivable suffering? We have no idea. It boggles the mind. To attempt to explain the great tragedies of history would be an insult to life and to God Himself. But let's not make the mistake of thinking that God doesn't care.

Reward and punishment means you get what you deserve. How does that jibe with the undeniable fact that the wicked have been known to prosper, and "nice guys finish last"? The biblical Job was an utterly righteous *tzaddik,* and yet became the very personification of suffering. Nowhere in the Book of Job does it mention how bad or how sinful he was, not even a slipup. We can dismiss, therefore, any assumption that suffering or success is necessarily indicative of a person's villainy or virtue.

There are times when we must pay the consequences of our actions, and the punishment ought to fit the crime. But the concept of reward and punishment can't come close to explaining what is happening when innocent people are dying or living unbearable lives. We may try to make sense of this, in desperation, by blaming the sins of others. But how is that fair or just?

The Jewish people suffered unspeakable cruelty in Egypt for 210 years as slaves to Pharaoh, after Yosef had passed. How can we explain this? What kind of sin could possibly account for 210 years of horrific bondage—men, women, and children—especially at a time when we had not yet received the Torah's codes of right and wrong? Were we all held responsible for transgressions against God's laws before they were given? Clearly we have to say that suffering, especially extreme suffering, can rarely be considered as punishment for sin.

Fast-forward twelve centuries or so through the Exodus from Egypt, the revelation at Sinai, forty years of wandering in the wilderness, and the establishment of our sovereignty in the Holy Land, to the Roman invasion of Israel some two thousand years ago. The Romans destroyed our Temple in Jerusalem, drove us out of our homeland, and the Jewish people were scattered around the known world.

There's a prayer in our liturgy that says, "It is due to our sins that we have been exiled from our land." Apparently we're taking the blame for all these centuries of bitter exile because two thousand years ago our ancestors couldn't keep their act together. Does this make any sense? How can any right-minded person accept such an assertion? Two thousand years?

But if we look closely, the emphasis here is that we were *exiled from our land*. We're not talking about inquisitions or pogroms or attempted genocide. It's the fact that *we are not on the land* that is the result of our sins. As a chosen people, a nation of priests, we had been given a mission that was grounded in our presence in the land of Israel. God's intention was that we should have a powerful and positive impact on the entire world; our divinely inspired purpose was to extend His wisdom, will, and blessings of peace and prosperity to all corners of the globe, without ever having to leave our home. Had we not sinned, we would have been able to accomplish our mission and influence global civilization from our place in the holy city of Jerusalem, as in the days of King Solomon's Temple—the golden age when the nations of the world came to Israel seeking guidance, instruction, and inspiration.

The fact that we have been and are still in exile after two thousand years and counting is because we forfeited that privilege. Our mandate had been to bring Godliness and holiness to everyone, everywhere in the world. Today the mandate remains, but the mission base has been relocated to wherever we find ourselves, to pursue God's purpose from our state of exile.

The suffering that comes as a result of sin has to be commensurate with the nature of the sin. The Talmud tells us that if you stub your toe, it's a punishment for sin. If you're frustrated because you reached into your pocket to get a quarter and you pulled out a nickel instead, that's punishment for sin. Not exactly comparable to a brutal inquisition or the expulsion from our homeland—that sort of suffering has nothing to do with sin, because no sin warrants that kind of suffering.

God created this world as a messed-up world. It's the lowest of all possible worlds. Chassidus and Kabbalah tell us that there are four kinds of worlds, which vary according to the degree of Godliness revealed. The highest of all worlds is a dimension in which the presence of God is so obvious, there is not an iota of possibility of questioning His existence. The lowest world obscures the presence of God so effectively, a person can go through an entire lifetime without ever acknowledging Him, rejecting and ridiculing the very concept of God. Chaos reigns.

This world is as low as it gets. Hypothetically, the next step down would be a world in which you cannot know Him even if you want to. But such a world cannot exist—there would be nothing to justify its existence. Here, we have the option of denying God, and we also have the option of getting to know Him.

In this lowest world there is also mortality. Adam and Eve's original home in the Garden of Eden was nowhere near the lower worlds, because there was no death. When they ate from the tree, they descended to this world, the world of mortality. And along with mortality came pain, at first associated with the fear of dying, an anxiety to which we are all susceptible. (Though viewed positively, anxiety could be reframed as a survival instinct.)

The idea that human beings are responsible for messing up the world is unacceptable to us. This world was *created* as the lowest world, the darkest world. Yet it's a world of great potential. We're presented with the opportunity to turn darkness to light and make that potential real. If we get it right, we can turn this world not only into a Godly place, but the Godliest of all places, where the greatest revelation of Godliness prevails. We come into this world knowing it's messed up, and it's our job to fix it.

There have been times throughout history when the world has shown itself as intensely evil, seen not just in the behavior of the people, in but nature as well—tsunamis, earthquakes, and plagues. When we encounter such unexpected evil it knocks us off our feet. Lack of Godliness is one thing, but with so much pain and evil, the world can seem beyond repair. We have no clue how to clean up such a mess. Temporarily, at least, we could fall into despair. After the destruction of the Holy Temple, we were overwhelmed, unsure whether we'd ever get back on track. Then came the sequels: the Inquisition, life in the ghettos and *shtetls*, persecution, concentration camps... too much to bear. We didn't know this was part of the deal. So for a generation or so after any given calamity, we've felt paralyzed, incapacitated, powerless, with no confidence in the future and no clear sense as to how things will get better.

I met a teenager whose life had been one long, miserable ordeal of neglect and abuse. She said to me, "I don't believe in God or *Mashiach*. The world is so, so bad. And all your Pollyanna answers about how it's all for the good, sorry, I'm not buying."

I said, "Okay, where do you go from here?"

She said, "Well, now that I know how bad things really are, when I get older I'll find a way to make things better."

"You're going to make things better? You just told me how terrible this world is. What makes you think it can get better?"

"It can always get better."

"You're the biggest believer I've ever met," I said. "You claim not to believe in *Mashiach* and God, but you're the ultimate believer. You know how bad things are, and yet you're convinced they can get better. Fantastic!"

We didn't start the fire. What we're saying is, the world is evil, but we didn't mess it up. It's been a mess since long before we arrived, and we know it's our job to repair it. We've been in situations where we thought we had lost the battle. We couldn't imagine handling such impossible tasks. Yet a generation later we're back on our feet, doing whatever we can to make the world a better place. Life is a process. Nothing went wrong. The *plan* has not been messed up; this *is* the plan. It's a very painful world, and we were given a painful job. But it's a good job, a necessary job, and we can succeed.

7

Facts, Truth, and Consequences

Our choices are our own. The results of our choices are not up to us.

Imagine that the first explorer ever to go to Australia comes back with a report: there's an animal down there that hops around on its hind legs and carries its baby in a pouch on its stomach. A person who has never been to Australia or seen a kangaroo might be too "intelligent" to accept this.

Today we know there are kangaroos in Australia. But it took an explorer to come back to the Northern Hemisphere and tell us about something we'd never heard of. That's what exploration is: to discover something you never knew existed.

Presented with a piece of news that seems like pure fantasy, we have a choice. We can either accept it until it's proven false, or doubt it until someone proves it true. It seems the latter choice is more popular. Skepticism is practically primordial. Try telling your average caveman, who has lived in the same cave all his life, that just over the hill he can see from his cave there's another hill. And beyond that there's a mountain.

"Ridiculous. *This* is the hill. What do you think, I'm stupid?"

"Oh and by the way, a bear went over that mountain."

"Don't make me laugh. What's a mountain? I never saw a bear go over a mountain, and I never will."

To the intelligent mind, every new piece of information is cause for celebration. We live and we learn. Conventional "wisdom" (let's be generous) is to distrust any idea until it's been proven true beyond a doubt. It may not exactly be a throwback to the age of the Neanderthals, but it's more a fear-based reaction than intelligence. It's protecting ourselves emotionally, by refusing to accept anything unless we're absolutely sure. Is that intelligent?

Let's rearrange our thinking. When we come across something we had never heard or seen before, the first reaction ought to be to acknowledge that we just learned something new. It may not necessarily be true, but the very fact that it's a new idea is reason enough to pay attention, and conversely there's nothing to be gained by doubting it. Doubt, actually, is totally unnecessary in life. You can go through life perfectly well without ever having doubts. Someone asks you whether you think there's life on other planets. You might say, "I doubt it," but you could simply say, "I have no idea"—which is undoubtedly true. Most of the time, when people say they doubt something, they could just as easily have said that they're absolutely sure they know nothing about it. And there's no doubt about that. In most cases when we say we doubt something, we mean we don't know. Would it hurt to say that? Why can't we simply say, "That's great," when we hear something new, instead of "maybe." Maybes don't add anything to our lives; they only restrict and limit us.

Science and life have different sets of rules. A scientist is governed by certain protocols. If he can't repeat the experiment, control all the variables, and get the same results consistently, he doesn't have a scientific fact. That doesn't mean it's wrong. Water runs downhill, we're told. Is it true? The scientist has to observe water under all conceivable circumstances to determine whether it's consistent or not. But water runs downhill whether the scientist can prove it or not. Proof is not absolutely necessary, or even helpful, in every situation. Proof is appropriate in the laboratory, but not in life. The scientist comes home, and his wife says, "Oh, I missed you," and he replies, "Where's the evidence? You can't prove that. You didn't miss me yesterday, so why today? Something is inconsistent here." The psychologist comes home, and his spouse asks, "Hi, honey, how was your day?" He says, "Do you really want to know or are you repressing something your mother said thirty years ago?" He's not going to stay married for very long.

What's right in the lab or the clinic can be totally wrong at home. Life is lived by completely different rules. In life we need to be enthusiastic, innocent, uncomplicated, trusting, and secure. If we think we need proof for everything, what we really need is healing. Maybe we've been lied to too often. Where does the skepticism and the doubt come from? From someone who told us there's a Santa Claus?

When we want to know what's real and true, there's a completely different set of criteria than for scientific fact. There are facts, and there is truth. They're not the same thing; the distinction is important, but tricky, because they're both real—just in different ways. Fact is reality as it is, or as it happens to be. Truth is reality as it is supposed to be, as it must be. Most human beings are decent and good. True? Yes, it's true. But it's not a fact. The fact is that many people can be horrible. That's a fact, but that's not the way it's supposed to be. Jews don't eat pork, that's true; but Jews do eat pork. That's a fact. Every mother loves her child, true; there are mothers who throw their babies in dumpsters. That's a fact.

When the fact and the truth are not the same, how is it resolved? The truth cannot surrender to the fact, because true is true: it *has* to be true. The fact is reality as it happens to be, but it doesn't have to be. Sooner or later the fact must surrender to the truth. Here's an interesting—and funny—fact: when the fact surrenders to the truth, we call it a miracle.

A person in a terrible car accident nearly dies, but survives and recovers. "A miracle," we say. "Thank God!" But what's the miracle? People shouldn't die; that's true (particularly inasmuch as death is not part of God's ultimate plan). But people do die in car accidents. That's a fact. In this case, the fact surrendered to the truth. We love when that happens.

The Jews left Egypt because they had an appointment at Mount Sinai. God wanted to talk to them at Mount Sinai. They're on their way, and all of a sudden there's a sea in front of them. The Jews said, "What should we do?" God said, "So what if there's a sea in the way? Go to Mount Sinai." They walked into the sea, and what happened? Miracle of miracles, the sea got out of the way.

But what actually happened? The sea was real. It was a fact that it was there. But it didn't have to be there—"So get out of the way! We have to get to Mount Sinai." When the fact surrenders to the truth, we call it a miracle.

Things should be the way truth dictates, not the way facts dictate. During the totalitarian rule of Joseph Stalin, the entire Chassidic movement together with the philosophy of Chassidus were severely threatened. Most Chassidim lived in Russia, and Stalin made it impossible for them to practice Judaism. Under Stalin it was impossible to raise a Jewish child according to the traditions and truths of Judaism. That was a fact. Some people stopped practicing Judaism altogether, because it was factually impossible. They abandoned their God, and their kids became atheists and Communists. Some pious people ignored the fact completely and continued to practice Judaism. They were "disappeared" in short order.

Chassidim didn't ignore the facts. On the contrary, they worked with them or around them. They built *yeshivas* for Torah learning and hid them underground. If in the city the Communists closed down the *mikvah*—the ritual bath that is central to Jewish life—Chassidim built another one in the suburbs, where "they won't find us so fast." In other words, Stalin is real; deal with the fact; don't ignore it. But always believe in the truth, and never start believing the facts. Stalin will die. Judaism will continue. Look at what's happening today in Russia. The facts have surrendered to the truth.

The coming of *Mashiach* will put an end to this division between facts and truth. Every fact will be the truth, and every truth will become a fact. Although it is true, as we said, that people are basically good, it's not yet a fact. It must become a fact. The facts must surrender to the truth. Then the world will not just be what it happens to be, but what it's supposed to be.

Now, who knows what the world is supposed to be? The Torah pretty much lays it out like an open book, so it seems like we who study the Torah may be the only ones left who have any idea of what the world should be. Our message to the world is this: we're not trying to change anything. We are trying to make the world what it is supposed to be, and therefore inevitably will be, because the truth will always win in the end.

The question is, when is the end? It's easier to answer that not so much in terms of when, but in terms of what the end will look like. One of the things that is going to happen when fact becomes truth is that suffering will end. Moreover, once we get to the truth, all the suffering that took place in the past will make sense. Because whatever surrenders to the truth becomes part of the truth. This points to another development we are looking forward to with the coming of *Mashiach*, which will be the ability to truly *heal* from all the pain of the past. Not by merely surviving or tolerating it, but by actually seeing the goodness in it, so there will be nothing left that is bad.

What was good, for example, about our having to suffer through 210 years of Egyptian exile? Whatever the reasons God had for sending the Jews down to Egypt, it was a strategic plan, part of what had to happen to repair a broken world. He sent us there because we had a job to do. But when God took us out of Egypt to liberate us, that wasn't just strategy. It was His personal pleasure, an expression of God's love, because we are *His*.

A king sends his people to war, and then he's thrilled when they come home. If he's so thrilled about it, why did he place them in harm's way in the first place? The answer is (assuming we're talking about a benevolent king or a genuine president), if you're the king you send troops out to war when it's absolutely necessary, in the national interest. But when you bring them home, it's not a strategic move, it's because they're yours. Similarly, God places us in difficult situations because there's a job at hand. It's what has to happen. When the obstacles are overcome and the job is done, what happens next is not part of the strategy, it's because He cherishes His troops. It's personal.

Must We Suffer?

What causes depression? What makes people give up on life? Is it pain? Rarely. Tragedy? Hardly ever. Because if pain and tragedy were to make people give up, we would all be gone by now. There'd be no human race left. What actually leads people to depression is the thought that something should not have happened—not just because the thing that happened was a bad thing, but because when something happens that shouldn't have happened, it makes everything unpredictable. What's next? There's no rhyme or reason; the anxiety is too much to bear, and we give up. Without that feeling that it shouldn't have happened, we can survive whatever happens.

A priest once said to me, "Why do Jews suffer so much?" I said, "We don't suffer, we live longer. Throughout history we have always been there. If you hang around for four thousand years you'll have a lot of headaches—giving the impression that we suffer more." The Romans didn't suffer. They ceased to exist.

"And by the way," I said, "have you seen our calendar, our festivals and holy days? I think we're having more fun." It's true. According to the facts, there's no way we can survive. But the truth is, we're more alive, because we're more in touch with truth than with facts. The facts are just going to have to surrender.

Have we ever been intimidated by facts? The bumblebee should not be able to fly. He has a big body and tiny wings. But nobody told him he can't, so he flies. That's Jewish. Jews are a tiny minority that the world tries to stifle and silence. But that's just a fact. The truth is, we are here to stay. We are here forever.

We now know that nothing bad comes from heaven. But can't *bad* be introduced through human behavior? Because we have freedom of will, we may cause suffering that wasn't meant to happen. If I freely decide to hurt you, something bad is going to happen.

This is where it gets a little complicated. The idea of free will can be misleading if I think I am free to do whatever I want. I am free to *choose*; it doesn't mean I'm totally at liberty to do as I wish and get it done. In other words, you can make your choice, but that's all the freedom you're going to get. Fine, you decided to rob a bank. That's it, that's your freedom of choice. But you're probably not going to actually rob a bank, because you don't know how to rob banks, and you're a member of a gang that can't shoot straight.

If you decide to shoot somebody and miss, your choice was made, that was your free will, but must your victim die? If you make your choice and fail, you can't complain to God. Your choice to kill makes you a murderer, whether or not he dies, and whether or not the charge will hold up in court. It's about the intended victim's destiny, and his destiny says, "Not today." If he were to die, that would be up to God. In God's eyes, the intent to kill makes you a murderer.

A man decides to commit suicide. He goes up to the seventy-sixth floor of the Empire State Building, opens the window, and jumps out. The wind blows him back against the building and he falls onto the ledge of the seventy-fifth floor. He is bruised and scraped up a little, but he doesn't die. Did he have freedom of choice? Yes. He chose to kill himself, and he acted on it. Did he die? No.

The outcome or the result or the consequence of your choice is not part of your choice. That's God's business. While God gives you freedom of choice, He doesn't guarantee you will succeed. If someone chooses to hurt you, that doesn't mean you'll end up a victim. This is a really significant concept. If you feel that you are suffering because of somebody else's bad choice, you're wrong. No one can hurt you, not even those who desperately try to devote themselves to it. The hurt can come only from God, not from another human being.

Yosef's brothers provide a perfect example: they made a series of bad choices, and nothing worked out the way they'd intended. At first they wanted to kill Yosef. Then they threw him in a pit, then they sold him as a slave. "Men plan, and God laughs." Not only did Yosef survive, he became the viceroy of the Egyptian empire, with unimaginable power vested in him. The brothers were sure he would take revenge, so they pleaded with him not to. What was Yosef's reply? "Why would I be angry at you? Sure, you had bad intentions, but God had other ideas. What happened to me was His plan, not yours." Interestingly, however, Yosef didn't let them entirely off the hook. "You did something evil? Better get some help. You need to straighten this out with God. But that has nothing to do with me."

If you decide to hurt someone and that person doesn't get hurt, it doesn't make you any better. You can't claim to be a nice guy because you failed at being a bad guy. You tried to do someone harm, and although you didn't succeed, you're still as bad as you're going to be. The only way you can become a murderer is by choosing to be one. After that, once you pull the trigger or let the arrow fly, you're no longer in control. But you're a murderer. Ironically, however, knowing that after you make *your* choice what happens will be entirely *God's* choice could conceivably influence you to think twice before you make your better choice. What do you think God would do (and *will* do) in this situation?

We listen to the weekly news about rockets fired by Hamas into Israel, nearly always without casualties. Does Hamas have really bad aim? Logically, more people should get hurt. This daily miracle is absolutely astounding. The rockets blow up and land in a garbage dump. If they do hit a building, nobody is ever home. That's why when Israel tells the United Nations that twelve thousand rockets were fired at us last year, the international community responds, "Well, nobody got hurt. So who cares?"

Firing the rockets makes them terrorists. The fact that God diverts the rockets into the sea is no credit to Hamas. They are as evil as people can get. This presents us with a much more stringent definition of morality: you're a murderer as soon as you pull that trigger. The significance is in the choice, even if the desired result doesn't come to pass.

Intention changes everything. If you meant well, God loves you for trying, even though you blew it. And if you meant evil, even though things turned out okay, He's not happy with you. Freedom of choice carries its own significance. It doesn't need to have consequences to matter.

We have no idea which acts of kindness are the ones God is waiting for in order to bring *Mashiach*. It could be the very next thing you or I do that tips the scales. We have to believe that every positive action, everything we do to prepare the world for

Mashiach, may prove to be the final tap of the hammer. The final redemption is embedded in God's plan; but a plan is not the same as an act. We've got to follow through on His plan with our action. It's exciting to think that after five thousand years of good people doing great things, all that's left to make all the difference in the world is for us to do one more tiny act of kindness. Think globally with every small step.

If we hesitate and *Mashiach* arrives one minute later, there will have been seven billion individual minutes of additional human suffering. How can we consider that acceptable? If we can bring *Mashiach* one minute sooner, can you see how huge the significance of that is? Maybe you or I can wait a week, maybe we're not in such big trouble. But your fellow man might be. He can't afford a week. And if for some reason you're not worried about the whole world, how about just the Jewish world? Fifteen million more minutes of Jewish suffering because of our hesitation to do a single act of kindness?

Twenty-four more hours of suffering doesn't cut it. We need *Mashiach* now, not tomorrow. The next *mitzvah* might just be the one to tip the scale. Maybe you're the very one designated to complete the task of correcting the world and getting it back on track. We're never going to be content as long as what *is,* is not the way it ought to be. If fact is different from truth, it doesn't sit right.

Life is good, and God is good, and since things don't happen that He doesn't make happen, bad things don't happen. There isn't another God lurking somewhere, and we don't believe the devil has an agenda of his own. If something happens that we don't like, and we don't know why, that too was meant to happen, because only God moves and shakes the world.

We're working toward a world in which the truth prevails, and in which all facts surrender to the truth. We won't need to explain anything, because there'll be no further questions. The purpose of

Creation is to rectify the wrongness, to make sweet that which is bitter, to bring light to the darkness.

Beware of Answers

Once a person understands, he often also ceases to care. It's the nature of the beast. Suppose I'm masterful at playing the markets and you ask my advice about a potential investment. "Don't do it," I tell you. But you go ahead and do it anyway, and before you know it you're in big trouble.

Now you come back to me and say, "Can you help me out with this? I really messed up here."

"I told you not to do it."

"Yeah, I should have listened to you, but now I've got a serious problem. I can't deal with this on my own."

"I tried to help you. I told you not to do it. And I was right. Let's see if you'll listen to me next time." What does that say about me? I don't care because I'm right? Because I understand why it happened, I have no compassion?

Elie Wiesel was often asked why there was a Holocaust, as though he should know just because he was there. Usually he would simply say, "I don't know." One time there was this rather obnoxious fellow interrogating him nonstop. "Sorry, I can't tell you," he said, and the guy got upset.

"Does that mean you know and you don't want to tell me?"

Wiesel looked up at him and nodded yes, and the guy was about to blow a gasket. "Why won't you tell me?!"

"Because if I told you, you would become a Nazi."

"What are you talking about? I'm Jewish! Why would I become a Nazi?"

Wiesel's answer was brilliant. "Look, you're asking me why there was a Holocaust because you're disturbed, it bothers you, you lose sleep over it. How could six million people be liquidated like that? What a horrible word, *liquidated*. Better to say *killed*. But they weren't just killed. They were liquidated.

"So you come to me and say, 'Tell me why. Explain it to me.' When I tell you, you'll say, 'Oh, hmm, okay, so that's why. Now I can sleep.' You've become a Nazi, because only a Nazi can feel comfortable with the Holocaust and sleep at night.

"So what was it you were asking again?"

When we ask a question like that, the last thing we want is an answer. Don't you dare answer that question, because by answering it you're saying it's okay And it's not okay. We don't want an answer, we want a change. We want the fact to surrender to the truth.

There's only one way to talk about a Nazi mindset, about how anyone could casually kill millions and then go enjoy supper with their family: they could do it because they "understood." It made perfect sense to them that the Jews needed to be killed. What could possibly be objectionable about something so logical?

When a civilian is killed we complain. What about when a soldier is killed? People in uniform deserve to die? What is this distinction between a soldier and a civilian? The truth is there should be no dying, there should be no suffering, there should be no war. Just because you're aware that if you put on a uniform you might get shot, doesn't makes it okay. Now that I understand the suffering, it should cease to bother me? No. The fact needs to surrender to the truth.

Again, the sages ask why the righteous suffer. It's a much better question than the "bad things/good people" canard, because it means I know that behind it all there's a reason, I know it's all for the good, I know it's meant to be. Yet it disturbs me.

There was a time when the church used to call midwives witches, and the church would burn them at the stake. Why? Because the Bible says women will give birth in pain, and these midwives were helping women ease their pain. How dare you take away the pain? In a similar vein, the Bible says if you see a poor man, feed him. How dare you? God made him poor. Who are you to interfere? Of course, it's absurd. The whole point of morality is that if people are dying, save them; if people are hungry, feed them; if people are ignorant, teach them; if people are in pain, take it away.

Sadly, once we know *why* there is pain, we get comfortable with it; now we're satisfied—and we lose our human sensitivity. That's neither moral nor decent. Even when we know why, we object; there must be a painless way. We wake up finding darkness and pain, and we plead for the bitterness to come to an end.

Here's a beautiful story. There were two elderly brothers I knew in Minnesota who would recite the entire *Tehilim* (Book of Psalms) every *Shabbos* morning. One of them explained their extraordinary custom: "We were in the concentration camp for three years. The Allies came in and liberated the camp. They came in, they opened up the gates, and they said, 'The war is over, you're free to go.' And we were standing there by the gates, totally paralyzed because we had no place to go. The *shtetl* was gone. Our family was gone. This is something people don't realize. We panicked. We stood there completely lost; we didn't know what to do."

Just then, a Polish woman came toward them with a big basket and handed them a loaf of bread. "My brother and I looked at each other," he said, "and we promised each other that for this kindness that God had shown us, we would say the entire *Tehilim* every *Shabbos* morning for the rest of our lives."

They were standing at the gate of a concentration camp, and they couldn't get over God's kindness? From where did they get this gratitude? And after all they witnessed and experienced, the first thing they did when they came to the United States was to get married and have children. From where were they able to conjure up such enthusiasm for life? How does this work? How did they not give up?

It was because they knew that the concentration camp was part of a divine strategy—a necessary, calculated move. But when God sends you a loaf of bread, that's personal, divine love.

The first and the last thing we must grasp is the plan. There will be a world. It will be an ugly, unGodly world, a world of pain. Our job is to make it better. So when you see something painful and ugly, don't panic or go into shock. This is our mission. Whatever pain we see, whatever ugliness we encounter, what can we do to fix it?

The Lubavitcher Rebbe, the sage of our generations, once said, "If you see something that needs to be repaired, and you know how to repair it, then you have found a beautiful piece of this world that God has left for you to complete. But if you only see what is wrong and ugly in the world, then it is you yourself that needs repair."

8

“Why Are We Here?”

Just because it’s uphill doesn’t mean you’re on the wrong road.

Throughout history human beings have sought to understand the purpose of life. It’s not just an intellectual or academic curiosity; people have an urgent emotional need to know why we’re here. But why? Do we really have to have a reason? If we haven’t figured it out by now, maybe we ought to give up and be satisfied with not knowing. We’ve been here for over five thousand years. This is our place. This is where we are. What’s wrong with just being here? Why are we still so uncomfortable? Can’t we settle down already? We are not going to find an answer anyway. That’s because the question is being asked out of order.

When we feel so strongly that the fact of our existence compels us to discover our life’s purpose, we’re actually getting it backward. In truth, the purpose comes *before* the fact. You don’t build a car and then figure out what it’s for. When you need to get speedily from where you are to where you want to go, you invent a car. The purpose always precedes the product.

The decisions we make *after* finding ourselves alive are not about our purpose in life. Some say their "purpose" is to become a doctor, or an engineer, or to travel the world. That's a made-up purpose, not an actual purpose. It may define and describe what we're going to choose to do, but it's not the reason we exist. The purpose of our lives must come before life itself; life is the result of that purpose. It's not something we can create after we are born.

What drives us to so unrelentingly search for purpose is the unconscious or subconscious instinctual sense that we must be here for a reason. Not knowing what that reason is makes us uncomfortable. It's akin to remembering that you have an important appointment, but you can't remember when, where, or with whom. You just know you have to be someplace, and it's urgent.

If life is purposeful—and it is, and always will be—it means we were created that way; and the purpose had to have come from the Creator. Like the guy who invented the car because he needed faster transportation, God created us with a purpose. That's why anyone who feels there must be a purpose to his life must also believe in a purposeful God. Had He not created us with a purpose, we actually wouldn't need one. Without this innate feeling that there's a reason for our existence we wouldn't bother to look for one. Our purpose in life, therefore, is His purpose.

Morality and Mission

Once upon a time (and maybe still, depending on where you look), people believed in a sort of situational ethics, in which anyone's individual values are perfectly acceptable as long as we live and let live. You have your values, I have mine, and let's all get along.

For two reasons that doesn't usually work. First of all, if your values differ from mine, if I think what you're doing is wrong, I'm not likely to let you live your way so harmoniously. I might get pushy, or at best, I'll ignore you and let you suffer if you get into trouble. In such a situation, live and let live is not only a faulty principle, it can in fact be cruel.

Second, if I'm not all that sure of my beliefs or values, with a little bit of pressure or bribery I'll easily discard my values and change my mind at the drop of a hat. I might as well not have any values at all. So to say we each have our own truth and our own values is more amoral than moral.

How then do we define a healthy, purposeful, moral human being? A holistic approach would say that a healthy person is someone whose body is in perfect balance, so that it doesn't interfere with the intelligent mind—allowing the mind to pursue the purpose for which we exist. By the same token, when you have an appointment you must keep but you wake up lame, that would be an illness. If you have no place to go and your legs don't work, there's no problem; you're not ill. Without purpose there can be no illness. And without God there would be no purpose.

There would also be no morality.

The medical world, ironically, does not really have its own definition of health. We do know, mostly from statistics, what it means to be *unhealthy*. Most people can walk, most people can hear with both ears, and most people can stand up straight. Therefore, anybody who can't walk, can't hear, and can't stand straight is statistically unhealthy. But we don't actually have definitive knowledge of what *healthy* means, which is cause for concern. If you're a doctor, how do you know when treating a patient whether you're leading him toward health or just getting rid of overt symptoms, and quite possibly making him weaker on a less obvious level?

In a more philosophical sense, a definition of *un*healthy might be a condition in which you're prevented from getting to where you're supposed to be—or in other words, unable to effectively pursue the purpose of life. Health, therefore, is what furthers God's purpose in creating us. This leads us to a corresponding definition of good and evil. *Good* means whatever advances the purpose for which we exist. *Evil*, or bad, is anything that interferes with or sets back our progress toward the purpose for which we exist. We can conclude from this that since our purpose is actually God's purpose, there is essentially neither good nor bad without a Creator to define them. *Now* we're looking at health through the lens of morality.

There was an atheist who wrote a book explaining and defending his atheism. At the end of the book he acknowledged that there was a problem with everything he had written. "If I truly reject the notion of God," he said, "then I cannot claim that certain things are intrinsically evil and others intrinsically good. Incest, for example. If I don't believe in God, the best I can say is that incest is a bit dangerous, because of its effects on the unborn child. The inability to say that anything is absolutely evil makes me uncomfortable. It goes against the grain and in fact prevents me from being an unequivocal atheist."

Therefore, without God or the Torah, whatever morality we are able to embrace will be a very tenuous and conditional morality, one that cannot satisfy the human need for an absolute sense of right and wrong. Is murder wrong, or is it just a little inconvenient to have people killed?

We've defined a healthy person as one who has a purpose in life and knows what that purpose is, and there's nothing preventing him from fulfilling that purpose. The same is true with morality. To be a morally healthy person is to be able to know what's *right* because it leads to fulfillment of God's purpose, and what's *wrong* because it interferes with that fulfillment. That's the ultimate gift of the Torah: God tells us what our purpose is, how to achieve it, and how to avoid whatever would prevent us from achieving it. It's not religion, just common sense.

By definition, purpose precedes the project: we don't have a purpose before we are created. Our purpose therefore must be determined by a Creator Who has a particular plan or purpose in mind—not just a global plan, but for each of us as an individual. That's not coming from any religious text. It's just the definition of who we are and how we function. Each of us feels compelled to figure out what our individual purpose is.

We can see this clearly from an example of when it's not working. When we fail, or feel as though we've wasted our time and our efforts amount to nothing, we tend to get very upset. It's not just that we haven't achieved a goal, it feels like we've failed in our purpose. It's no different from when you see your child hanging around doing nothing all day. It bothers you. Not because it violates some religious or moral principle, but because humans were created on purpose. There is something embedded in human nature that tells us we are here for a purpose, and it disturbs us when people act purposelessly. Why else would we get dismayed over our children doing nothing?

Look at what you are, where you are, and what is going on. You'll discover strong clues as to where you are best suited to make a difference. Where you will experience success is where Divine Providence leads you, which is where God leads you, and therefore where you need to be.

"You will bring your fruits to the place God has chosen, in order to make His name known," Scripture tells us, referring to the yearly offering of the first fruits of the harvest. The Talmud says *the place* refers to the *Beit Hamikdash,* the Holy Temple in Jerusalem. Chassidus applies the idea to one's personal experience, in all times and places. Wherever you go, be aware that this place where you have arrived is the place God has chosen for you to be. What is the purpose of you being there? To make God's name known.

Our original mission, as Jews, was to introduce monotheism to the world, both collectively and personally. It was a worthwhile undertaking, and by and large we have been successful. Most of the world has advanced toward basically monotheistic beliefs. But that was then, a mission more or less accomplished long ago. Today, our job is to take it a step further. What the world needs to know is not just that there is a God, but also what it is that God expects of us. This of course presumes that He wants, in fact *needs*, something from us.

This is not an obvious proposition. Nearly every religious teacher in the world will tell you that God needs nothing. He is infinite, eternal, perfect. If God is perfect, He cannot logically be lacking anything. And if He were lacking, He wouldn't be perfect. It feels, therefore, intellectually inconsistent and counterintuitive (if not blasphemous) to suggest that He needs something from us. It's an uncomfortable notion. Some may feel, moreover, that it would be beneath them to worship a God Who is in some way imperfect.

The real issue is philosophical: can God be perfect and still need His Creation? God was already perfect, eternal, and infinite before He created the world. Yet He went ahead and created us. What on earth for?

By definition, the Creator has some sort of relationship with His Creation. We can't just dismiss or ignore that relationship and insist that He needs nothing. If He needed nothing, nothing would have happened. Clearly, something happened and keeps happening. But why should He bother?

If we were only speaking about *wanting* something, that wouldn't present much of a problem. There are things God wants, and there are things God doesn't want. God wants you to keep the commandments; God wants you to observe the *Shabbos*; He wants you to keep kosher; and He doesn't want you to kill, lie, cheat, steal, or eat on *Yom Kippur.* We call that God's will. But where it gets complicated is when we *do* kill or steal or eat on *Yom Kippur*. These are things that happen that He doesn't want to happen, that are against His will. Something is going on here that overrules and overrides His will. Why else would He make something happen that He doesn't want—like allow evil to exist in the world? If God doesn't like it, why did He create it, and why does He tolerate it?

Quite simply, the goal for which God created the world is more urgent than His will. There is a greater purpose that surpasses His will. The only way to explain it is to say there is something He *needs*. It's not that He is needy or weak, in the way we might use the word to describe a human need. We use the word *need* in the sense that it is *necessary*. It is absolutely necessary that His purpose be achieved.

So again—who are you, where are you, what are you good at? What does God need you for? As imperfect beings, we sometimes have the thought that what we're doing is not exactly what we should be doing. It's safe to assume that we're never going to have 100 percent certainty, unless a sage with crystal-clear vision says, "This is your mission." That's not to say that we ought to allow that little smattering of uncertainty to sabotage us and end up doing nothing. What *could have* been or what *should have* been can drive any human being insane. Better to stick with *what is*.

Ask yourself, "What do I have to work with? What are my options?" They're not unlimited; not every possibility merits your consideration. You'll most likely be choosing between one or two or three things. If you see yourself going in a certain direction that's meeting with a measure of success, take the hint and continue. If God has a mission in mind for you, trust that He's not going to hide it from you—what would be the point of that? He's going to lead you in the right direction, and you have to be prepared to respond accordingly. In general, we should never say no to any good project we are capable of doing. Even if it should turn out to have been a mistake, it'll be a good mistake, a purposeful mistake. When something comes your way, don't look the other way.

Be willing to work with anyone who shares your inclination to do something good. You'll never regret working with anyone on a worthwhile project, even if the collaboration doesn't last over the long haul. Every small accomplishment is nonetheless great. Don't be hung up on knowing *this is it.* Go for it, and if it's the right one, you will succeed. Or maybe the project will build, snowball, and evolve into your true destiny. In the meantime, you will have been occupied and engaged in meaningful work. And just because there are setbacks, it doesn't mean this is not your mission; it just means it's an uphill mission. Uphill is good. There's nothing wrong with a challenge that will bring out your best.

The gifts you have are yours, not necessarily anyone else's; don't be shocked or dismayed when someone doesn't like what you do. We each have a certain amount of influence, on a certain number of people, in a certain limited range—and that's it! We do our share and have an effect on our little piece of the cosmos. Those who are unaffected may find us irrelevant, maybe even annoying. Nonetheless we work and blossom wherever we are.

The guiding principle is that you're here for another. In the course of doing one person a favor, you'll inevitably help a lot of people indirectly. You help a man make a couple of dollars, he succeeds in feeding his family, his family grows up and raises many more healthy generations. It's a ripple effect. That's the way God designed His world. Chassidus reminds us that even if you help only one man, that will justify a lifetime of eighty years. Of course, we will affect many more than one. Everyone does.

The Rebbe always cautioned against overplanning and insisted on the "doing." You can get lost in the planning, the worrying, the mental preparations. Don't get stuck. It's what you do that counts. This is a generation of action. "Well done" is much better than "well said."

The key is to push yourself a little bit beyond your comfort zone. When God gives you a dollar, expand your mind and think about five-dollar projects. Now your vision is worth five dollars. When you attain those five dollars, expand your vision to ten, and work at the ten-dollar level. You're not limited to the money you have in your pocket; it's only your imagination that sets limits. Of course, you're also realistic at the same time. You don't go about launching a project that's going to cost millions when you don't have even a dollar. Likewise, if you inspire a person you may think, *Wow, if I can inspire one, I can inspire a thousand.* No, reaching one person does not, by any reasonable calculation, suggest reaching a thousand. Not now, not yet. In any event, whatever it is you choose to do, whatever the scale, and whatever extra effort you bring to bear, that's precisely the blessing you will get: you'll get what you need. You will be neither overcompensated nor shortchanged.

9

Free Choice

Sometimes it's the misfits of the world who are best qualified to get it done.

The biggest mystery in all of Creation is the human being. Everything else in the world seems to know its place. Nature is perfect; everything has a function and functions more or less perfectly. If you look at nature, it looks like the purpose of life is merely to survive and to evolve. But humans don't fit that picture so snugly. A human being doesn't seem to know where he belongs. We don't want to merely evolve; we want meaning and purpose, content and quality. We're misfits. And the reason we're such misfits is because we have freedom of choice.

You might be thinking this doesn't make sense. God created the universe, divided mundanity from divinity, then gave us a Torah that describes Him, reveals Him, and defines His purpose: to elevate the lowliest of all things and unite them with their Godly source. True, He empowered us, as a nation of priests, to introduce Him to the world; but even so it seems that it's all about His choices, His likes, and His dislikes, from beginning to end. Does it seem plausible that He would set His plan in motion, permeate the world with divine potential, blaze a trail toward His sacred purpose, and then bestow freedom of choice upon a horde of flawed and unreliable creatures such as us?

If God had no particular preference, if good and evil were equal in His eyes, and He then gave us free choice to select good or bad, that would make sense. But if God is particular about right and wrong and the whole point of Creation is to reach a Godly place, why place it in our hands? A serious ambition calls not for options and alternatives, but a serious, single-minded direction.

If you think about it, freedom of choice granted to human beings is far from a compliment. We're proud of the fact that we have freedom of choice, but really, should we be? What does it mean that we have choice? I have the option of either being human or being a monster. Should I consider that an honor? When you hire a babysitter, you don't want him or her to have freedom of choice. You want to know for sure that anything and everything this babysitter is going to do will be for the well-being of your child. You're not going to pay the babysitter more because benevolence is optional.

Do we have a choice to be born or not to be born? Do we have a choice of being male or female, tall or short? Do we have the choice to exist in this era of history, or in some earlier or later epoch? Not at all. When you think about it, you have no freedom of choice regarding most of the really important things in life. Where does this concept of choice come from?

After the great flood of Noah's generation, God promised He would never again wipe out mankind because of their sins. His reasoning was that since man is born with an evil inclination, the inherent nature of mankind is such that He can't really hold it against us when we misbehave. That may sound like a condemnation, but in actuality He presented us with a challenge and an opportunity.

God expects us to be more than good; He expects us to be divine, despite our inborn evil character. And what we mean by evil is not something sinister or malevolent, but rather a natural, understandable selfishness. The evil nature of a child means having been born completely wrapped up in itself, its needs, and its wants. In effect, right from the get-go, no one else matters. And yet this utterly self-absorbed creature is actually capable of transcending that nature and becoming a vehicle for divinity. Our freedom of choice and our ability to act against our nature lies in the realm of morality. Human beings are not great problem solvers, as we might be inclined to think; many of our toughest organizational or technical problems turn out to be practically unsolvable. But when it comes to morality, human beings are well equipped to be moral decision-makers.

God sets the stage. We are born when we're born and created the way we are created, according to the gender, race, identity, and so forth we are given. These significant fundamentals of life define the parameters within which we will play our roles. Whatever one's role may be, wherever you are, whoever you are, and under whatever circumstance, there will be moral choices. There's right, and there's wrong. The challenge is to choose the right. "I place before you a choice," God says in the Torah. "Good and bad, life and death. Choose life." To *choose life* doesn't mean "don't die." It means "Breathe life into the existence you are given. Whatever the nature of your existence, rich or poor, strong or weak, loved or hated, that's the context. Now bring goodness into that context." Freedom of choice, therefore, is solely in the realm of moral choice.

What's fascinating about this is that the consequences of your choices are beyond your control. Once you let loose the arrow, you have relinquished control over what that arrow is going to do. You cannot determine whether or not your intended victim is going to get hurt. All you can do is choose to do him harm or not. You can choose right or wrong, and that's that. The consequences of your choice remain in God's hands.

When God says you are free to choose whether to be a killer or not to be a killer, that doesn't mean God is going to provide a victim. Nobody is going to die as a result of your freedom of choice; the death of the victim is up to God. Yet a victimless crime is still a crime. Even if you're not a very effective murderer, you are responsible for your choice. Good or evil is determined by your choice, not by the consequence.

This actually empowers and lends more significance to a human being than if we were to be focused on consequences. You can be living in an environment where everyone and all the influences in your life incline you toward evil, and yet you are free to be good. In fact if you choose good under those conditions, that is the *greatest* good, the truest expression of free choice. It's possible. We see it all the time. People surprise us. Those who have every reason to be evil suddenly turn out to be good. That's freedom of choice.

The fact that this freedom only exists with regard to moral issues is a clue to the reason why God gives us freedom of choice. Our choices pivot around one thing, and one thing only: are we into Godliness or are we not? Are we moral or immoral? Good or bad? Holy or unholy?

God is looking for a true relationship. In a true relationship, both parties have to be free to choose. God's desire for a relationship means that He chooses us and wants us to choose Him. And choice means we must be free to go either way. In a real relationship, if I'm willing to love you, I have to be aware that you might love me back, or you might hate me back; but I'm still willing to love you. If I were to love you only on the condition that you love me back, then I don't really love you, and that's not a relationship.

God may love you back, or He may not. He could actually hate you back. God knows that there are times when we might hate Him, but He loves us anyway, because that's what love is about.

God, of course, can make everything good, including us. But then where's the relationship? Giving us freedom of choice means that being good is not something we're given, it's something we choose. It's not easy, but we have a fantastic role model. Imitating God is one of the Commandments: "I am compassionate, so you be compassionate. Emulate Me."

God's love is for real—meaning, unconditional. That's one of the key divine attributes we need to imitate. The biblical account of Creation tells us how.

God created the world in seven days. On the first day he created the quality of kindness; on the second day, judgment; the third day, compassion; and so on, all because He wanted a meaningful, productive relationship. He's saying, "In order for Me to have you, in order for us to become truly one, I will create whatever it takes. I don't want you only out of love, because that wouldn't be unconditional. But if love will help, I'll create love." That was the first day of Creation. Then on the second day, He says, "If judgment helps, I'll create judgment," which by its very nature serves to highlight the commitment part of our relationship, keeping us accountable. Then comes the third day, and the realization that compassion is necessary. So, "I'll create compassion." It's quite a remarkable process, and far more substantive than any of those "God is love" platitudes. God says, "Before I create love, I'm creating you. Then, if love is necessary, I'll create love."

Imagine a relationship in which a man expresses to his girlfriend that he wants her forever. They need to be together. They need to become one. To make that happen, love is apparently necessary. So since it will help them be one, he'll provide the love. Love is not the condition; love is the tool. What *is* the condition? The condition is the need. He needs her. They have to be one.

From whom do we learn this? From our Creator. God first decides to create us. Then He produces love as a tool, as a support. When love turns out to be not the most effective tool (it happens),

God can be tough. When being tough doesn't work, God can be compassionate. When that doesn't work, God is simply loyal.

We are told that with the seven attributes that correspond to the seven days of Creation, God created the world according to His divine plan. What's the plan? To put it concisely, we must be one, and we will be one. If that's God's plan, it must succeed, and it will succeed. Why? Because God gives us freedom of choice. If we didn't have the option to choose *not* to participate in that oneness, it wouldn't be the real thing.

Naturally, God wants us to do the right thing. The right thing means getting closer to Him. If you're getting closer to Him without freedom of choice, that's not closeness—it's just robotic programming. When we do the right thing, we truly are becoming one. We are elevating and perfecting the world, completing God's plan.

What kind of world will we have when we finish our job and the relationship is consummated? What is a perfect world?

10

How to Bring God Home

You're proud? You're egotistical? You have ulterior motives? No worries. Self-improvement is beside the point.

The *Tanya*, a small book with enormous impact, comprises the guiding philosophy and the practical principles of Chabad Chassidus. It was published over two centuries ago in response to a demand, a hunger that existed at the time. Hopefully that hunger still exists today: people want to know how to serve God. It's not written for skeptics, or the disaffected, or the doubters, or the turned off. Its target audience is made up of people who simply want to serve God and really don't know how.

Back then, people would travel long distances to the Alter Rebbe in desperate need of his advice and guidance. After a while, the questions that came up most frequently began to form a pattern, and the Rebbe wrote a pamphlet addressing each question with his instructions regarding that problem. Eventually all these pamphlets were taken together and turned into the book that we now know as *Tanya*. It is as relevant today as it was when it was written, perhaps even more so. Serving God is synonymous with having a purpose in life; and since one's purpose must always precede the life one lives, knowing what it means to serve God is essential to a life well lived.

The world's existence is born by divine purpose, and is therefore completely receptive to the purpose for which it was created. It follows, then, that the world is capable of living up to God's expectations and fulfilling that purpose, just as a carefully designed machine will function the way it's designed to function.

The same is true of human existence. We were created, each of us, with a purpose and for a purpose. And we are certainly capable of fulfilling that purpose. Though that's encouraging and inspiring to know, how do we do it?

It's long been assumed among people of a spiritual persuasion that in order to fulfill your purpose, it's necessary to transform yourself into something saintly or otherworldly. You have to disavow your earthliness, or escape your earthly character and worldly personality in order to become angelic. Even if it were to work that way, this is a long, arduous path. Not everyone is capable. It's also possible that after all the effort it took to become a spiritual, holy, and refined person, you still will not have fulfilled the purpose for which you were created.

Could it be that your purpose is not to become heavenly or spiritual, but rather to bring Godliness into the physical, ordinary, everyday world? If that's true, if the pursuit of sainthood is the wrong (and probably futile) plan, then what exactly *is* the plan?

There is nothing heavenly about the Ten Commandments. "Honor your parents," "Don't kill," "Don't steal," "Don't covet your neighbor's wife," etc.—all pretty earthly. Even "Don't take God's name in vain" and "Don't worship other Gods" are more about human behavior, our speech and our deeds, than spirituality. It's obvious from even a cursory look at the Commandments that our immaculate sanctity is not what God is after.

There is physicality, there is spirituality, and there is Godliness. The physical world needs to be repaired; the spiritual realm can be a training ground, but the goal is to be Godly. *Godly* means embodying God's interests, God's will, in the world we live in right here. It means making this world the way He wants it to be. A person should train his children, for example, to be kind and sensitive to the needs of others, so that when he gets older he will actually give to charity. In simple language, this is what we mean by serving God.

An alternative approach would be to give a lot of charity, so that down the line you'll develop a more charitable and generous personality. Which of these two scenarios is more Godly—developing yourself into a generous person so that you will eventually give charity, or giving charity in order to transform yourself into a more generous person?

The *mitzvah* is not meant to make you a better person; you should become a better person in order to do the *mitzvah*. Which in turn, of course, makes you an even better person. The goal is not necessarily to improve yourself, but to serve the higher purpose for which you were created.

Self-help advice as to how to refine yourself can be very uplifting, spiritual, even elegant. But it's not the end goal. The mandate is not to become a *mensch*, per se, though you might need to be a *mensch* in order to fulfill the goal. But even if you're not a *mensch*, you can still give charity, without preconditions. That's Godly. Godliness, unlike spirituality, is available to everyone at all times and under any circumstances. Thus, even if by personality and disposition you happen to be a very stingy person, you can give charity anyway. When you do, it's magnificent! The fact that you're by nature tightfisted does not in any way diminish the Godliness of the *mitzvah* of *tzedakah*.

Any condition that we impose upon morality is in and of itself immoral. It's akin to saying that we will have a good society only when everyone becomes highly educated, refined, or artistic. As soon as we say we'll be good once we put in place certain conditions, that's already immoral. Because you can be good right now, without conditions.

The finest human being is still not divine. Serving God transcends the best of human qualities. The *mitzvah,* the fulfillment of God's will in this material world, is divine, even though you're not.

Human beings who are very far from divine can do divine things. That's the awesome message of the revelation of Torah at Sinai: ordinary people can perform extraordinary, Godly deeds. This is possible because divinity is so true, so real, so *present*, it has no prerequisites. Generally speaking, if you're trying to achieve something wonderful, you need to educate and train yourself. When we're talking about an accomplishment that is cosmically true, however, there are no qualifications or requirements, no specifications of time or place. A person can readily do what is Godly because Godliness is absolutely true. Truth is true everywhere, and it's true all the time.

It's true that holiness manifests on different levels. There's a ladder that stands on earth; its head reaches up into heaven. You can climb that ladder and improve yourself endlessly. But then there's the view from above. What does God see when He looks down at the world? What is He interested in? What is His purpose or intention in creating the world?

Truly spiritual, holy, and refined souls don't do *mitzvahs* in order to climb the ladder. They do *mitzvahs* because they know that's what God wants, and they're here to serve Him. When God calls upon the great characters in the Torah, the patriarchs and heroes and holy men, they say, "How can I serve You? Whatever it is You want, I'm ready. I'm here, let's go. Your desire is all I need."

Love and fear of God, though sublime, are immaterial when God wants something done. You're given an immediate opportunity to do a *mitzvah,* because He's waiting for it. Getting it done turns out to be the noblest of all intentions, greater than awe, greater than love.

Real growth means transcending yourself in action. The Rebbe teaches that if you devote yourself to what God needs rather than what you need, you will succeed in ridding yourself of ego not by a process of elimination, but by adding something positive to the world. Just put all your energy into doing what He needs, or what the community needs, or what your fellow man needs, and you will speedily accomplish your goal and fulfill the purpose for which you exist.

Skip the preliminary stuff—your egotism, your ulterior motives, your selfish impulses and pettiness—and go right to the top. Find out what God needs, devote yourself to that, and all those extraneous faults and foibles will scatter themselves like so much dust in the wind. Instead of fighting and focusing on everything negative and undesirable in yourself, focus on the joy, the beauty, and the pleasure of serving God. In so doing you will reap the benefits of becoming a refined person almost automatically, and lightening your own load.

Why should I have to humble myself in order to show my respect for God, when I can respect God and thereby become humble? Humility doesn't require feeling insignificant and worthless. Humility means realizing that I'm important, I'm valid, I'm worthy of the privilege of serving God. Why struggle to eliminate the negative when we can accentuate the positive?

The Chassidic message to the world is actually universal—a clarion call to all nations, races, colors, and creeds: you were given life, and it's your life. But it's not for you.

You weren't given love so that you can enjoy love; you were given love so that you will offer it to someone else. Whatever fabulous wealth may pass through your hands was given to you, but it's not for you to keep. It's for you to share.

Does that seem counterintuitive? Of course it does. It's not easy to convince ourselves thoroughly and comfortably that our lives are not for ourselves. We tend to think, maybe even by default, that our lives and everything we've been given are for the sole purpose of our own enjoyment. But blink your eyes for a moment and return to the idea that there is a purpose to your life. Your purpose was established long before you arrived on the scene. To truly realize that is so liberating, so mentally and emotionally healthy, it could put all the psychiatrists out of business.

I have to get comfortable with the idea that my body and everything I think I own are not my possessions. Even my needs are only there for the sake of other people's needs. If that seems confusing, it's because I've always assumed that my life is about me, and it was never about me.

This is the beginning of all decency and morality. In some ways, environmentalists have come to that realization: this planet is not for us. Therefore we have no right to corrupt, pollute, or destroy it; it's not our planet, it's not our world. That's a very specific philosophy, and it's essentially Godly. It's like the idea of what wisdom means—that when you see a beautiful sunset, you know Whom to thank. If we know God and what His plan and purpose are, we know Whose it is, and we know where we're going.

Who would you be if you didn't have an ego? How would you behave if you were not selfish by nature? Whatever that may be, why not act as though you were already there?

This is not hypocrisy. It's not hypocritical to give more charity than you feel like giving. It's not hypocritical to be polite when you're not feeling polite. It's only hypocritical if you're doing it to fool people, to take advantage of them. If you're doing it because it's good to be polite even though you're not into it, that's not hypocrisy. That's goodness.

Of course, we do our best to be consistent. But it's perfectly human and understandable that we have our ups and downs. The goal is to be really there for Him consistently. It's a process. We work toward it, and we don't give up. If you're not there today, you'll be there tomorrow.

Life is not about us, nor is it for our own purpose. We don't need to be here. We were created against our will, we live against our will, and we will die against our will. Our purpose today is only to assist God in fulfilling His purpose for creating the world.

11

Modesty: Meet the Real Me

What you see is not what you get.
Most of the time it just gets in the way.

If God is everywhere and He is everything, how then is it possible that we cannot see Him? If His existence, as the sages assure us, is more true and more real than all the things He creates, why is it we can see everything *but* Him? Surely He's more real than the chair you are sitting on; yet you can see the chair, and you cannot see Him. Is God only in heaven and not on earth? How does that make any sense? *Everywhere* means everywhere.

Some say we don't see God because He is pure spirit, invisible. Some say that if He *were* visible, His presence would be so overwhelming it would take away our freedom of choice. Or some would say that we're the problem: we don't see Him because we are so unholy, we are lacking in the merit and the refined sensibilities required to see holiness. Still others suggest that we don't see God because, as compared to the things He creates, He's like the thought that precedes the Creation—and thoughts cannot be seen. But no. He's not thought. He is more real than thought.

The Torah presents many examples of prophets who had encounters with God, heard His voice, or experienced visions of spiritual entities that represent His presence. It's true of the great ones—Elijah, Ezekiel, Isaiah, and company—as well as of the evil prophet Balaam, who tried to spite and defy God even after He had appeared to him in a vision. Moses, the greatest of prophets, uniquely spoke with God face to face; but like the other prophets, Moses did not *see* His face.

The reason we don't see God is because He doesn't allow it. He hides from us. In Kabbalah, the veil behind which He hides is called the *tzimtzum*, self-limitation. He makes room for finite creations to exist. But esoteric explanations aside, the question remains *why*? What reason does God have for hiding and preventing us from seeing Him?

Seeing might sound like a good idea, but it gets in the way of intimacy. That's what's wrong with seeing. The eye sees only *things*—external images. The image doesn't let you know its inner quality. Our eyes see only the *things* that describe the appearance of a person—weight, height, size, eye color. But a person is not a thing. Can you see love? Intelligence? Integrity? No matter how long you look at a person, you won't know who he is. You may stare at someone for years and not get to know her any better.

It is only natural that we should want to see God; and we should always want to see Him. But God Himself wants to be heard, not seen. Would it inspire us if we saw Him? Yes, of course. Probably for about a month. What usually happens when we are excited about people who are strikingly beautiful in our eyes? We're beside ourselves, thrilled, overjoyed, delighted to see them. Until we get used to them. Then the excitement fades and they become ordinary.

By not allowing us to see Him, God is saying, "If you see Me, you will be very impressed with My magnificence. Possibly even overwhelmed. But I don't want that. I want you to know Me. Know who I am. Understand Me. Ask Me why I created you. Ask what I want, what I don't want; what I like, what I don't like. Ask what gives Me pleasure and what makes Me uncomfortable; what makes Me happy, what makes Me sad. If you see Me, you will never learn these things. So I am not going to let you see Me. I want to be known, not seen."

Because we don't see God, that's why we've been busy getting to know Him for over three thousand years and counting. We never get tired. As far as God is concerned, it doesn't matter how long it might take, as long as the relationship is strong, intact, and not superficial. Seeing may be helpful in a working relationship or a transactional arrangement, but that's not what God wants. He wants an intimate, personal relationship. Knowing is intimate; seeing is not. God wants to be *heard*.

When the Torah describes Adam and Eve's relationship, it doesn't say Adam took one look at her and fell in love. It says Adam *knew* Eve; and then she was with child. For a marriage to be fulfilled, to remain fresh and fascinating, we need to know each other. And there will always be more to know. Thus, intimacy between husband and wife should happen only in the dark. Because intimacy can't be seen.

This is called, in Hebrew, *tznius*, modesty. Modesty means I am not a thing that you can see with your eyes. I am someone you have to hear and understand and care about. God practices *tznius* and asks us to do the same.

In the world around us there is immodesty more or less wherever you look. But even there it's recognized that this lack of modesty prevents real growth and connection in relationships. Today's relationships tend to be superficial and artificial. No one knows how to get personal anymore. "If you look good, I'm interested. If not, I'm not." People break up because they've lost interest: she's not as pretty as she used to be; he got older or slower; someone else is more appealing, better looking, or more exciting. It's tragic.

Like the guy who came to speak with me and said, "I'm getting a divorce. I don't need this." *This*? He's divorcing her because he doesn't need *this*? Is he married to *this* or to her? I said, "If you don't need this, whatever this is, get rid of this. Why are you getting rid of *her*?" It was a totally new idea to him. He had married her because she was a good-looking woman. Now he doesn't need this, so she's out. Never mind that she's a human being. He had never thought of her that way. That's what immodesty does. A lack of modesty is like pornography: it means looking at a person because you want *it*, not her. Not a relationship with a human being, just *it*.

Sometimes this same coldness exists between parents and children. Most teenagers understand this well, whether or not they can articulate it; because deep down, this is what a teenager wants: "Do you hear me? Do you get me? Do you accept me for who I am? Get to know me!"

And if these bonds are not in place, then it's "So what if she's my mother? I have my own life and she has hers." Or "I really don't care what my dad thinks." And from the parents' side it's "I have no idea what my kids are up to. I'll just let 'em go." It's as though their lives don't touch each other, and as a result people are suffering. Because we desperately need these human connections.

Fashion Statements

The topic of modesty in clothing has become a huge issue, especially between teenage girls and their mothers, and even more so in traditional Jewish communities. One girl complained to me, "My mother is crazy. She's a grown woman, and she makes such a big deal about the buttons on my blouse!" To which I replied, "You're right, that's crazy. Just button another button or two." She looked at me like I had just told her to wear a forty-gallon plastic bag. "No way!" So now we have two people hung up over a button.

If, according to a mother, *tznius* is defined by the placement of a button or the length of a skirt, everybody is in trouble. This is not what modesty should sound like, and she is certainly not teaching modesty to her daughter.

Almost every *mitzvah* we introduce to our children carries a feeling, an unstated implication, that it's not only the right thing to do, but it is Godly, exciting, and uplifting. When it comes to modesty, however, we treat it like the house rules. "You can't dress that way in *my* house." The other *mitzv*ahs—keeping *Shabbat*, or *Kashrut*, or visiting the sick, take your pick—they are all beautiful. They're presented as a way of connecting with a higher and more inspiring desire, with the divine will. It's easy to get enthusiastic about being with that program. Then when it comes to teaching *tznius*, all of a sudden we adopt an offended, judgmental, shaming tone. "You can't walk out of here looking like that!" Does that sound like a *mitzvah*? More like the imposition of a community standard. This is no longer about God; this is "I can't let you dress that way." So of course we get pushback. Unlike other *mitzvahs*, modesty stands out like a sore thumb, which is precisely the opposite of what modesty actually represents—a refined, quiet, subtle beauty that bespeaks inner value and doesn't call attention to itself.

If we listen carefully to the kids who are having a problem with *tznius*, they are telling us exactly what their problem is. They don't get the point of being preoccupied and obsessed with *things*, which is what buttons and hemlines are. They're not buying into the idea that because we're ashamed of how we look, we have to cover up. Sarcasm ensues. "Fine. So I'll button up. Now everything is wonderful? You're happy now?" But we're not listening. Listening is a talent. If we make a genuine and concerted effort to listen to our teenagers, it makes all the difference in the world to them. Even if we still disagree, it doesn't matter. We listened. Now we've earned the right to have something to say.

Here's an approach: tell them their own story in practical terms. You get up in the morning, you look in the mirror, and think, *Should my skirt be a little longer or shorter?* That's not a life. You are hung up on the wrong thing. And what's worse, you're using the language of *should* in a disempowering manner. It's fear based.

How about waking up in the morning, and if your clothes fit, you put them on and go? How liberating would that be? When you don't have to think about what to wear, you can live your life. You could even treat it like a uniform. It's just not something to think about. This, by the way, is why in some Jewish circles, men all dress alike. We think of them as conformists, with no individuality or personality; but in reality it frees them to put their attention somewhere more meaningful than *things*.

With some teenagers this might be a hard sell. A common response to the topic of *tznius* is, "I don't understand all these stupid rules. My clothes are an expression of who I am. Why can't I dress the way I want?" The simple answer is yes, everyone can (and *does*) dress the way they want. But the better question, the deeper question, is not "Why can't I?" it's "Why shouldn't I?" And here the word *should* means something else entirely.

Some people are nasty and very skilled at hurting other people's feelings. Should they rein it in? Suppose someone were to tell you to be generous. "Why should I?" you may say. "I was born a tightwad. I gotta be me. Can't accept me the way I am? That's your problem." We are what we are. A snake is a snake. Snakes bite. Yes, you can be true to your bad character. But you shouldn't. Imagine if we all were just what we are, as is, and stayed that way. Ouch.

On another level, *should* can be understood in terms of fear of consequences: you should be nice to your friends, or you're not going to have any friends. If you want friends, you must be friendly. This is logical and well-considered, but it is self-serving.

Then there's a third rationale, more in keeping with your true identity. You were created for a certain purpose. You should fulfill that purpose, or you will have wasted your life. *Should* here applies to the things you were created to do. A Jew should keep kosher. A non-Jew has no such obligation. We should be who we are. Similarly, a man puts on *tefillin*, a woman should not. *Tefillin* are necessary for one and not the other. One should do what one is designed to do and that for which he or she was created. In its most positive sense, the word *should* indicates that if it's meant for me, I want to do it, and if not, I don't.

Why then should I be obliged to dress modestly, if it's not me? Or is it? Who is the real you? Is the real you modest or immodest?

Attention, Please

People whose manner of dress tends not to be *tznius*, whether by nature or by habit, frequently complain that no one takes them seriously. They may be very popular and well-liked, but they are perceived to be lightweights, all about fun and games, far from thoughtful.

There was a woman in Minnesota years ago who lamented this very issue. Because she cared about the education of her children, she would go to school board meetings to convey her opinions as to how the school system should work. It was important to her that she be heard; yet no one would consider her input, because she was very obviously into her looks. She didn't understand why people didn't take her seriously. She later told a story that revealed a core identity issue.

Her eleven-year-old son came home from school one day with a classmate. They sat down at the table and she served them snacks. She then heard the classmate say, "Where's your mom?" And her son said, "That's my mom," pointing to her. The friend said, "No, come on, really? She's not old enough to be your mom." The friend thought she was the older sister. This woman said that made her wildly happy. She was complimented that she didn't look like a mom. Here is a concerned mother who would prefer not to look like a mother. So what does she want?

Does she want people to think she is the mother of her son or his sister? Is it possible that nobody takes her opinions seriously because she hasn't made up her own mind? The question then is, who is she really? Is she a person concerned only with her looks and what people think of her, or is she the mother who is genuinely concerned about her child's education? Obviously she is both. She's not faking either one. But she should figure out how she is coming across to others.

The idea that you can be who you are, yet dress in a way that's not consistent with who you are, is flawed. You want to look good, be popular, and feel free; but you also want people to take you seriously, respect who you are, and consider your point of view worth listening to. It's an inherent inner conflict. It doesn't serve you well.

There was a girl I was counseling who had been severely depressed for quite some time, to the point of hospitalization. During one of my visits she confessed that the reason she was depressed was because no one noticed her. She felt as though she was invisible. "I'm so insignificant, when I walk into a room nobody sees me," she said. She was genuinely hurt.

There was a guy who had similar issues, but in reverse: he was so self-conscious he thought everyone was constantly reacting to him. He said, "Every time I walk into a room, people walk out." He was totally preoccupied with himself.

Then there are people everyone notices, but no one has the slightest idea what they're actually about. Nobody knows and nobody cares what bothers them or what *they* care about. That hurts just as much.

What do we want most? Do we want to be noticed, or do we want to be understood?

There are things the eyes enjoy and like to see. There are things the ears enjoy and like to hear. There are things that the mind enjoys because it likes to know, and things the heart enjoys because it likes to feel. Of all these sensory modalities, seeing is the most shallow. To see beneath the surface takes work. It's said that we have two eyes, in order to be able to differentiate between deep and shallow; but still, eyes can only see *things*, and human beings are not things. *Tznius* helps us compensate for this visual disability.

Oftentimes people dress a certain way to express their individuality. They don't want to just follow the rules like everyone else; they want to reveal something about themselves that will be noticed, to be appreciated for who they are. The problem is that it produces the opposite of the desired result. When you're dressed immodestly, nobody will ever know who you are, because all you've done is draw people's attention to something that's not you.

A girl asks, "What's so wrong with a little more skin?" The answer is "Nothing. That's why you shouldn't be known for your skin." At the risk of citing a somewhat unrefined example, picture a girl whose clothing is very immodest having a conversation with a group of boys who are paying her a lot of attention. When she leaves the group, what sort of impression has she left them with? Do they now know who she is? Or were they more likely distracted by her provocative appearance? The distraction only gets in the way.

Actually, every teenager knows this intuitively. They get it: there's got to be more to *tznius* than buttoning buttons or covering parts of the body. If that's all modesty is all about, they're not interested. If a teacher or a parent stands there with a yardstick measuring their skirts, they will resent it no matter how well it's explained. On the other hand, if we were to teach our teenagers what real modesty is, *that's* something they could love.

They want something better, and we're not offering it to them, so they rebel. Yes, everyone should look attractive; but there's more to them than that. They are bigger than that, deeper than that. Nobody is showing them how much more meaningful modesty can be, so all they're left with is some absurd concept of *tznius* being nothing more than the number of buttons or the length of a skirt.

Some people are inwardly modest, but don't give much thought to the way they dress. They want to be heard, not seen; they want to be *known*. But they haven't yet put that together with the fact that when they dress modestly, they are proclaiming loud and clear, "I am not a *thing*. If you want to know me, listen to me. Get to know me. Understand me."

Who determines whether this or that article of clothing invites being seen, or being known? It's a good question, and there's no one simple answer. In truth, only the Torah can make such a fine distinction. The Torah is very sensible about it, and its rules are a good place to begin. The parts of the body that are engaged in intimacy should be reserved for intimacy. An intimate embrace takes place in privacy, and there are borders that separate private from public. It's so natural and reasonable.

Will a longer skirt ensure that people will want to get to know you? Of course not. Or not necessarily. But the better question is, who are you? And is that well represented by the way you look? What exactly are you advertising? Don't assume that the deepest part of you will be discernible if you dress immodestly. Anyway, sooner or later, as you mature, your priorities shift and you stop caring so much about what you look like on the outside.

Imagine speaking to some teenager and saying, "You know, I hate to have to tell you this, but your mother is not so *tznius*. She unbuttons her *whatever*—and she—"

"Stop! That's disgusting!" the kid exclaims. Why suddenly so appalled? Because when you talk about your mother's *tznius*, you're not talking about buttons. You are talking about *her*, a person.

If your daughter enjoys wearing less-than-modest clothing, and talking to her about it is likely to spoil her enjoyment and make her unhappy, it's not worth it. You have a happy child, why ruin it? Before suggesting she might want to change her clothes, tell her how glad you are to see her happy. Your child needs acceptance, not judgment. You don't want to give the impression that her happiness is making you miserable. Our children have enough misery at school and elsewhere; they don't need it at home. Better to focus on building a happier home, a happier community, a happier street.

Schools too need to make modesty pleasant. Other *mitzvahs* are not strictly enforced rules and regulations; take for example the ritual washing of hands, which hardly triggers any resistance. And if a child refuses to wash his hands before lunch, would you throw that child out of school? Unthinkable.

The message we want to impart to today's generation is: When you raise your standards, people will be much more interested in knowing you. Lower your standards, and they'll lose respect. Even God does it this way. He doesn't want to be seen; all He wants is to be known. And He acts accordingly.

Don't underestimate your teenagers. Assume they will embrace the highest standards when they realize that it's consistent with who they are, and you'll be pleasantly surprised. Expect too little, and you'll get nothing. Take the high road.

12

Sexual Harassment: No Trespassing

God created a world of inequality.
That's why He introduced morality.

Contemporary society has underestimated the volatile nature of sexual tensions to the point where abuses, or accusations of abuse, have become commonplace. It's a complex and sensitive area of human interaction, and widely misunderstood. Having been rather negligent about it, people are now beginning to realize that it calls for more diligence and care.

It's not only in the workplace, with its inherent power differentials, that these issues between men and women have come to light. It is true everywhere, and it affects all sorts of people, not just high-powered personalities who abuse their authority. In a wide range of situations, people find themselves, at least potentially, at war with the opposite gender. Each one is afraid of the other, and wary of being hauled in front of a court.

Sexual harassment is thought to be about the trespassing of boundaries and the violation of someone's space, without having been invited in. For more than three thousand years, Jewish Law has set down intricately detailed rules to safeguard these human interactions. Only recently, however, have people begun to see that these seemingly old-fashioned ideas may in fact offer some profound insight.

The rules of modesty advocated and taught by the ancient rabbis were not for the purpose of avoiding litigation or out of respect for people's rights. A man and a woman who are neither married, nor related to each other (as in brother and sister or father and daughter) are simply not allowed to be alone in a room together behind closed doors. It is reasonable to assume that this is because placing themselves in a private space conducive to intimacy leads to the possibility of a misreading of the intentions of one or the other or both.

Additionally, it's not a good idea to create an intimate context when you have no intention of being intimate. At the office, unless your workplace has a glass door or walls, leave the door open while conducting an interview or a meeting. To say that we're able to close the door and not be tempted toward intimacy is naïve, at best, and denies reality. The very significance of a closed door is that it generates an atmosphere of intimacy.

Likewise regarding your children. If you don't want them to be sexually active, you have to furnish them with a lifestyle that will support that expectation. Provide a context, an atmosphere, and an environment in which avoiding physical contact or sexual tension is easier, rather than more difficult. If you were to say to your teenagers, for example, that they're allowed to be alone with someone of the opposite sex on sleepovers, you are not doing them any favors. And again, it's the same with adults. If you're going to be intimate, then an intimate setting is appropriate. If you're not going to be intimate, it's not. It's actually cruel to tell your children that they can go "halfway," and then expect them not to go "all the way."

For the same reason, Jewish Law requires people to dress modestly, and forbids affectionate physical interactions, even handshaking, between men and women who are not related. It also prohibits discussions of intimate personal subjects between men and women who are not married to each other. There are things that should be kept private, personal, and not shared in any way, not even with a gesture or a glance. Simply put, anything that is a characteristic part of intimate life between husband and wife is never shared with anyone else. It is set aside, reserved, and respected as something sacred. Even for married couples, we only express intimate gestures when it's time for intimacy, never in an unsuitable moment, nor in the absence of appropriate feeling, because casual intimacy is deadening.

The purpose, the reasoning behind these laws, is to establish a lifestyle that supports an intimate life between husband and wife, so that they are not left dependent on the treacherous uncertainty of their sexual energies or their capacity for self-control.

All of this is reasonable and practical. The laws of modesty are also necessary for legal purposes. A major problem today in the courts is that there is no clear definition of harassment. Let's say a man and a woman working in the same office are taking a coffee break. They go over to the coffee machine and he puts his arm around her and says, "So, how's it going?" She recoils. "You wanna get arrested?" He says, "Lighten up, I'm just being friendly." She says, "Get your hand off my shoulder or I'm calling the police!" He says, "Whoa, take it easy, what's your problem? You're just overreacting."

Conversely, in another instance, it's after office hours and a woman walks into her male coworker's private office. "There's nobody else here now," she says, as she closes the door. He says, "Excuse me, but please leave the door open." She says, "What are you afraid of?"

Now, if any such cases were to be brought to court, what's a judge to say? Is this harassment? Or is the ostensibly harassed person just a little too edgy and uptight? Is it just imagination working overtime? Should the judge recommend they see a therapist or a counselor or a life coach? She says he's harassing her. He says he's only being friendly. How is a judge supposed to decide? Even in more severe forms of harassment, when the harassment appears to border on violence, for example, there often is a lack of clarity.

Consider the Clarence Thomas confirmation hearings for Supreme Court Justice in 1991 and the accusations of inappropriate banter and sexual innuendo brought by Anita Hill, his assistant. The tension was so extreme, the entire country got caught up in it, with everyone taking sides as to who was telling the truth and who was lying. What was the crime we were talking about? Whether he said what she said he said, or whether he didn't say what she said she heard? What exactly are we discussing here? And most importantly, what are we left with as a society?

The effect is that we are intimidated, and not necessarily only by the "harassment" itself. The fact that we just saw on public television a case laid out about harassment, and yet we have no concrete definition of what *constitutes* harassment, is frightening. The career and the life of a Supreme Court Justice hangs by this thread. How are we to identify and prevent harassment when society hasn't even defined intimacy?

Sexuality is among the most sensitive, all-consuming aspects of our lives. As such it renders us extremely vulnerable. If we abuse it, we risk dreadful consequences. But if we don't, if we're able to approach sexuality mindfully, it can bring wonderful rewards.

Human beings in the civilized world have labored long and hard to attain a level of dignity that distinguishes us from the animals. Though our physical body is similar to that of an animal, we do not live by the dictates of the body; we take great pride in the fact that we are guided by our intellect. We don't eat all the time, even though the body would like to. We eat only when our intelligence tells us it is appropriate to eat. We are physical beings with physical needs, yet we rise above them when the occasion calls for it. A mother may be utterly exhausted, but if her baby is crying, she finds the energy to tend to the child. A man may be weak, but if he sees someone pinned under a truck, he will be able to lift the truck, not by the strength of his body but by the strength of will that resides and abides in his *neshama*, his soul.

We live in accordance with our *neshamas*, to the degree that we can. That's our claim to fame; it's what defines us as human. Hence, as any given human being grows and matures, he or she is gradually shifting the center of gravity from the physical aspect of existence to the mind and the soul, with a sense of purpose, so as not to live like an animal. Sometimes we're successful at this. Sometimes not so much. So the civilized human being works very hard at bringing his or her sexuality under control. Its power can be overwhelming. It can take years to learn to regulate our sexuality with consistency, so that we are in charge, rather than under its influence. People who have finally more or less reined in their sexuality don't appreciate anyone coming along to upset the applecart and disturb the order they've established for themselves. They need other people's consideration and respect.

Sexual harassment in its most violent form, as in rape, is different from any other violation. If someone hits me over the head, I am a victim of his violence. It has almost nothing to do with me; it's *his* violence that has made me a victim. If someone breaks into my house and steals my belongings, I am a victim of his greed, but it's not a moral failure on my part. I've just lost some stuff. But if someone interferes with my sexuality, whether in an overt attack or by harassing me sexually, it's not just his or her sexuality that I'm a victim of; I am a victim of my *own* sexuality having been disturbed. That's why it is a much more intimate violation. I'm not just a victim of something bad within you; you're violating and traumatizing something that resides within me.

Harassment, therefore, is merely a subtle form of rape. You're forcing me into a sexual encounter, knowing that I am vulnerable, because we are all sexual beings and you're taking advantage of that.

To use a somewhat vulgar example, take the boy who says to the girl, "Oh, come on. You enjoy it as much as I do." Well, that may be true, but that's precisely why we need to get a handle on our sexuality—all the more reason not to harass her, because he knows very well that she's vulnerable in this area. In other words, her sexuality is her weakness, and in that regard she may well be weaker than he is. She may not even be fully aware of what's happening, being either too young or too naïve to know what her sexuality is all about. To take advantage of her weakness is the epitome of immorality.

Every human being has a certain model or conceptual structure within which he or she frames sexuality, depending on one's values or morals or upbringing, and that framework provides the basis of how we bring our sexuality under control. We spend our lives trying to master this nature. We should be in charge of our sexuality rather than the other way around. We should want to be a *mensch*, a person of integrity, not an animal. But if we don't think our way through it and put these ideas into practice, if we fail to control or master our sexuality, we will in fact be diminished to the level of an animal.

Loss of Innerness

Where does the expression *sex object* come from? When a person says, "Don't treat me like an object," what kind of object is he or she referring to? A toaster? An alarm clock? No, we're talking about the human body. Yes, the body is an object, and if you look at me solely as a body without considering the soul, then all you are seeing is an object.

There was once an old man who was very ill. Fortunately, the woman living next door was able to go every morning to his little hut and spoonfeed him cereal. The old man was appalled. In desperation he wrote a letter to his son, saying, "You must come immediately. Something terrible is happening. A woman keeps coming into my house. It's not right."

The son came rushing over and, after investigating and appraising the situation, said to his father, "I'm not sure what you're panicking about. You're eighty-four years old, and you're sick. You are so weak you can't even get out of bed. She's eighty-seven, and she comes and feeds you cereal. What's to worry about?"

"I see you don't understand human nature. Don't you know that *desire* could suddenly make me well and her young?"

A human being is sexual twenty-four hours a day, from the moment he is born to the moment he dies. That's a definition of a normal, healthy, red-blooded human being, and that's the nature of our sexuality.

Harassment means, first and foremost, the callousness that allows you the audacity to take advantage of my disadvantage. It's *chutzpah*, and it's immoral. And second, to add insult to injury, you're treating me as though I had no soul. You insist that I'm probably enjoying it as much as you do. But that can't be true, because even though our bodies might be on the same page, our souls are not.

Now the question is, if the body says yes and the soul says no, to whom do you listen? Which part of you is more important? There are plenty of people who think the soul doesn't count, the soul doesn't know what's good for it. It's what the body says and wants that matters. How could you say no to what the body wants?

It feels good! When you say no, you must not mean it—why would you say no to something so enjoyable?

To take this a step further, sexual harassment isn't just when somebody walks in, gives you that sly grin, and closes the door. If you were to put a little boy into a kindergarten classroom where the rest of the class consists of little girls, that's also harassment. Nobody would go to jail for it, but it's still harassment, because in that context the little boy cannot behave naturally. It makes him uncomfortable to be surrounded by girls. It oppresses and stifles him. He needs to suppress his emotions to fit in. Then when it's time for high school the boy becomes the quarterback on the football team, and he's surrounded by cheerleaders. That too is harassment, because if you're a normal teenage boy and you're surrounded by cheerleaders, you cannot breathe, you cannot smile, you're afraid to make a move lest you make a bad impression. You probably don't even recognize it, but it's a terrible kind of harassment that makes you feel neither normal nor natural. And yet we expect him to handle it.

A group of seventeen year olds once consulted me on the kosher dietary laws. They wanted to know what kinds of food to pack while on a camping trip. I asked them who was going on this excursion, and they replied, "four boys and four girls." I promptly told them I could not help them, because four boys and four girls on a camping trip together is already not kosher, never mind about the food. These very clean-cut and no doubt good kids were offended. They said, "Rabbi, we've been doing this for years. We grew up together. We went to the same school together. We've known one another since kindergarten. Nothing inappropriate happens! In fact last year my sleeping bag caught fire and I had to share the sleeping bag with a girl. And nothing happened."

"In that case," I said, "you don't need a rabbi—you need therapy."

Is it not a tragedy when a seventeen-year-old boy can share a sleeping bag with a seventeen-year-old girl and nothing happens? Obviously they shouldn't share that sleeping bag, but if they do, they are bound to have some strong feelings. Why was he proud of the fact that nothing happened? Who did this to him? Who did this to *them*? Who did this to an entire generation? Since when is this a virtue? This is not the way God created the world. It is a sad loss.

A man and a woman alone together is itself a sexual event. Even if nothing else happens, not even an unholy thought, it is nonetheless a violation of modesty. We are sexual beings. If we no longer have normal sexual responses or reactions, this is not an indication of our sophistication or heightened state of spirituality; it's a sign of decadence. And it drives a society to pornography, because if not with a real person, then with what? Some artificial, unnatural, ridiculous, imaginary form of sex? What happens when pornography becomes commonplace? What's next?

What's happening in our society in general is that we've turned ourselves outward so much, particularly since the 1960s, that what used to have great *inner* significance has lost its meaning. That which used to be shared only in intimate circumstances and with focused intention has lost its intimacy and its focus. It's as though we have nothing left that is so private and sacred that sharing it constitutes genuine intimacy.

The idea of modesty, the preservation of intimacy so that our sexuality remains meaningful, is of biblical origin. It saves us from becoming jaded or callous. Our grandparents had it. It has been that way for thousands of years. But in recent times we have tested it. We've been subjects in a vast experiment to see what freedom can produce. We're expected to be open and casual and sharing, letting it all hang out, expressing every feeling we feel (or imagine we're feeling) with anyone and everyone, whether they want or don't want to listen. We've lost something in the process. We're now discovering through our own painful experience that our ancestors, though they may have seemed a little bit rigid, were on the right track.

Some people have argued that being rigid and closed is detrimental as well, as in what's known as the Catholic school girls' syndrome, wherein they rebel at the first whiff of freedom. It was this backlash, they say, that triggered the sexual revolution. The idea is correct to an extent, but it's been presented in such inflexible and harsh terms, without explanation, context, or nuance, that no one appreciates the how and the why and the wherefore. They base it on the erroneous assumption that people are inevitably going to misbehave if allowed to do so. But it's not principally about the misbehavior. It's about the fact that when something is truly understood to be sacred, special, and intimate, we will treat it with respect.

An Antidote

Harassment means we don't understand the dynamics of human sexuality. We think we can turn it on and turn it off whenever we want to, but we can't. It's always there, just under the surface, and because we are moral, decent, intelligent, sophisticated, and spiritual human beings, we keep it under the surface. But when you harass me, you're basically forcing my sexuality to the surface when I'm not prepared for it. I don't want it, and I don't like it.

The antidote is to gain respect for intimacy. The problem is not a lack of respect for women or men, or simply abuse of power, because many of these men are not power hungry, and they do genuinely respect women. And women are often just as guilty or ignorant for the same reason. What they lack is respect for intimacy. "What? We were just having fun!"

Another facet of the solution is to be sensitive to another person's dignity and feelings, to be respectful of the weakness that you see in another person. How do we respect a weakness, you might ask? If it's a weakness, shouldn't we work at it, fix it, correct it? Not at all. Not even between a husband and a wife. If the husband has a weakness, the only time his wife ought to discuss the weakness is when her husband brings it up for discussion. And vice versa.

For example, a wife comes home and says, “I’m so stupid. I blew it. I have a problem. I don’t know what I’m gonna do.” Or “I am so disorganized, I can’t get it together. I keep forgetting where I put things.” And the husband says, “Why don’t you . . . blah blah blah?” She is insulted. In her mind, she thinks, *I didn’t ask you.* In his mind, he responds, *Well, you brought it up.* But what she really means is “I mentioned it. I was reflecting on it. I was not inviting comments.” We can criticize ourselves, without inviting comments. “I’m allowed to comment, but you’re not.”

There’s a story in the Talmud about a woman who dragged a man to the Jewish court and sued him for humiliating her in public. She said, “We were out in the market and he pulled off my *sheitel*, my wig, from my head. He embarrassed me in front of everyone.” The court looked into it, found him guilty, and ruled that he had to pay damages for the insult. They settled the case and as the two were walking home she stopped to buy some beans. They walked along a little farther, and the bag of beans split wide open and the beans spilled all over the ground. She whipped off her head covering and started gathering up the beans in her wig. He was infuriated and dragged her back to court. “I want my money back,” he cried. “She says I insulted her when I took her wig off, and here she took it off for beans!” The court debated and came back with their decision: she may, you may not.

Similarly, when a person comes home and says, “You wouldn’t believe how stupid I am!” and the spouse says, “Ahh, yes, I know,” that’s harassment. If I’m willing to confess my weaknesses, don’t you take advantage of it. Don’t kick me when I’m down. If I talk about my faults or my weaknesses, you’re not invited to comment, even if we’ve been married for forty years.

Sensitivity to other people's weaknesses means to give due deference to their foibles. They are entitled to their weaknesses. Yes, they should overcome them. Yes, they should see someone about the problem, especially if part of the problem is that they don't wish to talk to you about it. But it's not for you to say. For example, if a wife goes to a marriage counselor and says, "My husband has a very serious problem. He never shows his emotions," the counselor should say, "It's none of your business. You married him as he is. Love him as he is and get off his case." That's good marriage counseling, albeit unprofitable.

Now, if the same husband of the same woman goes to the same counselor and says, "You know, my wife is really upset with me because I can't express myself," then the right response to him is, "Why don't you try? Open up. Grow up. You live with a person; you are torturing her. Do the right thing. Talk! Work on it." In other words, the husband's inability to express himself is a weakness, a human failing, a kind of emotional paralysis that calls for therapeutic assistance. It's the therapist's job to help him change. Yet the wife has to not just tolerate it but respect it.

Every person has a moral right to his or her weaknesses. We have to respect the space they create to protect themselves. If we don't, we're basically being immoral. Morality says that when you see a weakness in someone, don't take advantage of it. Walk carefully around it, avoid it, support it, and respect it. The person has worked so hard to get their fragile life together. Don't disturb it. Don't step on it. Don't enter where you're not invited.

If we could all cultivate this sensitivity, it would make us better and more decent people. In many ways, our ancestors understood this; they wouldn't call attention to another's failing or stick their noses where they knew it might hurt. It wasn't that they put up with each other because it was unfashionable or unthinkable back then to divorce. It wasn't because they lacked intelligence or sophistication or lived emotionally stifled lives. No; they were simply honorable, dignified human beings. They saw all the faults in one another and took care to tread lightly. That's what it means to be a *mensch*.

A Respect for Gender

The issue we are discussing here, which the media have been addressing so eagerly of late, is the abuse of power. Or perhaps more accurately, the injustice and hurtfulness of people who use their power to abuse others. Many people with power assume their might gives them the right to do things to others that for anyone else would be simply unacceptable.

It is, of course, a moral concern. However if all we're able to do about it is pass legislation to make certain acts or words illegal, that is not necessarily a moral advancement. It would be rather awkward and utterly unnatural, for example, if our laws were to look upon any attention that a man shows to a woman *because she is a woman* as offensive.

Let's consider what the Torah had to say concerning this topic over two thousand years ago. In the Talmudic tractate *Pirkei Avot*, the Ethics of the Fathers, one of the sages tells us, "Do not speak too much to the woman. This is said with reference to one's own wife; how much more so does it apply to the wife of another. Hence the sages have declared, 'whoever indulges excessively in conversation with the woman causes evil to himself.' "

The first question all the commentaries ask is, "What constitutes *too much*?" And how would one measure this? It's an open-ended, puzzling statement, or so it seems.

Some translations render it, "Do not gossip with women." But this is not helpful, because the Torah of course forbids gossip between men as well. Another translation renders it as, "Don't speak overmuch to women." But how much is overmuch? Are we talking about counting words?

What is even more difficult to understand is the logic behind the statement that speaking too much to women "causes evil to himself." Are they serious? Where does such a seemingly presumptuous notion come from?

What then is the deeper meaning of the admonition not to make conversation with the woman, not even with your wife, and certainly not with other people's wives—in other words, with women in general? What does it mean to "make conversation" or speak too much?

And another question, perhaps the most mysterious is, "What is the reason for the term the sage uses, *ha isha—the* woman, not just women, but *the* woman?"

There is a tendency among men to carry on the sort of conversation with a woman that he wouldn't necessarily have with another man. The reverse is probably true as well; if a woman is attracted to a man, she might contrive a conversation she wouldn't otherwise engage in if she were speaking to a woman. By Jewish Law, neither one of these is kosher.

A modern-day example: it is not unusual for two men to sit next to each other on an eight-hour flight without a single word being exchanged between them. If a guy is sitting next to a woman, however, suddenly he finds something to say. It doesn't matter what it is. If he asks her, "How long is the flight?" that's more than likely too much, because he's making conversation when he actually has *nothing* to say.

So the question is not really about *how much* conversation; it's whether the conversation is legitimate. Would he ask or say that to a man, or is this a conversation invented for some extraneous motive?

This is astoundingly ahead of its time. The Talmud is saying, "Do not talk to a woman as though she were an object." Why would you make conversation when you have nothing to say? Because you are not talking to a woman, you are talking to *the* woman. You have objectified the person. This, we are told, is forbidden. Plainly, we are not allowed to make this sort of conversation with any woman, not even one's wife, since a woman is not an object.

On the other hand, the sage is not telling us not to notice that a woman is a woman (which suggests another problematic trend that sows confusion in our society today). Rather, he is saying that there are human beings; some are males and some are females. Treat a man like a man and a woman like a woman, but never like an object.

We might be tempted to try to train ourselves not to notice the opposite gender in order to avoid accusations of abuse (as if once you notice, there's bound to be some kind of misbehavior or micro-aggression). It would be really sad if a compliment addressed to a woman were to be considered sexual harassment. Women might have to resort to covering themselves up completely, where you not only can't discern whether she is good-looking, you can't even know whether she is a woman. That is far from the Torah's intent. There might even come a time, God forbid, when if a man were to say to a woman, "You look good today," he'd go straight to jail, however innocent the compliment may have been. You noticed that she is a woman. And you don't usually tell men that they look good. You are, therefore, guilty as charged.

How, then, do we establish a healthy, respectful standard of behavior, one that is balanced and natural, neither denying nor abusing our respective genders?

The first thing is to acknowledge, as the secular world has now begun to discover, that it is neither natural nor realistic to expect that men and women can have platonic relationships. It doesn't work, and it shouldn't work. Imagine if a man were to say to a woman, "I am very comfortable with you. I don't even think of you as a woman." Well, if you don't think of me as a woman, just whom are you befriending? I am a woman.

"We can't have platonic relationships" does not mean that the only way you can relate to a woman is sexually. What it means is, you cannot have a relationship with a woman without respecting the fact that she is a woman. *Platonic* suggests indifference. Indifference is never good for any relationship, and moreover it is profoundly detrimental to the human condition: it causes us to die inside.

A man in a healthy relationship with a woman is conscious of the fact that she is a woman, acknowledges that she is a woman, and treats her accordingly. To attempt to maintain a platonic relationship is to ignore or deny that she is a woman.

There was a man running for the presidency who was accused of being in a hotel room with his secretary overnight. He said nothing happened. Being alone in a hotel room is nothing? That's too platonic. What he means to say is nothing sexual happened; but being alone is intimacy. That's either appropriate or inappropriate. But it's not nothing. Being alone in a room with a person of the opposite sex is something. You can't call it nothing. If it *were* nothing, when would it begin to be something? When one of you is offended? Conversely, a husband and a wife going into a room together should never be nothing; it should be the beginning of intimacy. Being alone together is intimacy.

Platonic means attempting to ignore the fact that a man is a man and a woman is a woman. That breaks down the whole male/female dynamic, which is the very source of life, the energy that keeps all life growing and multiplying. If that gets ruined, never mind going to jail, we are going to become extinct.

The recognition and acknowledgment of our respective genders are absolutely essential to our survival. Trying to be completely platonic is not only perilous, it's insulting. That does not mean it's okay to feel we have some right to cross a boundary uninvited. Not noticing and not respecting a woman are two different phenomena, and they're both wrong. How do we balance this? How can we be keenly aware that a woman is a woman and a man is a man and nonetheless safely avoid being offensive or trespassing?

We can't clearly understand harassment, intimacy, or sexuality without recognizing that what is sexual is not necessarily intimate, and vice versa. Consider what's going on at campuses around the world among young people today. We used to read about how teenagers were out of control with their raging hormones and hyperactive sexuality. Today, although they are doing things their ancestors would never have even thought of, it's utterly casual. Even many of the things sexual predators are being accused of are not actual sex. It's more like grown men playing doctor, acting out all sorts of childish fantasies. If it were sex, there would at least be some modicum of respect. It's as though in place of a man saying to a woman, "I am sexually attracted to you," he's saying, "I want to expose myself to you." It's downright disrespectful. The insult is worse than the injury.

What's happening today more and more is that sex without intimacy—described in the 1960s as free love—has lost its appeal. What people are doing is what used to be called pornography. They no longer are willing to pay for pornography, because people are now living pornography.

As a result of years, decades, and generations of failing to heed the counsel of our sages, our boundaries today have become scrambled. Even when harassment is not the issue, we seem to have lost sight of how to be intimate when intimacy is positive, necessary, and appropriate. The result is that we now trespass boundaries when we ought to be honoring them, and we're not sharing intimacy when the borders should be open.

The good news is that it's become painfully obvious that it's time for change.

13

I'm a Terrible Person

Okay, so you had a nasty thought. Or you did something you knew was wrong. Welcome to reality.

It is absolutely essential, *Tanya* teaches, to serve God with joy, with *simcha*. *Simcha* is nonnegotiable. To attempt to practice Judaism without joy is not only unacceptable, it's not even the real thing.

How, then, are we supposed to be joyful, when there are so many reasons to be miserable? We are constantly assaulting ourselves with nasty thoughts, negative emotions, and deplorable desires. What chance do we have?

A major loss of joy comes from the remorse we feel over our failings. Each of us harbors an awareness of our misdeeds and faults. It's an inner voice that says, "How could you have done such a despicable thing? Look at this mess you have made! You blew it!" We want to do good, yet we are drawn to do exactly the opposite.

There is good guilt, and there is bad guilt.

Teshuvah is generally translated as repentance. The conventional assumption about repentance is that if you did something wrong, you should feel bad and sad. Your conscience tells you that when you commit a sin there must be a price to pay. And the price, most would agree, is that you now have no right to happiness. Show us you're miserable, and we'll know you are truly sorry.

The Alter Rebbe, author of the *Tanya,* says otherwise: repentance is not at all about misery. "Serve God with joy" remains the watchword. This is not a popular idea among religious people, who believe that all sins are punishable by gloom, and that sadness is a mandatory part of the deal.

A young man writes to the Rebbe, discouraged, disheartened, giving up—because he is *really bad*. The Rebbe writes back. "Think positively. Be optimistic. Serve God with joy."

So he writes again. "If the Rebbe knew how bad I am, he would not tell me to be happy."

The Rebbe answers. "I doubt whether *you* know how bad you are. And I'm still telling you that you should be happy."

This is the moral of our story: if you really knew how bad you were, you would stop being bad. *Feeling* bad does nothing to make you better. On the contrary. Are you feeling bad about your misbehavior? How bad is it? If all it does is make you feel bad, you couldn't be thinking that it's all that bad. If you truly understood *how* bad it is, you wouldn't feel bad. You'd become better.

This is what the Alter Rebbe says in *Tanya*: a person who is depressed over his sins thinks his feeling bad is a sign of virtue. He has a conscience. He thinks he's doing *teshuvah*. But it's really just part of the sin. There's a part of every sin that depresses you. And that can be worse than the sin itself.

Religious misery is the worst kind of misery, and it can afflict even nonreligious people. The guilt, whether conscious or subconscious, can be gut-wrenching. In the time of the Baal Shem Tov, the founder of modern Chassidism, good people everywhere had been suffering for naught, miserable because they thought they were supposed to be. The Baal Shem Tov came along and offered a glimpse of hope. And two generations later his successor, the Alter Rebbe, clarified these teachings in ways that have become universally accessible.

In essence, he says to us, "You have done some really bad stuff you weren't supposed to do. Do *teshuvah.* Resolve to set aside some time to work on yourself, instead of indulging in negative feelings about your misbehavior. Guilt is not measured by how bad you are; it's how much pain you caused, and to whom. Is there something better you can strive for? You were created with a purpose, a significant mission in life. Why let sin get in the way? You have so much to do that is noble, valuable, and important. Can you be a proactive part of something worthwhile?"

This is why God gave us *mitzvahs.* Now you can do something useful, notwithstanding your nastiness. That would be real *teshuvah.* And you do *teshuvah* with *simcha.*

You have a Godly soul, which is the fullness of who you are; and then you have an unGodly soul, this annoying little pest called a *yetzer hara*—an "evil inclination"—that's all trouble, all the time, and won't leave you alone. Godliness means doing for God what He needs and making Him happy. It might as well make you happy too. If it's your desire to do something for Him, why do it with a frown? If God invited you into His palace, put on a smile before you go.

How to Beat the Blues

Maybe you're feeling bad about yourself, not because of anything you did, but because you're just a grubby character. Could be you don't like yourself at all. You're upset because you are riddled with nasty thoughts, vulgar feelings, petty impulses, foolish attractions. It doesn't make a difference that you didn't *act* on them; you're bothered by the fact that you are *tempted* to sin. But this isn't about sin. So it doesn't call for *teshuva.* It calls for a personality change.

This melancholy is more difficult to overcome when you think it's justified: you should be ashamed of yourself. And you are. Shame permeates your entire sense of who you are and defines your personality to the core.

Here too *Tanya* weighs in. There's nothing positive, humble, or admirable about these abject feelings of worthlessness. It's not humility, says the Alter Rebbe; it's arrogance. Why? Because you are imagining that you ought to be a *tzaddik*—a flawless, infallible, impeccably righteous specimen of human perfection. Whatever gave you this idea? You are neither capable, nor expected, nor destined to be a *tzaddik*. If you're utterly astounded at your own unholy thoughts or feelings, you are out of touch with your own reality. It shouldn't come as a surprise. You need to get over yourself and be all you *can* be.

Your mission, should you choose to accept it, is to be subject to all these negative, sinful thoughts and to subdue them. You think you're a lowlife? Do something that affords you a sense of purpose, something slightly more noble and more respectable than you're accustomed to doing. With one small act of integrity you can override and rise above your lowliness. If you have evil thoughts but you don't actually sin, you should be happy that you're successfully accomplishing your mission. You're doing exactly what you're created to do.

Imagine a guy who goes for marriage counseling and says, "I have no idea how to make my wife happy. I've tried and tried and I'm clueless. I am a terrible husband, I'm a loser, and I'm miserable." So the counselor calls the wife and says, "What does your husband need to do to make you happy?" And she answers, "Me? What are you talking about? I'm perfectly happy." Turns out, when he says, "I'm so upset because she's not happy," he really means himself. We do the same with God. We have a hard time being joyful because we think God is not happy with us. We beat ourselves up because He's angry at us. We assume He'll never forgive us so we can stay depressed. It's yet another scheme of that pesky old *yetzer hara*.

But here's the deal. Who made us like this? God created an evil inclination and gave it to you. Was it a trap, a setup? Don't you think that given His infinite prescience, He knew you'd surely fall prey to its seductive charms? Yet He did it anyway. You're *supposed* to have this *yetzer hara*. Your "fatal flaw" is designed precisely and exclusively for you, because when you do manage to overcome temptation, even if it's only once in a while, it makes Him very happy. This is the darkness which only you can transform to light.

Regret is something else entirely. Don't confuse it with misery. Whereas sadness is lifeless, regret is a symptom of being fully alive. It's the beginning of the change you need to make. *I did it. I regret it. It was wrong, and I won't do it again.* That's true remorse. It signifies movement: you're flowing and growing—quite the opposite of feeling stuck and miserable. To choose to be miserable without real regret is to remain stagnant, until you're ready to acknowledge the need to change.

There's an eye-opening story about the previous Chabad Rebbe that illustrates the difference between misery and regret. When he first came to America in the early 1940s, the Rebbe had a doctor who used to come to his home and give him injections to treat his paralysis. They became friendly, and the doctor would often come by just to sit and talk with the Rebbe.

On one such occasion the doctor noticed an ashtray full of cigarette stubs. The Rebbe was at the time a very heavy smoker. The doctor then mentioned that current research seemed to indicate that smoking was detrimental to one's health. This was long before this became common knowledge.

Later in the conversation the doctor, who was himself a smoker, took out a pack of cigarettes and offered one to the Rebbe.

The Rebbe declined, and said, "I don't smoke." The doctor registered surprise, and the Rebbe explained, "You told me, not even a half hour ago, that it's not healthy to smoke. So I don't smoke."

That's called regret. Having realized it was wrong, to the Rebbe it was immediately out of the question. From that moment on he no longer smoked. There was no "Really? I have to stop? Can I have at least one last cigarette?" Or "Maybe I could smoke less and less gradually over time?"

When the Rebbe said, "I don't smoke," he meant "I am free."

This is the true meaning of freedom of choice: *I can liberate myself. I am free to assume whatever identity I desire. I can choose to see myself having the character and capabilities that will serve me well.* The reason we are often miserable about our failings is not because we failed, but because we refuse to *think* of ourselves as failures. There are times when the ability to reframe or alter our self-image may in fact be imperative.

When you decide you're going to be better, it cannot result from some dark and dismal process. True regret means simply that the person who used to do whatever it was you used to do—smoke, party like a rock star, eat nonkosher food, work on *Shabbos*, whatever—no longer lives inside your mind and heart. It can happen in an instant. You have the freedom to choose who you want to be, and what identity you wish to take upon yourself. Nobody can take that away from you.

Is that not reason enough to be joyful?

A woman who came to one of our programs told me she had been miserable for most of her life. At some point she figured out that this had begun when she was six years old. There was an incident where her mother punished her, at which time the thought crossed her mind that she'd like to take a knife and kill her mother. It was just a fleeting thought, and it passed, but she couldn't live with herself, thinking she was some kind of monster. She was distraught at the notion that she could actually imagine something so horrible. This triggered a depression that lasted for forty years, even though she hadn't acted on the impulse, never said it out loud, and most of the time didn't think about it at all. You see something in yourself that is totally unacceptable, and you plunge into despair. It doesn't take much more than that. And there's no human being in the world who doesn't suffer from something like this.

In order to survive such a basically self-made trauma, our mind plays a little trick: we turn our negative feelings inside out and project them toward the other. Throughout years of therapy, all this woman talked about was how angry she was at her mother and how she had to quell the anger and forgive her mother. The therapist tried convincing her that her anger was justified. It helped not one iota, because neither her mother nor her anger was the issue. Her real issue was that she couldn't accept herself, because she was a monster. And the more they talked about it, the worse she felt. How do you escape the sort of sadness that no apology will assuage? You can't say, "I'm so sorry I'm the kind of person who long ago had a fantasy that I could kill my mother."

Chassidus sheds light on such situations, and it's pretty straightforward: those nasty, unholy, evil deeds you keep thinking about? Wrestle them into submission. Continue to dismiss them and breathe a sigh of relief. God's plan is not that you should never have bad thoughts. The plan is to have bad thoughts and not act on them. Your flaws are the very character traits that empower you to fulfill God's purpose—which is to increase goodness and defeat darkness. Serving God saves us from ourselves.

Imagine a person who wakes up in the morning, opens his eyes, and discovers a hammer in his hand. He wonders why he has a hammer. Maybe he's supposed to be a carpenter. If he's supposed to be a carpenter, that's probably why he has a hammer. If you wake up with a calculator in your hand, what does that tell you?

You're probably supposed to be an accountant. If you wake up with tremendous anger inside, guess what? You're supposed to master the anger. Anger is a nasty and unholy trait, but that doesn't make you the devil. God needs anger fixed, and He gave you the job. Fix it. The same is true of jealousy, greed, whatever. They're given to whomever they're given, to refuse, deny, and reject, until they are diminished, denied, and weakened.

It's not your fault, and it's not your mother's fault. You weren't misbegotten or born evil. You were born with a job. There's no reason to be sad, ever. If you're unhappy, it just means that you haven't yet reached the core awareness that just as you were given money to invest, love to share, and knowledge to spread, you are given anger and greed to control and subdue. And you're doing it.

14

Transforming the Past

Even if it is broke, why fix it? Celebrate how great it is. And will be. And was.

What's done is done, conventional wisdom confidently proclaims. As surely as the clock ticks, as relentlessly as weeks and months and years fly by, we cannot change the past. Or can we? The answer to this may not be as obvious as it appears. In fact there are discussions in the Chassidic literature suggesting that we can change the past—not just as a plot device in some science fiction fantasy, but in light of a certain mysterious philosophical concept of time. Even assuming this is true, however, what difference does it make? Practically speaking, doesn't the question seem irrelevant? Whatever happened in the past, today remains today. That was then; now is now. And the same is true for whatever may unfold tomorrow. What's important and necessary is that we handle, today, the day-by-day demands of the hour. But let's come back to this after revisiting an all-too-common emotion we touched upon in the previous chapter: regret.

Regret comes in two flavors. There's regret for what could have been, and there's regret for what should have been. If I regret not having purchased a piece of real estate thirty years ago because it would be worth a fortune by now, I'm regretting what could have been. If I regret not having given charity to that poor guy and leaving him to suffer instead, I'm regretting not only what I could have done, but what I should have done.

There are two differences between them. Number one: validity. If we regret what *could* have been, are we even sure there's anything to regret? A guy says, "I could have bought that building for nine dollars thirty years ago, and now I'd be rich." Is that true? How do we know it's true? Maybe something would have happened to that property, to that location, or even to the real estate market, and the guy would actually just be out nine dollars, period. What he thinks he could have done might have been the absolute worst decision. There are no guarantees. Whereas, when we regret what *should* have been, the regret is valid by definition. Yes, you should have been nicer. Yes, of course, you should have been kinder. Yes, you certainly should have been more respectful. What's the question?

Then there's difference number two: does the regret effect any change? Will it improve anything at all? "I really, truly regret that the building isn't mine." Can this wish that he had done what he could have done, but didn't do, make the building his? Maybe slightly? A little bit, a tiny bit? No, not at all. "But I regret it *very* sincerely, deeply, with all my heart!" Nope, sorry, nothing has changed. The building does not, will not, *cannot* become a little bit his.

Whereas when we regret what should have been—"I should have been nicer to my friend"—the regret itself makes me nicer. If we truly, sincerely wish we had been more sensitive, then we have become more sensitive. If you really regret having been disrespectful to your mother, you have become a more respectful child. This kind of regret accomplishes something. It moves you to where you ought to be.

If you're gonna have regrets, skip the ones about what could have been. The only valid sort of regret is about what should have been. By regretting what should have been, the regret itself brings you closer to your goal. You are now more of what you should be. It was worth the effort, worth the expenditure of emotional energy. It was time well spent.

History and Vision

There is a famous story about a government minister in Russia who paid a visit to the Alter Rebbe while he was imprisoned by the tzar for alleged treason.

The minister, who was something of a Bible scholar, asked the Rebbe, "What does it mean when after Adam eats from the Tree of Knowledge, God asks him, 'Where are you?' Does He have to ask? Doesn't the Almighty already know where His creations are?"

"God is always asking us where we are," answered the Alter Rebbe. "Since the beginning of time, in the Garden of Eden, God has continually been asking each of us, all His creations, '*Aiyeka?*' Where are you?"

At the time Adam had been ten hours old. God wanted to know (or rather, wanted Adam to know), "So, what have you accomplished thus far? What contributions have you made? How have you advanced in the mission and the purpose for which you were created?"

This fundamental question echoes through the chambers of time and continues to be posed to each one of us, every moment of our lives. Indeed, if we were here for a month, a year, forty years, eighty years, God would keep on asking us what we know now that we didn't know yesterday. Where are we? What do we think and feel today that we didn't think or feel yesterday?

Human beings are such creatures of habit that if we don't consciously ask ourselves this question, we could be having the greatest of experiences yet remain unmoved and unchanged. Our habits can be so stubborn and strong, they draw us right back to our routine, and we lose the transformative power of progress.

What if our honest answer to the question is that we're somewhere we shouldn't be? How can a person make up for lost time and lost ground, stumbling down ugly roads? Can we actually transform our past? Are we really capable of making lasting changes?

Let's roll back a couple of chapters from Adam's conversation with God to the sixth day of the Creation story, the Friday of the first week. After having brought everything into being, including humanity (i.e., Adam), God saw all that He had made, and it was *very good.* Until then His assessment of His handiwork had been merely "good." Why add *very* all of a sudden?

It was because with the creation of Adam, as perfect and complete as God's Creation had been until now, *change* became possible. On the one hand, the world God creates is good; yet in a certain sense it is not yet all it can be. With Adam in the picture it can fulfill its great potential. That's *very* good.

Of course, for the world to be improved, it needs the ability to stop being what it is and start being what it is becoming, which is why God created time. Since He creates everything *in order to be changed,* if there were no time, change would not be possible. The world of a moment ago no longer exists, because the world of a moment ago is now the past. But a moment from now is yet to be. Therefore we have the power to make it what we want it to be. The world has become fluid and flexible, awaiting our improvement. We can overrule the rigid expectations of what will be tomorrow, and have an *effect* on tomorrow. As God's partner in Creation, as junior creators, we can bring out the potential that exists within everything God created. We can see this clearly in the Hebrew language, in which the word for year is *shanah,* which means *change*;

and the word for month is *chodesh*, which means *new*. The nature of time is that it's always new and always ready for change.

This doesn't change the fact that apparently we still can't change yesterday. Bygones are bygones. According to the nature of time we've just described, we can't fix what was, because it isn't anymore. It's gone. And yet, we *can* rectify the mistakes we have made, which is an essential part of fulfilling the potential within our world and in our lives. By working with what *is* and changing it into what is *yet to be*, we can remake what *was*. The secret of transforming our past is literally by transforming the present.

This ability is unique to humankind. We are the creatures who are able to remember the past and foresee the future. The Talmud says, "Who is wise? He who can see what is being born." We are endowed with the capability of seeing what is to come, not through prophecy, but through wisdom, and understanding, and knowledge of consequences.

Change and rectification are part and parcel of *teshuvah*, which, as we've discussed, is better translated as *return* rather than repentance. Return to what, you might ask? Good question. The short answer is, return to our original self; or more precisely to that aspect of ourselves which is and always has been in a state of perfection and in need of no change. This is the Godly soul, and since it's the need for change that necessitates the existence of time, the soul is not affected by time. That's in effect what *Godly* means: that it always was and always will remain unchanged, just as God is/was/will be. When it comes to the Godly soul, there is nothing new.

Teshuvah used to be understood on the basis of the idea that as humans, we are riddled with personal issues and deplorable character traits that we need to fix in order to undo whatever damage we've done. In our times we've seen a radical readjustment of our entire notion of *teshuvah*. The emphasis is not on what's horribly wrong and needs to be repaired, but on the Godly soul, and our ability to choose to be Godly in our actions, our perceptions, and even our feelings. We have the option of choosing morality or immorality, Godliness or its opposite. The theme of today's generation is that we don't need any new inventions, and we don't need a do-over. We have everything we need; we already are everything we need to be. Therefore don't try to fix what isn't right. Celebrate the Godliness that is. Today, change means just be yourself, in the fullest sense of who you are. And if you find yourself in the habit of doing something that's not consistent with who you are, just stop. It's almost like saying that the biggest change you can make is to stop changing.

Because God desires a genuine relationship with us, and a real relationship cannot be coerced, He gives us the prerogative to decide whether to accept or reject Him. With each passing day, with every choice we make, we get either closer to or further away from our Creator. We are either more willing or less willing to do it His way. As a result, we *perceive* Godliness either more clearly or less clearly. It's a living relationship that is ever-evolving and ever-changing from moment to moment.

There are of course some things that are and will remain beyond the scope of freedom of will. Moral issues and Torah laws are among the principles we cannot and are not required to decide for ourselves. Not that we have no choice exactly—there's always the option to rebel—but consequences are what they are, and not in our control. And destiny is destiny. We'll look into that more in depth when we get into the topic, or topics, of marriage.

The Secret of the Sixth Day

Speaking of marriage and of ever-evolving relationships, let's go back once more to our Creation story in the biblical account. We'll discover an intriguing and useful parallel between our relationship with Godliness, and the dynamics of what goes on between a husband and a wife. And we'll see how all that sheds light on what's really happening when we do *teshuvah.*

"Let there be light," said God, and sure enough there was light. Heaven was created on the second day; grasses and herbs and trees on the third; and the sun and the moon and the stars on the fourth. (Right here, by the way, is irrefutable proof of the divine Creation of the world. Only God could get away with saying, "Let's first have the grasses and trees and *then* the sun.")

After the creation of man on the sixth day, God looks over everything He has made and declares, as we've said, that it's *very good.* Wonderful. But soon thereafter He says, "It is *not good* for man to be alone. I will create for him a woman." Hold on a second—what just happened here? Did the Almighty change His mind? Did God just pronounce that everything is good and then suddenly remember, *Oh, wait, it's not actually so good after all*?

The Talmud explains that when God said it was not good, He didn't mean that it isn't good for *Adam* to be alone; God was referring to Himself: "It's not good for *Me* if man were to exist alone. The natural world, in and of itself, doesn't need the existence of woman," said God, "but *I do.*" Why? Because God's intention in creating the world was *change.* He had created a world that was perfectly imperfect—perfectly prepared to be transformed into what He needs it to become. And Adam was His designated agent of change. But man can't handle that all by himself. What God was saying was, "I will now create someone who will help Adam change the world; not to help him with *his* needs, but to help him fulfill *My* needs. My need is to bring holiness to this world. I need man to make this world a dwelling place for holiness." So God created woman to help man do what God needed the two of them, together, to do.

Reading between the lines we can infer that there's a fundamental difference between a man and a woman with respect to *change.* In very broad strokes we could say that man is himself in need of improvement, whereas woman is created precisely as she needs to be. Take for example the blessing a woman makes each day in the morning prayers, thanking God for having "created me in accordance with His will." She may desire or need to grow, to become a better person, a better friend, or a more nurturing mother, but not to become *more of a woman*, per se. She is a nurturer by nature. She does not need to change the essence of who she is.

A man, however, lives with a deeply embedded anxiety that he needs to become more of a *mensch*, whatever that may mean. The male ego lives with a ghost that haunts him, telling him that no matter how much he has accomplished, his net worth is zero. Ceaselessly taunted by existential questions—*Who am I? What have I become? Am I there yet?*—he fears that he is dust, he is dirt, he amounts to nothing.

Even the strongest, wealthiest, most powerful and successful of men can find themselves living with such a demon. Extreme examples abound: Howard Hughes, for one, who achieved everything a man could possibly achieve. Or so you'd think. A billionaire magnate in the aviation industry, a Hollywood movie mogul, considered the most financially successful businessman in the world, Hughes's inescapable feeling of insignificance plunged him into a paranoid, obsessive-compulsive nightmare of a life.

And another, still more extreme, and infinitely more malevolent man: Joseph Stalin. Stalin's personal demon was born of abject poverty in childhood, ridicule, shame, and betrayal. His paranoid inferiority complex drove him to a life of criminality, cold-blooded murder, and eventually mass exterminations, as one of history's most maniacal totalitarian dictators. Untold millions were killed at his command.

Even for us average guys, it can be a daunting task for a man to outgrow the internal anxieties he faces, let alone be truly happy and healthy. From his very first rite of passage as an infant, his circumcision, we see how a man is born imperfect. And so it goes, milestone by milestone, for the rest of his life. No sooner does he mature beyond being "Mommy's little boy" than he begins to bond with his father, then struggle to step forward, onward and upward, toward his own identity and greater and greater independence.

Eventually he will need to leave home to seek his fortune, the way all coming-of-age stories are told—to travel, explore, and wend his way through all sorts of adventures to discover himself. Is he then done? Is he man enough? Not likely. There is always more to becoming a man. If he fails to make certain turns at critical points in his life, he may remain stuck in his little-boy-hood, or simply become a grownup with no purpose or direction. He senses the danger and lives with this fear of annihilation, dreading the prospect that he may never become anything at all. So a man spends all his time and energy trying to comfort himself with great achievements, macho posturing, impressing all the girls, and beating up everyone on the block, all to prove he's a something.

A woman, on the other hand, might consider herself anywhere between a one and a ten, but she's never a zero. She's more grounded from the time she was born. She doesn't feel the sort of pressure a man endures to undergo fundamental change. She can move on confidently from being "Mommy's little girl" to becoming a mommy herself; a girl doesn't have to go far in a quest for transformation to claim her identity. She may fear mistreatment or abuse, but she has no fear of annihilation. And because she's not preoccupied with a demon, as men are, she is readily available to others as a nurturer. A woman is created complete, as a model or an example of what God wants man to achieve, with her help. She's his indispensable associate. Only together with her does a man have what it takes to fulfill God's vision of His world.

What a man needs to do is give up on the idea of ever being anything but a zero. He needs to recognize that he started out as dust and will return to dust. It's what's known in Chassidic philosophy as *bitul*: the more you accept your own nothingness and stop fighting it like a demon, the more you can accomplish. You don't have to *be* great to do great things.

Accepting this fact is his key to liberation, and, ironically, empowerment. Once he makes peace with his ghost and realizes he is entirely in the service of his Creator, he can finally find focus, sharpen his attention, and take that complete turn toward change for the better. He stops being hung up on his own survival and begins to become a nurturer.

When men stop grappling with their demons and are no longer preoccupied with their existence, they become better able to empathize with and demonstrate sensitivity to the needs of others. Such men can be incredible nurturers, sometimes even more so than women, who are born nurturers. A mentor who has attained this stage of self-development can show a young man what it means to be a man, and introduce him to a life free of ghosts. The Rebbe is an unparalleled example and role model in this regard.

The nurturing mentor's job is first to validate the young man's struggle, to win his trust entirely without being judgmental or intimidating; and then to say, in essence, "You're a man. Stop fighting and start living your life. Do something useful." A mentor's support can be pivotal to a boy. If he expresses disapproval, even inadvertently, it can be shattering; if he endorses him, the boy is blessed. Whatever it takes—sometimes all it takes is a smile—the young man has to hear "You're okay. You don't need to become; you need to do." Then he can let go of his demon. He is ready to make a difference in the world.

A Country Bumpkin Comes of Age

A fascinating theme can be seen in nearly every classic fable or fairy tale, those seemingly silly stories that have been remembered and repeated over hundreds of years.

A powerful king is confronted with a grave problem. His daughter, the princess, has been kidnapped, and the king is devastated. To save the princess a dragon must be slayed. The king exhausts his great armies and mighty warriors, but all to no avail. Along comes a simple country bumpkin, who in his innocent, blundering way manages to slay the dragon and save the king's daughter. He then marries the princess, and they live happily ever after.

These stories demonstrate a profound psychological gimmick. They appeal to a boy's subconscious, and subliminally, every boy gets it: he is that country bumpkin who has yet to become a man. He waits for the opportunity to serve the king, to do something for an important person and gain his approval. That's how a boy becomes a man, by serving someone who is already a man. And now he's in: he's not only the dragon slayer, he gets the girl. He discovers his own feminine side. He can now be a nurturer. He is still that same country bumpkin, a nothing who has won the day.

Today's superhero stories generally fail to encourage our sons to serve or to earn their manhood, let alone develop the virtue of humility. To set them up for success in life we would do well to instill in them the wisdom of service, rather than the "I am the biggest and the best" fantasies they are accustomed to. The reality, of course, is that every boy knows he does not become a man by breaking through brick walls, flying faster than a speeding bullet, and fighting off multiple meanies with special-effect ninja moves.

Stories aside, as important as they are, there is really no substitute for an effective mentor. Not a superhero or a sports hero or a politician or a CEO; some of these people haven't yet become men themselves. They're still sparring with their own demons. A boy needs a positive role model whose approval will be meaningful and uplifting, who will help make him into a man.

A man, once he embraces his nothingness, is as comfortable as the woman, his role model who embraces her somethingness.

Now he can accomplish extraordinary success in life, sometimes more effectively than a woman.

This male/female phenomenon reflects a more spiritual dimension of the same reality. The Godly soul, unchanging, pure, and eternal, is analogous to the preeminent feminine characteristic of a woman: she too is by nature unconstrained by an obsessive need for change, such as we find among men. As we discussed above, she is essentially as God intended her to be. It's no accident that our Godly soul is called in Hebrew the *neshama*, which is grammatically a feminine word. And in the lyrical language of the *Midrash*, we see that when God speaks to the Godly soul, He calls it "My daughter." Whereas when He addresses the Jewish people in embodied form, signifying the masculine aspect of who we are, He says, "My son."

Men are subject to all sorts of struggles to effect the transformations we were put here to complete. Sometimes we even have to resort to violence to become victors instead of victims. It's a "guy thing." The feminine aspect of the universe, however, has no need to go to war or force its way to completion. A woman may appear to be a member of the "weaker sex," but we can see empirically that her hidden strengths can surpass the bravado of a man. How unfortunate it is, in fact how tragic, that even in our relatively enlightened times the masculine world can still have so little respect for feminine qualities. It's directly proportional to the way a materialistic society can show so little regard for the Godly soul.

Women are sometimes tempted to compete with men. If she gets no respect for being a woman, she may well choose to act like a man. "Anything you can do, I can do better." Jews are often tempted in this way as well, vis-à-vis the surrounding non-Jewish culture. If it's not popular to be Jewish, they'll adapt. "If you can't beat 'em, join 'em." This is a big mistake for women, and a grave mistake for Jews.

Following this train of thought, Chassidus teaches us that the Godly soul, the part of us that doesn't need fixing and represents the feminine side of the *Jew*, is by the same token the feminine aspect of *God*. The Godliness embedded in the essence of the soul doesn't need to be elevated, improved, or changed. It is already in a state of perfection. And this idea can in turn open our eyes to the true nature of *teshuvah*.

Like the word *neshama*, *teshuvah* too is feminine, both in the grammatical form of the word itself and in its meaning. *Teshuvah* means return, get back to that original essence that doesn't need fixing—in other words, the part of us that is feminine, complete. Celebrate the unblemished perfection of what is and always has been good, and that in itself will fix what is bad and broken. Rather than fight the darkness, bring in the light.

To do *teshuvah* is to move beyond all the remorse and regret and celebrate who we are. The only thing we are missing is appreciation for what we have, which is unquestionably a feminine quality, because men are not built to be content. We look at someone who is content and ask, "What do you know that we don't know? What are you so pleased about? How do you get to be so comfortable with what is?" But when a man gets past his demon and no longer has anything to prove, *then* he can be content.

Being content doesn't mean being passive. A guy can go to work every morning at six A.M. and work all day and be content doing what he does, because he is being who he is. This is a trait we all need to acquire. Jews too need to be content with being Jews. Not because of any particular activity or school of thought or allegiance to such and such a sect, but simply because we're Jews being Jewish, proudly caring about a fellow Jew, with no need for embellishment.

Why was this concept not revealed until relatively recently? Because until now the world has been very masculine. It needed to be masculine, because of all the monumental changes that needed to take place. The land of Canaan had to become the Holy Land. There were battles to wage and wars to win. However, as we draw closer to the coming of the *Mashiach*, there are fewer and fewer changes we need to make. We now need to get comfortable with and excited by the idea that what is good is good, what is right is right, and we no longer need to be in the repair mode that once dominated our lives.

That's also why *Shabbos* is known as the *Sabbath Queen. Shabbos* is feminine; it means that today there's nothing you need to fix. No need to be so masculine. And that's why the era inaugurated by *Mashiach* is called the *Permanent Shabbos*. Change will no longer be required. The world will be as it needs to be.

When we do *teshuvah* and return to the innocent state we once knew, we will be in harmony with our Godly soul. From that place of connectedness we'll become empowered to change anything that needs changing. We'll also gain the ability to rise above the limitations of *time*. Our lives will no longer be fragmented into past, present, and future; we will have learned to bridge those differences, to the degree God needs us to. What makes it possible? It's the feminine side of Creation, which lives within the Godly, feminine aspect of each of us. Our Godly soul is complete, and therefore completely beyond time, beyond all need for change.

15

Happiness

If an unhappy person shrugs and says, "I can't complain," believe him. He's lost his right to whine.

A family invites you into their home, and you accept. They usher you into your room and bring you everything you might need—a comfortable bed with turned-down sheets, a warm blanket, a sumptuous meal—and ask for nothing in return. They don't even let you wash a dish or make the bed. They barely know you; and you've done nothing to merit such extraordinary hospitality and generosity. You smile, of course, and express heartfelt appreciation. They're happy to have you and you're more than happy to be there. To have shown anything other than gratitude would have been unthinkable.

We are guests in God's world, before we have done anything to be deserving of reward. Whatever *mitzvahs* we may have to our credit are meager and few. Even if moved to do something special to deserve His hospitality, we're not really sure how or what that might be. But imagine if we were to moan and groan and complain about the littlest thing—that would certainly fall short of being good guests. The least we can do in His presence, in His home, is to show a little gratitude. Just being here is reason enough to be delighted we've been invited in.

To be happy we need to have at least some idea of what to be happy about. Sometimes we forget or get so caught up with life's dramas we can't stop thinking unhappy thoughts. But though we may not have everything we want, we have what we need. We didn't deserve to be born, and yet we were born free. Is it not enough that we are alive?

Happiness is not merely an obligation; it simply makes sense. Suppose a person says, "I didn't ask to be born. I didn't ask to be invited, I don't want to be invited, and I am not happy about being alive." He can say it, but it can't be true. Everyone, even in the midst of the direst straits, wants to live. In fact we want so *desperately* to live, we cannot stand it when life is not perfect. So all we do is complain. Does that not show how much we really want to live?

A story is told about a couple who had been happily married for many long years.

The wife was just about the ugliest woman in the world, but her husband didn't care because he was blind. The husband was rancorous, hypercritical, and horrendously foul-mouthed, but she didn't care because she was deaf. They lived together blissfully, until one day a famous doctor came to town who people said could cure anything. They went to him, and he cured the husband of his blindness, and the wife of her deafness. Some weeks later the doctor came to their door to collect his fee.

To his surprise and dismay, the couple attacked him. "You've ruined our lives!" they yelled. "We were happy before, and now we are miserable! Look at what you've done!" The doctor apologized profusely. "I'm so terribly sorry. Please come back to the clinic, and I will make you blind and deaf again." At which they screamed, louder than before, "No! That's the last thing in the world we want."

"In that case," the doctor replied, "you have to pay me. Here's the bill."

More succinctly, the dialogue goes like this: "I didn't ask to be born," says the unhappy fellow.

"No problem," says God. "I'll take your life back."

"Oh no! I didn't mean that at all!"

The appropriate response to life is first to offer thanks for what we do have. When we say thank you for what we have, we are essentially saying life is good. Having done so, we may complain about what we don't have. But if we don't care enough about life to say thank you, what right do we have to complain?

There was an old and very bitter man in our synagogue, a survivor of the Holocaust. Every *Shabbos*, rain or shine, even in the freezing cold Minnesota snow, he would show up in *shul*. Not to pray, mind you, because he was not a believer. He came for the singular purpose of telling us how he doesn't believe in God.

One day in the middle of a *Shabbos* morning we found out that he had become a grandfather. Everyone went up to him with big, warm congratulations of *mazel tov*. He remained sullen, showing no sign of joy, let alone gratitude. I took him aside and said, "If you're not happy that your grandchild was born, then you don't have any right to complain that God allowed six million people to die in the Holocaust. A God Who let people die is perfect for you, because anyway you don't love life."

You can be upset when life is not perfect to the precise extent that you love life. Loving life goes hand in hand with the hope, perhaps even the expectation, that life will be perfect. But if you deem life not to be good, then death is not so terrible. If you don't love life, how can you complain about death?

It's not difficult to understand what pure unadulterated happiness looks like. All we need to do is have a look at very young children. They are naturally, spontaneously joyful, for no reason at all. What do they have to show for themselves? They have no accomplishments to be proud of, no need to count their blessings. They're getting life for free. That alone is worth celebrating. They're simply happy to be, and blissful in their bones.

For grownups it gets a little stickier. The clear and innocent awareness that someone gave us life for free is usually harder to come by. For us, happiness comes from doing the right thing, not from mistaking *free* to mean free to do whatever we want. People do what they want and are not happy at all, stressed to the breaking point, addicted to distractions or deflections or drugs. But escape is rarely anything other than short-lived. If not suicidal, then they're at least subject to the desperate need for denial.

If you know your purpose in life—in other words, what you are needed for—you can be the happiest person on earth. If you are not doing what you are supposed to, and what you *are* doing is immoral, you can be the most miserable person in the world. There's only one way to be truly happy, and that is to have a clean conscience.

How do we acquire a clean conscience? By knowing and doing what is expected of us. This is where the blessing of Torah becomes evident and relevant. It tells us why we are here, how best to behave in this world, and how to make even this lowest of all worlds a holy dwelling place fit for God. Clear directives rescue us from the need to second-guess our roles and missions in life. Inner peace and happiness ensue.

Happiness, Contentment, and the Pursuit of Pleasure

We often use the words *happiness* and *contentment* interchangeably. They're not the same. "I am content to live in this house" is different from "I'm happy to live in this house." Let's define our terms.

Contentment means I am accepting of my burden. I may not have what I want or need, but I recognize that there's a method to earning it, so I am content to do the job that will bring me the things I need or want. I'm willing to assume the responsibilities of the work in front of me. If I work hard, although hard work might exhaust me, I can get there.

The person who resists his job or his lot in life lacks contentment. If you don't want to be where you are or do what you're doing, and you feel you have no choice in the matter, that's discontent.

Contentment is in many ways related to maturity. It takes a certain maturity to say, "Okay, this is what I have to do, and I'm willing to do it." You follow the rules in the Army to become a good soldier. Maturity and wisdom say, "If this is what you are, and this is where you are, this is what you need to do." Well then, let's get to it. Being content allows you to do the best you can at what you do.

Contentment also calls for a measure of humility, an acceptance of one's role in life, not because of anything personally lacking but because of being needed for a purpose that might seem inconsistent with one's own needs. But if that's what I'm needed for, that's what I'm going to do. Every other creature on earth is humbly content with its assigned role: an animal is content being an animal, a vegetable is content being a vegetable, and a mineral is content being a mineral. There's something almost mystically nonnegotiable about it. If God's creatures were not content to be what they are, nature would break down. The world would be in a state of utter chaos and dysfunction.

Who breaks the rules? Only a human being wreaks havoc on his own contentment. A person can be miserable, not because he doesn't want to exist at all, but because he can't handle existing in the situation he's currently in. He wants to be somewhere else, anywhere but here. He doesn't want to live in the now. His sights are set on some distant future, like the person who wants to remain a child and refuses to grow up, or the child who hasn't even turned twelve but craves being an adult and pretends he is.

All of these miseries are forms of discontent. It's understandable; life can be difficult. It's easy to become cynical and dissatisfied. All the more reason to cultivate the maturity and humility it takes to find contentment in your mission.

Unlike contentment, however, happiness has nothing to do with your performance, your job, your obligations, or your purpose in life. Happiness is the door prize you get when you cash in your free ticket into that theme park called the world. You're ushered in and you get to go on all the rides. It makes you feel like you're getting a free gift you did nothing to deserve. We don't earn life. We don't deserve it, or even ask for it. It's a gift from God.

The more we're aware of how undeserving we are, the deeper our perception of the gift, and the greater our happiness can be. Here's this wretched person who thinks, *I'm a sinner. I'm failing at my mission in life. I destroy everything in my path.* This guy actually has more reason to be happy than someone with an average or above-average measure of self-esteem. Happiness is in direct proportion to the feeling that, despite an utter and complete lack of any merit whatsoever, you're given *life* in all its vivacious glory, monumentally undeserved—not just as a one-time windfall at birth, but every day and every moment of your existence. And the fact that this gift is given to every creature on earth ought to multiply that happiness many, many times over.

An unhappy person has had his right to complain revoked. A happy person, however, can complain bitterly about his role in life and the situation he finds himself in, and still do so happily. "I love my life. I'm happy to be alive. But I hate living in this country, in this city, in this nine-to-five job from hell." Being discontented does not mean you're not happy. It's an important distinction, but nonetheless there's no contradiction.

Take the character Tevye the milkman in *Fiddler on the Roof*. He's not content with his poverty, with the squalor of the *shtetl*, with the Cossacks who torment his people, or with his young daughter's choice of a boyfriend. But he loves life with a passion that is robust and infectious. It's what makes him so endearing and so memorable. "If I were a rich man," he sings, unabashedly complaining to God. "Would it spoil some vast eternal plan, if I were a wealthy man?" A malcontent with major problems, whether or not his problems are legitimate, is not necessarily unhappy at all. Happiness is a different experience from contentment. If every time we were discontented we were also unhappy, this would be a very sick society indeed.

Happiness is not one of the 613 explicit *mitzvahs* enumerated in the Torah. And it's certainly not one of the quintessential Ten Commandments on which all these particulars are based. Nor is there a specific injunction prohibiting sadness. It is simply that sadness is lifeless, and happiness is life. Although happiness is not an individual *mitzvah*, it is a precondition for all *mitzvahs*; and though sadness is not a sin, it's a precondition for all sins. When God says, "I place before you today a choice between life and death; choose life!" He means "Be happy. Don't be sad." Because when you start to lose interest in life, then you're drifting away from everything good and holy. Whereas happiness is a channel for everything Godly.

The verse in Psalms that says, "Serve God with joy" doesn't mean "smile and be happy while you're serving God." It means "serve God by being happy." If you wish to serve God and there's no particular *mitzvah* within reach at that moment (or even if there is), simply by being happy you are serving God.

What's there to be happy about? Be happy to be His guest, to be invited and included in His world. Whether or not you're a *good* guest is a question worth considering; but the first question is "Are you happy being here?" Serving God with joy means being happy to be included in His Creation. That in and of itself is a Godly state of mind.

God gives us a planet that works. It's warm because of the sun; it's romantic because of the moon; there are stars by which to navigate. Not to mention the trees, flowers, fruits, and vegetables. And consider this—He could have made the world in black and white, but He gave us *colors* that not only make life livable, but so richly enhance the experience. There are blessings we recite thanking God for bringing bread out of the earth, for creating such marvelous phenomena as oceans, stars, lightning, and thunder. These are just the details; behind it all, and within it all, is life itself. And it's all for free.

Speaking of freedom . . . when Thomas Jefferson proclaimed "Life, Liberty, and *the pursuit of Happiness*" (italics added) in the US Declaration of Independence, he was on the right track—it was certainly an improvement over the "the pursuit of property" touted by some of his forebears—but he sort of missed the point. To make happiness a *pursuit* suggests that life itself is not good enough, that we need to find something to make it better. It implies that living and breathing is not reason enough to celebrate. The soul, which is the gift of life, ought to be celebrated and enjoyed with every breath. The Hebrew word for breath, *neshima*, is directly related to the word *neshama,* soul. Happiness is not a pursuit. You don't have to do anything or go anywhere to find happiness. If you feel the need to pursue happiness tomorrow, if the ability to breathe doesn't make you happy right where you are today, it's a day wasted.

To take it a step further, the pursuit of happiness is actually—subtly at least—a variety of idol worship. What's idolatry? You take a piece of wood and fashion it into a statue of some sort. So far so good. Then you find it so aesthetically pleasing, so symbolic and uplifting, that you assign some significance to the statue. Uh oh, trouble ahead: now it represents something you're reaching for, something you want that you don't have. But you already have it! God gave you this piece of wood, and you are intrinsically superior to it; yet you're reaching for something it stands for that is actually already yours.

Life is given. Pursuit is a form of worship. The sun, created to keep us warm and give us life, is worshipping *us*. How did that get turned around to where we worship it? The sun, the moon, the fruit, the flowers—we don't have to behave in a certain way or go somewhere far away to attain what has already been created and given to us. The suggestion that we have to pursue happiness is tantamount to idolatry.

Happiness means saying to God, "You included me, and I am thrilled. If I do a good job, I'll be even more thrilled, but when I do a lousy job and *still* continue receiving life, wow, how much more am I delighted!" Happiness is the appreciation, the gladness, the rejoicing, the recognition that we are a part of the plan. The rest is commentary.

Although our predecessors originally came to this great country in pursuit of happiness, somewhere along the line that changed. We don't just want to be happy, we want to indulge in pleasures. As a result, even happy people frequently feel the need to experiment with sex, substances, or other instant gratifications. It seems happiness alone is insufficient. We need the rush that pleasures bring.

The pursuit of pleasure is idolatry, without a doubt. It bears all the signs and symptoms: it is never what you think it is or will be; it does not make you healthier, stronger, or better; it only depletes you; you become dependent on it. It can also make you antisocial, because it's a completely self-indulgent endeavor. *Your* pleasure is not something anyone can share. Happiness is infectious; by its very nature it's shareable. But pleasure removes a person from family, friends, and society to the point where one can drown in one's own narcissism.

Pleasure and happiness are not at all the same. Happiness is when you have more than you deserve; pleasure is when you have more than you need. Unlike the pursuit of happiness, which may have subtle idolatrous overtones but at least has some virtue, the pursuit of pleasure is hedonism undisguised.

You sat and ate meat and potatoes, the staples you need for nourishment, to satiate your hunger. But then you want dessert. What's dessert really about? You're not still hungry. If you were, you'd have had more meat and potatoes. Dessert is strictly for your taste buds. You no longer need nourishment, so the dessert is more than you need.

Wealth is a pleasure. A person with a bank account that meets all his needs is comfortable; when the account far exceeds his needs, that's pleasure. Of course, how much a person actually needs is always subject to a judgment call. Does it give you pleasure? Some people simply can't enjoy wealth. They ruin it by imagining they need it—*If I have it, I must need it.* But people of modest needs are frequently happier, and enjoy greater pleasure, than people whose needs are great.

Once upon a time, righteous Jews would never allow money to remain in their homes overnight. It'd be given away at the end of the day, because if they hadn't spent it, they didn't need it; and since they didn't need it, someone else in need should have it. True, you can always make the argument that you need to keep everything you can get for a rainy day. *I may not need it right now, but I'm going to need it soon.* But where's the pleasure in that?

A little wisdom and maturity can cut down on one's needs dramatically. Children's needs are endless. They need everything, and they need it now. But no matter what you give them, there's no pleasure. You buy them a toy and they soon become bored and want a new one. As adults mature, however, they begin to realize they don't need as much as they thought. It can be true of anything. You can have more love than you need. You can have more food than you need. You can have more money than you need. You can have more space than you need.

Happiness, healthy happiness, means I am happy to be part of God's world. *Contentment* means I am happy to do the job God gives me, even though it may be challenging. *Pleasure* is the feeling that I'm rich, because I have more than I need.

When serving God with joy, there's no need to *pursue* happiness and run the risk of falling into idolatry. The same is true, and even more so, with regard to the pursuit of pleasure. Just having been invited into God's world is reason enough to be happy, to be grateful. We simply rejoice in having been included in the plan and with the gifts we have been given. Happiness may or may not bring contentment. Pleasures are always optional and are not necessarily a sign of happiness. Happiness and gratitude, however, are inseparable. One cannot exist without the other.

PART TWO

Marriage Matters

16

The Jungle of Dating

Selflessness is an admirable character trait in virtually every human interaction. Except when seeking a soulmate: be selfish.

Human marital relationships are hard, and getting harder. People are struggling just to get along; marriages are more easily derailed than ever. It's practically an epidemic. Even courtship and engagements have become a challenge. It's a jungle out there. How is one to survive without a proper map or compass? Sometimes it seems as though we need some sort of emotional combat training.

To survive the jungle of dating, there are a few things you must know. The first is that dating is the polar opposite of marriage. People who are adept at the dating game are likely to have a more difficult time navigating the transition to marriage. There are those who find that they enjoy dating so much, they end up as perpetual, serial daters, with no intention of marrying whatsoever. Once dating becomes a comfortable and rewarding lifestyle in and of itself, what they're comfortable with is something that's basically antimarriage. And if they do manage to marry without knowing how to adjust their respective roles from man and woman to husband and wife, marriage will be at risk from the beginning.

Surely, you may protest, there must be some intrinsic value to dating even when marriage is understood to be the goal. Yes, but it's still not easy. How is one supposed to know if a person is the right match without dating for an extended period of time? After all, commitment to marriage is a monumental life decision. "What if I made a mistake?" "What if I missed the boat?" "What if he or she is the wrong one?" The crushing uncertainties can be mentally and emotionally exhausting. *What if... what if.*

Fortunately for us, Jewish "dating" is a far less stressful way to select Mr. or Ms. Right from an infinite pool of Mr./Ms. Wrongs. It's different enough from conventional dating that it's not even all that accurate to call it *dating* per se. For practical purposes, however, we'll use the word *dating* going forward. We'll also take the liberty of occasionally using limiting pronouns—*he/she/his/hers,* etc.—to refer to both genders, interchangeably, to avoid overindulging in those often awkward and grammatically problematic *they, them*, and *their*.

When dating you need to know that to succeed you have to be totally selfish rather than self-effacing. You don't need to worry about what kind of impression you are making on him or her. You are not there to make an impression; you are not there to win him over; you are not even there to show her a good time. You are there to check him out, period. So don't wear a mask, don't overdress, don't put on a show, and don't go to extraordinary lengths to try to impress. Don't even wonder what he thinks of you. Don't do his thinking for him. Your attitude should be that if he doesn't like what he sees or hears, he can go home.

Another important point to remember is that dating for the purpose of marriage needs to be a very neutral activity. It should never be up close and personal. You don't become deeply involved or attached in any way. It's almost like window shopping—you are only there to look things over; whereas in more casual dating a couple may spend hours, weeks, or months together and become personally and emotionally entangled. They frequently end up getting hooked on each other before they're even close to a decision whether they're right for each other. By then the decision is out of their hands. They've both become so invested and attached, they wouldn't know how to break up even if they wanted to, so they might as well just get married. Or if they do break up, one or both may fall into depression and suffer undue pain. This is insanity. You have to stay neutral in order to be able to think clearly.

It's also not uncommon for people to reverse the order of dating and marriage. While dating, some people act as though they're already married; and after they're married, they interact as though they're still dating. For example, a guy once said to me, "I was in a restaurant with my wife the other night and I noticed that she has this annoying habit of..." Wait a minute, you're noticing this about your wife *now*? You're supposed to notice things like this when you are dating. Once you're married, what difference do her habits make? She's your wife! He is clearly confused, reacting as though he were still dating her, when the reality is they're married. They've got their situations switched—a disaster.

Many women give themselves wholeheartedly and without reservation to a man before they are married. This has caused women everywhere untold pain. Sadly, these same women may cease to see the importance of surrendering themselves completely once they *are* married. For whatever reason, or for no reason at all, they may feel the need to hold back, or to not be as available as they were before they were married. What's wrong with this picture?

To cultivate a close relationship with anyone to whom you are not married, to reverse the order of the sequence of dating and marriage is a serious mistake, not to mention less than completely kosher. In Judaism, it's not done, which is why we say rather bluntly that we don't "believe" in dating. It's neither helpful nor healthy for anyone looking to develop an intimate, long-lasting, and committed relationship.

The *Zohar* tells us that forty days before you are conceived, a heavenly voice announces whom you are going to marry. We call this prenatally designated spouse your *bashert*. The word *bashert* means a divinely foreordained soulmate. It's for this reason that we don't date as in the secular sense; we merely meet to see whether he or she is the one.

We also know from the *Zohar* that there are seven different souls that you could possibly marry, each one corresponding to one of the seven levels of your own soul. You are destined to marry one of them, and once that's determined, the other six become irrelevant. It's a decision that's not in your hands; only God Almighty, the ultimate matchmaker, knows which one is your *bashert*. There is simply no way for you to know until it happens. Since it has been decided for you, it's not your job, nor are you expected to figure out on your own who that person will be. The dating process is the way of unveiling what has already been ordained. When you meet someone you like, all you can say is, "I hope he/she is the one!" That's your part; the rest is up to God. If it is meant to be, it will be.

The very institution of marriage was God's idea in the first place. There's a holiness about it, an unfathomable divine wisdom behind it that makes it too important a decision to leave to us. So He decides. *Bashert* means it is destined to happen, and it must happen. There is no way around it. Therefore we can know beyond the shadow of a doubt that there has *never been a marriage that was a mistake*. If you imagine you may have "lost" your *bashert*, then it wasn't really *bashert* at all.

A further insight of the Kabbalah can render this admittedly striking concept more understandable. Marriage is seen not just as a union of two separate people, but rather as a reunion of two parts of a single soul. God divides each original soul into two parts, male and female, and when they finally meet in holy matrimony, the bond is restored. If it were just a question of unifying two disparate entities, you wouldn't necessarily need a man and a woman. You could make a union between two men, two women, two dogs, or even a cat and a dog. But a reunion of two parts of one soul can only happen in a marriage, and it cannot happen unless the two are predestined soulmates who find each other. That's the simple yet profound explanation of what marriage is according to Judaism.

You do, however, have the option of refusing to marry altogether. That *is* your choice. Should you decide to accept the challenge, you are going to marry the one preselected for you. You could even make a list of everything you're looking for in a mate, but it won't be a determining factor, because your husband is already who he is, and your wife is already who she is.

It is true that your marriage to your soulmate could end up in divorce. If the marriage were to become a source of unbearable difficulties for one or both of you, you have the option to end it and go your separate ways. Divorce exists because even if you are married to the right person, you may not be able to sustain the reunion. In fact under such circumstances where the differences are irreconcilable and the suffering intolerable, divorce is actually a *mitzvah*. God, in His mercy, provides a way out for you and instructs you to get divorced. Although God has put together the precise pair, He does not necessarily expect every person to be able to fully carry out His will at every stage of his or her life.

A subsequent marriage, then, will be a reunion with a different aspect of your soul, another of the seven levels. Thus, even a person's second or third marriage is also a reunion, between two parts of a soul that match each other on another plane, according to their spiritual standing at this phase of their lives. If you marry the person, he or she is your match—known as a *zivug sheni*, a second pairing—and here too it has all been planned out precisely. Once again, you cannot marry the wrong person.

In the instance of a marriage between a Jew and a non-Jew, where they are obviously not two parts of the same soul, they would be creating a union, not a reunion. This would apply to a same-gender marriage as well, which is an expression of free choice rather than predestination.

Matchmaker, Matchmaker, Make Me a Match

A *shadchan* is a person who assists with the dating process between two people— popularly known as a matchmaker. Does this sound primitive or patronizing? On the contrary, this time-tested system has long been established to preserve the dignity, integrity, and self-respect of the individuals. It is designed to eliminate the pain, suffering, abuse, complications, and heartbreak that can so often be shattering and devastating to a couple—either one or the other or both. There are no words that can suffice to fully portray the wisdom and the importance of using a *shadchan*.

Shadchanim, in the plural, are not at all the stereotypical old-fashioned characters you may have seen in *Fiddler on the Roof*. They are skilled, sensitive, professional facilitators, and they're paid for their work. Those who foolishly try to avoid consultation with this expert intermediary are setting themselves up for needless troubles. The prevailing practice of simply exchanging phone numbers and jumping right into a casual, self-made dating game invites unnecessary emotional distress. Until you are standing together under the *chuppah*, the wedding canopy, the *shadchan* is essential.

When a *shadchan* is involved, you do not ask for his or her phone number and nervously place the call. The *shadchan* who suggests the match manages the initial arrangements after both sides agree to meet. You don't ask your date if she would like to go on a second date; nor does she ask you. That can be awkward. The *shadchan* will inquire with each of you, and if you agree, will convey your answer. If at any point you decide you are no longer interested in seeing this person, then again, the *shadchan* serves as the intermediary. You never have to "break up" face to face—as if there were anything to break. This method ensures that these exploratory meetings will never become so intense that something will need to be "broken."

There are those who employ the *shadchan* only for the initial introduction and first meeting, and after that they call each other directly to set up subsequent dates themselves. This is generally foolish, and can in fact prove to be cruel. How do you call it quits without someone getting hurt? Imagine a couple who have been dating for a while without a *shadchan*. The guy decides he doesn't want to marry the woman. The honorable thing, of course, is to tell her face to face that he wants to break up. Naturally she wants to know why, and being a man of integrity, he tells her. She may well become traumatized. What at first seemed comfortable and spontaneous may end up being hurtful.

The system of using a facilitator is wise, dignified, and refined. It works. With a *shadchan*, there is a buffer. As outmoded as it may seem, using a *shadchan* is the single most significant rule of dating. Most significantly a guy should never propose to the girl without the *shadchan* first informing him that now is a good time, that she is ready and amenable to the match. He should never be placed in a position of proposing, only to be turned down. Again, until you are both under the *chuppah,* a *shadchan* is absolutely indispensable.

Concerning the predestined nature of soulmates, here's a funny, true story.

A *shadchan* in California arranged a *shidduch* for a woman she knew. After the first date, the woman said she was not interested in the guy, because he was losing his hair. She declared that this was the one physical trait she absolutely would not tolerate in a man. "No problem," said the *shadchan*, who proceeded to keep looking for someone else. Finally, she found a guy she thought would be a terrific match for her client. Unfortunately, he was already bald; but being a good *shadchan*, who knows never to pass up a possibility, she decided she had to try to match them anyway. She set up a meeting for the two and firmly instructed the man not to take his hat off during the date.

The two met, and the *shadchan* called each of them after the date to see how it went. She called the woman first to see if she was interested enough to go out again. She said, "Yes, absolutely." Then she asked the man, and he said, "Yeah! It went very nicely. Oh, by the way, I did take my hat off. Was that okay?" The *shadchan* was of course concerned, so she called the woman back and asked if she was sure she wanted to go out again. The woman said, "Yes! I'd very much like to go out with him again!" The *shadchan* asked, "Even though he's bald?" The woman said, "He is?" She hadn't noticed.

Because this was the guy preordained for her, his missing hair hadn't even registered. When something is *bashert*, it's no longer our decision to make. You may also be comforted to know that no matter what mistakes you think you may have made on your date, no matter what bad impression you believe you might have left, if he's supposed to be your husband he won't notice. Even if he does, he's *still* going to marry you. For this reason it would be unwise to waste time and energy analyzing every blunder or misstep. Rest assured that if he is the one for you, you will end up together. When it's not *bashert*, you will notice no virtues; when it is *bashert*, you will notice no faults.

Every marriage is made in heaven, and as such is powerful and holy. You cannot marry someone who is not your intended, just as you cannot have children who are not yours. In fact you practically cannot avoid marrying your *bashert*. Knowing this you can relax and see the wisdom of how best to find your soulmate. With your *shadchan,* you and your spouse are in good hands—and the three of you are in God's hands.

17

The Comedy of Marriage

A funny thing happened on the way to marital bliss.

When people come to me for counseling and say, "My marriage is not easy," I think, *What did you expect? Marriage is more than difficult. It's impossible.*

You are two human beings trying to live like angels. How hard could that be? Being married is a Godly and holy endeavor. And we are not so holy. It's more than a little awkward; it's laugh-out-loud comical that two people would even attempt to live together in holy matrimony. At the very least it calls for patience, with each other and with oneself. Above all it requires a sense of humor.

Consider the expression, "a match made in heaven." Well sure, in heaven everything works. In heaven, we would all get along very nicely. The real question is, "How do we make it work here on earth?" Humans have always solved their problems more effectively with wisdom than with might, money, or medicine. We are what we know. So we're going to need a whole lot of wisdom, along with a healthy appreciation of the absurd.

There was a time when marriage was pretty much a given, and people didn't need a reason or an excuse to take the plunge.

Marriage was for having children, and the world needed to be populated, so if you had children you were considered successful. That was also the time when polygamy was accepted, so having two, three, or more wives was not all that uncommon (notwithstanding the obvious challenges to a family's internal emotional support system. Not to mention the costs).

In earlier generations, marriages between husbands and wives weren't quite as personal as they have become today. As relationships became more private and individualistic, polygamy became unacceptable, thank God—it wasn't working for the husbands or the wives. More to the point, however, more and more marriages were no longer primarily about the kids.

Is it possible that the nature of relationships has changed once again? Why are so many marriages in trouble? People have been getting married for thousands of years, but in recent decades, it seems people have forgotten how to make marriage work.

What we have now is a watered-down version of marriage. It's no wonder people have become uninspired and perplexed. Today, just as following time-worn traditions doesn't seem to satisfy the longing for a personal relationship with God, so too in marriage: the attitudes and norms that once worked can't continue to sustain us. What was apparently good enough a generation ago is no longer enough. Fortunately, something positive is happening today. Couples are seeking a deeper understanding of what it means to be married.

There are myriad programs and books advising people on how to make their marriages work. Many are based on modern psychology; others are a product of the sort of experimentation that began with the sexual upheaval in the 1960s and evolved into newly minted therapeutic strategies. We have learned that we cannot experiment with life, with people, or with children. Attempts to fool Mother Nature invariably result in disappointment and confusion.

We have all been seriously, dangerously misled concerning the fundamental facts of life. What we need is not more psychology, but the time-honored, divine wisdom of our sages. The whole world desperately needs the stability and sanity a healthy marriage can bring. Its benefits are not just life-changing, they are life-*saving*.

Reconcilable Differences

The Torah tells us how humans were created: man was made from dust, and woman was made from man. In simpler, more useful terms, man is created out of nothing, and woman is fashioned from a living human being. On the principle that the Torah does not present even an iota of irrelevant information, it follows that this must be something we need to know. Understanding our respective origins is crucial in helping us understand the difference between male and female mindsets.

Since the male psyche has a memory (however subconscious) of having originally been nothing, men have an understandable fear of turning out to be nothing again. If anything or anyone should suggest or remind him of his inner nothingness, he panics. His survival is at stake. It doesn't take much to make him feel like nothing; he already suspects that he may very well be nothing, even without reminders. Because of his fear of annihilation, he has a fragile ego.

Chances are you've heard the famous story about the man who came before Hillel the Elder and demanded, "Teach me the whole Torah while I stand on one foot." Hillel answered him, "What is hateful to you, do not do to others." This was not some vague, open-ended message that is subject to creative interpretation. It doesn't mean that if you hate chocolate, don't let anybody else eat chocolate either. "What is hateful to you" is not a question, it's a reference to something you know you hate. What then is this thing that every man hates? It's to be reminded of his nothingness. No woman can understand this uniquely male terror, because no such fear exists in a woman's psyche. A woman might consider herself a ten or a one, but, as I said, she's never at risk of becoming a zero. So if you treat a woman as though she's nothing, it simply doesn't compute for her, because she's never been a nothing. But a man was created from dust; treat him like he's nothing, and he's easy to convince.

Being a zero is not just an insult; it means total annihilation. When you put a man down, you're destroying him. That's why men are often so sensitive they can't tolerate any criticism, because every critique reminds them of the ultimate critique. "You're not so tall," you say; and he thinks, *Here we go, I know where this is headed. First I'm not so tall. Then I'm not so smart. Then I'm not important, and finally I'm not necessary. You mean I'm nothing!* It may not be a conscious thought, but it's a suspicion that haunts every man. It takes a whole lot of time and energy to keep this demon in the closet. Men will overcompensate with all kinds of macho bravado to keep that door closed.

The proof of this is how disproportionately men respond to compliments. A simple compliment will make his life worth living. A wife says to her husband, "You changed the light bulb? I didn't know you could change a light bulb!" Every husband knows that it's a silly compliment. But he goes off to work feeling like a million bucks.

If he tries to return the compliment, however, he's in trouble. "You made these eggs? I didn't know you knew how to make eggs." She thinks he's lost his mind. It doesn't work for her. Women need to feel appreciated, but frivolous compliments they can do without. Changing a light bulb is better than being nothing, but scrambling an egg doesn't make her a ten. That's why the worst thing a wife can say to a husband is, "That's okay, I can do it myself." What he hears is, "I'm totally useless. I'm nothing." This has been the predicament of men since Creation, and it's gotten worse since the feminist movement destroyed any remnant of hope men had to feel needed.

The Talmud tells us that a man should honor his wife more than himself. It's not just because she is more deserving of honor (which she is) but because women are extraordinarily sensitive to injustice. But who among us is not sensitive to injustice? What it means is, whereas men can't tolerate criticism because it makes them feel like nothing, a woman cannot abide the *injustice* when treated as if she were nothing. She doesn't feel threatened, she is indignant.

Because of these distinctions, men and women will never truly understand each other. They're not even good for each other. Never mind Mars and Venus; men are from dust, and women are from humans. A woman who has a man in her life is miserable. A man who has a woman in his life has nothing but trouble.

That's why God created marriage. Marriage is not a precarious relationship between a man and a woman. It's a relationship between a husband and a wife.

The Purpose of Marriage

Marriage is a magical institution that transforms a man into a husband and a woman into a wife. It is a powerful and dramatic change. Before marriage, men and women could easily be better off without each other. In marriage, a husband and a wife cannot exist without each other. They define each other.

How come our ancestors' marriages, which were more often than not *arranged* marriages, worked better than today's? Largely because they had learned to put marriage first.

When God created mankind, He did not command us to love someone. He said, "Get married." Where does love fit in? You don't necessarily marry the person you love; but you should love the person you marry. That's why it is more important to find out what a potential mate thinks of marriage, rather than what he or she thinks of you.

Marriage is not a mere exchange of emotions, as in, "I love you and you love me, so let's get married." There is no intrinsic connection between love and marriage, and they certainly don't "go together like a horse and carriage." Marrying for love is a Hollywood invention. We get married for marriage, not for love. Qualification number one is to marry someone who shares your ideal, someone whose vision of life matches yours. Marriage means "let's make a life together."

If you get married because you want love, you'll never grow beyond yourself; you are still indulging yourself. Not that the self is insignificant; however, in marriage you define your *self* by focusing on what you can do for the other. It's not *I'm nothing without you.* It's *with you I become everything.*

Even God—perfect, infinite, eternal, all-knowing, and all-powerful—is not content by Himself. So He creates us in His image, and in the presence of our imperfection He becomes One. Marriage is like that. We too experience the abysmal discontent of being alone. "I gotta be me" is not enough. So we introduce another person into our lives.

Get past yourself, and your greatest pleasure will be in taking care of the most important person in your life—who will become your reality.

Giver or Receiver?

We get married because it is the divine way to be and the divine way to live. There's nothing bigger or greater than marriage. Humans were created that way; that's life. Not convinced? Then don't get married. In order for a marriage to succeed, you have to believe marriage is necessary, not just a possible way of living. It cannot be a byproduct of any other desire or need—not to relieve loneliness, not for a tax deduction or a green card, not even for love. You cannot make a lifelong commitment to a byproduct. For marriage to work, you must have the conviction that it is necessary, and everything else is negotiable. Will there be problems? Probably. But the problems will not be extraneous or unnecessary. The problems you now have will be the healthy ones, like the inevitable challenges of childrearing.

There's a pervasive but false notion that marriage is a matter of give and take. No; there is no *taking* in marriage, only giving and *receiving*. To take from another human being is abusive. Nor is marriage about dividing everything equally, split right down the middle, whether with regard to possessions or shared responsibilities. That's not a marriage, it's a living arrangement.

God designed the universe in terms of the principle of male and female, giving and receiving. We spoke about this in a previous chapter as the dynamic relationship between *mashpia* and *mekabel*, giver and receiver, in Chassidic terminology. The same idea is discussed in Kabbalah in terms of light, and the vessel that contains the light. It's the key to all interaction in the natural world; it's the yin and the yang. Rain bestows its life-giving power of growth upon the earth, and the earth blossoms forth with life in response. A philanthropist is inspired to perform acts of kindness and generosity; and the recipients accept his gifts, enjoy their benefits, and respond with gratitude.

It's common for people to think of a receiver as being weak or passive. In truth, however, receptivity lies at the root of all energies. All existence begins with a demand, a need, or a hunger. Without demand, supply is irrelevant. Receptivity is a feminine quality, and the dance of life begins with a woman. A man's life begins with his wife, because without her, he can't be a husband.

Women often misconstrue the meaning of being a receiver. To be a receiver is a woman's birthright. From the very beginning of Creation, God described the first woman as yearning for her husband. That's the beginning of all life. That's why Adam named his wife *Chava*—in the original Hebrew, the Mother of All Living Things. In English we know her as Eve. A mother is literally the source of all life. Her receptivity, her very *passivity*, nurtures her unborn baby in the womb. Even as she sleeps, life blossoms within her, without her having to do anything.

Even a husband is created by the wife. A man finds a woman's yearning irresistible; without it, his desire to provide, produce, and protect is for naught. Women's receptive, nurturing qualities are passive, but it's a passivity that is so powerful, it creates husbands. A wife who embraces her role as a receiver relinquishes her need for control, leaving her exquisitely vulnerable. In turn she not only becomes more attractive to her husband, she makes his life meaningful. He is needed, his existence is vindicated, he is here to give. It all begins with the woman. In her receptive presence he feels like a man, which leaves her feeling like a woman.

A husband must provide the security and stability that enables his wife to confidently surrender herself. This will happen only when she trusts him fully. Like a teacher attuned to a student's desire to learn, a healthy man is extremely sensitive to a woman's hunger. When we say a man is a giver, it doesn't mean giving is his *job*; it means his ultimate pleasure comes from the act of giving. Men find fulfillment in generosity. When a man knows he has given of himself effectively, he feels like a man. He may be successful in many other ways, but those achievements are irrelevant to his masculinity.

A woman's greatest fulfillment and pleasure is found in receiving and nurturing. When she receives fully and completely, she feels like a woman. There are relationships in which a woman is a giver, but in a feminine way of giving: her strength emerges from her openness and vulnerability. And conversely, there are times when a man is a receiver, but in a masculine way: his openness and receptivity is cultivated within his strength. Both give and both receive; yet in marriage they give *of* each other as well as *to* each other, sharing their respective innermost and essential qualities. When a woman can surrender to her husband, she become a wife. When a man can give himself completely to his wife, he becomes a husband. It is a true marriage. They have blended and become one.

Which, as we've said, is impossible—if we take ourselves too seriously. We have to remain lighthearted, taking *marriage* seriously, but not ourselves. People are funny; marriage is not. With all our foibles and pratfalls, we are comical, if not downright hilarious. Nonetheless marriage—however far-fetched—is for real, and for keeps.

18

The Confounding Power of Love

Be very careful when marrying for love. You might be marrying the love and not the one you love.

There is a much-lamented, catastrophic trend in modern marriages that has sent divorce rates soaring and has made marital counseling a thriving profession. It's not difficult these days to spot a troubled, dysfunctional relationship. But the key to the crisis can often be seen more clearly in seemingly happy, healthy marriages. Even an apparently well-adjusted husband or wife will privately admit that something is missing, that there are moments when he or she feels completely alone in the world. This should not be happening, and the usual symptoms—blaming, shaming, lack of communication skills—offer only superficial explanations. Poor role models are not a very good excuse either.

Deep in the reservoir of wisdom and information that has been gathered and cultivated in the Torah for over four thousand years lie profound, time-tested solutions to complex marital and family issues. The deeper one digs, the better it gets, and the more effective the remedies that can motivate and guide us to rise above our problems.

One of the things that destroys marriages in America is our obsession with love. Americans worship love. As we discussed in an early chapter, subtle forms of idolatry afflict our generation, as they have for many generations. And love is among the most seductive idols in today's culture. In the name of love, and for the sake of love, we will do anything. We will lie, cheat, steal, kill, and even kill ourselves, all in the name of love. It has become almost a religion unto itself. And like every idol throughout history, love will disappoint when we discover that it's neither what it pretends to be nor what we hope it to be.

When a marriage is floundering, we believe that love is the solution. If we already have a lot of love and it's not working, then we need *more* love. With enough love, everything will work. But contrary to the messages we receive nonstop from Hollywood and Madison Avenue and the Amazon bestseller list, love is not the answer to our problems.

If you married for love, your relationship is on shaky ground. There is something coming between you, and it's called love. There's me, there's you, and there's love. It's a love triangle.

There was a time when marriage was founded on family, or practicality, or the lifelong benefits of commitment in order to achieve a total union, to become one. Today, virtually every marriage originates in a love affair. Are marriages better now than they were before? Love has not made marriage stronger, better, or more satisfying; it has made it flimsy. Essentially, if you marry for love, then you marry the love, not the person you're supposed to be loving. This is why even in a loving relationship couples can feel alone in the world: because they're married to the love, not to each other.

If you are lovesick or lovelorn—if you desperately need to be loved—don't get married. If our goal or desire in marriage is to be united, love can't do that. If I don't *need* you, then no matter how much I love you, we're not united. We're simply enjoying each other. When the enjoyment wanes, so will the relationship. We see this in marriage counseling. She says he doesn't love her; and he says, "Of course I do." Is somebody lying? No, they're both telling the truth. He does love her—*what more could she possibly want?* But she sees it differently: no matter how much he professes to love her, it's not enough. And he's climbing the walls. *I didn't marry you for your personality or your opinion. Just shut up and let me love you, okay? But no, you have to ruin it by having an opinion.*

We often hear people say, "We got divorced because we fell out of love." That is to say, if the love is gone, your spouse is no longer needed. This is not a basis for a successful marriage. Marriage is supposed to offer stability, permanence, and security. If you base it on love, you'll end up with a shaky, fragile arrangement and a mountain of anxiety.

He: "Will You Marry Me?" She: "Why?"

A better perspective might begin here: "I need you. Sometimes I love you, and sometimes you get on my nerves. But we belong together."

The purpose of marriage, the reason you introduce another person into your life, is to go beyond yourself. If you marry because you want love, you're not getting bigger than yourself; you are still indulging yourself and your needs. People worry: "If I make my spouse the essence and center of my life, won't I lose my sense of myself, my identity?" No. When a spouse becomes the core reality of your life, it doesn't mean, "I am nothing and you are everything." It's, "I am everything *with you*, not without you. It is my pleasure, my role, my *identity* to take care of you." It does not eliminate you; it defines you.

Talmudic sages distinguish between a love that is not dependent on anything and a love that depends on something other than the loved one. It's rather obvious: if I love you for your money, your looks, your status, your intelligence, and you lose one or all of them, I am bound to stop loving you. The same is true when the extraneous thing is love itself. "You don't love me enough. You don't love me this way, or that way, or the right way, or my way." This is a love that will destroy itself.

Is it that you want this person in your life or that you want some of the things they have to offer? It's a fundamental question. A husband and a wife should have no "thing" between them. It is just them—him and her—and nothing else. If you introduce extraneous things, you're not married to a person, you are married to all these things. It's polygamy. And you have ruined the relationship. You are no longer one.

A relationship that is real is never for *something*. It's the relationship itself that is precious. A husband does not need love from his wife; he needs *his wife's love*. It's very different. "My love becomes significant when you wish to be united with me, not because you need love."

You don't need love from your children. That'd be totally immature. (If you do think you need that kind of love, go back to your mother.) What you do need is *your children's love*. Why? Because your children are necessary to you. Therefore everything about them is precious, desirable, important.

Imagine a man who says to a woman, "Please marry me. I can't live without you." Should she marry him or should she run away? If he means what he's saying, he's a very sick person. If he can't live without you, he needs therapy. Why would you want to marry him? You don't want to be his nurse. Or maybe he doesn't mean what he says. Then why would you marry such a man? He's a liar! If a man says he can't live without you, wouldn't you be curious to see what happens when you say no? And if he says he *can* live without you, tell him okay, go right ahead.

What should a man say? A man should say, "Please marry me. I can exist without you, but without you it's meaningless. It's not a life." This means he's not looking for love, he is looking for *you*. What is happening in our society today is that love has become larger than life, more significant than the person with whom you live.

Two Types of Love

When you love someone, what you're feeling is a desire for closeness. Someone appeals to you, for whatever reasons, and you want to come closer. Love is not a fixed state or a completed project, so saying, "I'm in love" really makes no sense. Love is always a pursuit, and you never get there.

If after being married for many years there is no feeling of a need to pursue, you may be tempted to say that you've grown as close as you can get. Whether or not that's true, what is happening is that love has faded to the background somewhat, and pleasure has taken its place. You're not feeling the *love* for each other so much as you're experiencing the pleasure and the comfort of having each other in your lives. Elderly couples will often say they simply enjoy the pleasure of each other's company; the only sense of pursuit lies in the desire to spend more time together and get to know each other even better than before. Love needn't be earth-shattering, dramatic, or overwhelming. In mutual acceptance, in presence, you come alive.

The Hebrew word for love is *ahava*. In Judaism we speak of *ahavat Hashem*, love of God, and the expression has two distinct meanings. Sometimes it's used in the sense of desiring to grow closer to Him, by serving Him well and knowing Him more and more deeply. This is a form of pursuit, and it's not unlike the love we have for our fellow man: we're not satisfied just to be comfortable with the natural connections among all human beings. With a spouse we want a greater closeness, seeking stronger and more meaningful bonds.

There are other instances in which the words *ahavat Hashem* describe a love that is not a pursuit of closeness, but a sense of appreciating and cherishing the preciousness and the presence of God. There's no pursuit, as in the passionate longing to come closer from a distance. The first type of *ahava* has a fiery, almost romantic energy. This second kind is more like the tranquil pleasure of a lifelong couple delighting in each other's company. It is also akin, in a way, to self-love.

What is self-love? When you love yourself, are you running after yourself to get closer to yourself? Self-love doesn't mean that you love yourself with passion or desire. It's not a pursuit. In fact it's somewhat misleading to call it love at all; rather, you are precious to yourself. Self-love, by the way, is really the origin of all love. If you didn't love yourself, you wouldn't know what love is.

Did you ever roll off the bed and fall to the floor? Children will sometimes roll off the bed, but adults usually don't. How come? To use the example I gave earlier when we touched on this topic, let's say you normally sleep on a double bed, but you visit a friend and sleep on a single bed. How is it that you don't roll over in the middle of the night and fall off, mistakenly assuming (in your sleep) that it's the double bed you're used to? It's an amazing phenomenon. The brain adjusts, and we roll a little less that night. Even while deep asleep, we are somehow aware that the bed has a boundary, and we don't go past it.

That comes from self-love. But you can't say it's because you want to be closer to yourself. Self-love makes you precious to yourself, and because you're precious to yourself, you are innately careful not to hurt yourself. If there's danger, you'll wake yourself up. And if you're on the bed, you'll know when to stop, even when completely asleep.

Self-love, however, is not unconditional love, any more than marital or parental love should be. Human love is always conditional. We love someone lovable, and if they're not lovable, we don't. To attempt to love people unconditionally—whether a child or a spouse or yourself—is to deprive them of their accountability, to rob them of the motivation and the strength of character it takes to *merit* your love.

What *unconditional* means is that you are mine, and you are important to me, even when I hate you. You might sometimes hate one or another of your children, depending on how they behave. Nevertheless you're still their parent. Do you love them? Not at the moment. But they are yours. You belong together, and they're stuck with you. That's unconditional. Not unconditional love; unconditional *commitment*.

Love is the spirit and the spice with which we live out a relationship. If we can place love in its healthy context and realize that love cannot carry a marriage, the marriage will succeed. From a biblical perspective, love is not important; it is the feeling you should have for those who are important. Whoever is important to you, even if you don't love them, they are still important. Conversely, if they are not important in your life, no matter how much you love them, they are still not important. We have to convince a boy that the brother he hates is more important than the dog he loves.

When the Torah says, "Love God with all your heart," it doesn't show how important love is; it shows how important God is. The same is true of loving your fellow human being as you love yourself: not because love is important, but because each and every one of God's creations is precious and important.

Did God create us out of love? To our great comfort and good fortune, no. For most of our history we haven't been very lovable. He has hated all our sinful ways, been angry and even at times disgusted by us. How do we explain that? We are important to Him. *You are My children. You are precious to Me. You are Mine. You belong to Me, and I belong to you, even when I hate you.*

And in this way, He models for us what marriage should be. Love comes and goes; marriage is permanent. You combine the two by finding the person you are going to marry, and if love is necessary, cultivate love. To feel needed, to be necessary, to be indispensable is infinitely more significant than to be loved. This was how our great-grandparents married—in many instances, without love. They became *important* to each other, and love followed. Maybe not right away, but that's what we mean when we say love will grow.

Love is a gift. There's a brief teaching of Chabad Chassidus that exemplifies what love is like: *You're dragging your feet down the street, overburdened with troubles and cares. The load is heavy, the problems too many to bear. Unexpectedly you run into someone you love. Suddenly your footsteps are lifted, and your burdens cease to weigh you down.* Such is the nature of love.

These Are a Few of My Favorite Things

Among the ways you give yourself to a spouse is with love. Another way is with respect, another is with devotion, and still another way is with money. These are all *things*. If he or she has no money, you don't care. You say, "I don't need money from you. But if you did have money, I'd need it, because it's *yours*."

Suppose you have a husband who doesn't love anyone. You're not missing anything. He is giving you everything he has; he just doesn't have this *thing* called love. If he has no love to give, fine, he still belongs to you. If he does have love, but won't give it to you, now something is wrong. You are not connected. If he or she "ain't got a barrel of money," you don't care. But if he or she *has* money and doesn't give it you (or is giving it to someone else) then you've got a problem.

If you're a husband, do you need your wife to make you breakfast? No, you can make your own breakfast, or go without breakfast, or go out and buy breakfast. But if your wife *will* make you breakfast, what a delight! Because it's her gesture, her gift, to the man she cherishes. Not because it's breakfast.

Imagine you are married to a guy. He's wonderful, but he doesn't have a boat. Are you going to divorce him for this? If he doesn't have it, you don't need the boat. All you need is him. Everything about him, you need.

Marriage is God's invention. We model our marriages after His unconditional commitment to each and every one of us. As humans, it doesn't make much sense to be married. What, you're going to devote yourself to one person for the rest of your life and you expect to love each other continuously and forever? You won't. Don't even try. But in being married, our human frailties are beside the point. We are engaging in a divine institution. Love each other forever and ever? Get serious—out of the question. Our *marriages*, however, are eternal.

When people say, "I love you," *I* is the word that comes first, *love* is next, and *you* is last. It's in the wrong order. It's tantamount to saying, "If it's not you, it could just as easily be someone else." What we should be saying, rather, is, "You, I love." Under a Jewish wedding canopy, at the moment of truth, the groom says to his beloved, *Harei at*... meaning "*You* are hereby (sanctified unto me)." His meaning is clear as day: this is about *you*. It's not about how I feel, what I want, or what things I need. The same idea prevails when we make a blessing to God. It begins *Baruch Atah*, "Blessed are You." We are addressing *You*, God. The rest is commentary.

It's become commonplace that when a man wants love and he's not getting it from his wife, he will go looking for someone who will love him. This is the excuse used by every man or woman who is unfaithful to a husband or a wife. When you're looking for love, it's dangerous. "My wife doesn't love me; *this* person does." Does that justify what he did? Yes, it would, if marriage meant finding love, but it does not. Just as you don't need and can't expect love from someone else's child, you can't get the love your husband isn't giving you from another man. You want *his* love, because he is important to you.

This unfaithful husband figured when they were both single that since things were good between them, he'd give marriage a try. Well, now it's not good, so he decides to try something else. She was just a tool. Had he genuinely connected with her, he'd never want to lose her. Connecting, being close, means creating an opening in your heart that wasn't there before. It's a different channel, a whole new experience. You discover a previously untapped love with a quality of energy you've never used before.

Before marriage you don't have each other, all you have are the things you know and feel about each other. Love is an emotion, and emotions are unstable. They're up, they're down; sometimes you feel them, sometimes you don't. But your spouse is your spouse.

A guy is running frantically down the street. "What's the matter?" you ask.

"My wife is not feeling well. I'm running to get the doctor."

"Wow, that's so special, you really love your wife."

"Who said anything about love? She and I haven't spoken for a month."

"So then why are you running? Take your time, you'll go for a doctor later."

"That's crazy, she needs a doctor."

"But you don't love her."

"What's love got to do with it? She's my wife."

The preciousness and the importance of your relationship never change. Feelings are fleeting, but you always have each other. If someone is important to you, you should make an effort to love. And if you don't? Try tomorrow. Maybe next week. As long as you are important to each other the love will resurface. The essence and the purpose of marriage is unity, not love. Marriage and intimacy mean merging and becoming one. What is vital in a marriage is embodied in the statement, "Be mine." If you're mine and

I'm yours, we are one. It's not meant in the possessive sense; you don't belong to me, and I don't belong to you. We belong together.

The Three Pillars of a Relationship

People sometimes ask whether they ought to hone their relationship skills. No, for the most part skills are not what you need. You need kindness, respect, and sanctity. These are the three pillars on which a marriage stands. They will support and transform not just marriages, but lives. Taken together, these three constitute an attitude, an intention, a frame of mind that will produce the proper feelings, that will in turn bring the right words to your lips. It's true that there are people who have the right feelings but lack the skill of expressing them verbally. These skills can be developed. But far more often, what's missing are motivation and wisdom. We need to go to the source of the relationship, the core principles, and everything else will fall into place. It's like refreshing your memory, reconnecting with the reason you married, what marriage means, and what your life together is about. Learning new tricks won't help.

Every relationship begins with kindness. Kindness is the single most significant quality that makes one ready for marriage. Kindness is embodied in a good heart, a benevolent eye, a predisposition to judge another favorably or not at all. Kindness in marriage is expressed in words and gestures that say, "I care." Generosity is how you express kindness. The greater the generosity, the happier and more loving the marriage. You have to be generous with your money, your time, and your space, as well as with your words and your judgment. Some people are generous with their money and their possessions, but not with their time: "Take whatever you want, buy it if necessary, but leave me alone." Some people are generous with their time, but not with their space. Generosity in space means you allow another person to invade your life; and even better, to enjoy each other's presence—and show it.

There are those who are generous with their space, but not with their words. If you're feeling grateful to your wife, say so. Put it in words. Don't be stingy. A husband once told me that his wife did something wonderful the other day. "Did you tell her?" I asked. "No," he responded. "It just didn't come up."

Be kind and generous with your words. It's crucial to keeping a relationship alive. Don't just think it, say it. Your spouse needs your verbal expressions of thank you, and I love you, and I appreciate you.

The second pillar that supports a relationship is respect. Kindness and generosity bring you together; what *keeps* you together is respect. Two people who are kind to each other can live together, but two people who are respectful toward each other can live together forever. Many divorced couples can look back and clearly see that it was a lack of respect that brought the marriage to an end. Without respect, the relationship deteriorates. It can even get nasty.

There's a prevalent assumption that respect is something one must earn. "I'll show him respect when he shows me he deserves it." In other words, I only respect people for a reason, when they do something admirable, if not awesome. But respect should not be something you hold back until someone yanks it out of you. It doesn't have to be earned, it comes from you, free of charge. It is a form of generosity. Some people are generous with their respect, while others are stingy with it unless you dazzle and impress them.

For example, we offer respect to the elderly. Why? Because they're feeble? Because of their achievements and renown? No, it's just appropriate. It's the right thing to do. We show respect by honoring people's dignity; it is simply proper to give respect to the elderly, to parents, to scholars, to people of authority. We don't ask what they did to deserve it.

In the same vein, how much more essential is the respect you must bestow upon your spouse—for example, by not invading his or her space or privacy. A thousand years ago one of the great sages of our tradition taught that one should never read a spouse's mail without an invitation to do so. Great advice, and it hasn't changed with the advent of email and text messages. Equally important, if not more so, is the care we ought to take not to lower our standards of decency and modesty in the presence of a wife or a husband. You wouldn't answer the doorbell without getting "decent," out of respect for the person delivering your pizza. But with a spouse, you think you don't have to be decent? Does the pizza guy deserve more respect than your spouse?

Modesty is more important at home than on the street, to preserve the dignity of the home. It's common for a father to say to his daughter, "You can't go out dressed like that." What he should say is, "You can't be in the *house* like that." Why should the street be more important than your house? There's an adolescent assumption that when you're in love you can let your hair down, be at your worst behavior, and you'll love each other anyway. But it's not true. That is the very familiarity that breeds contempt. Walking around in your underwear does nothing to preserve your dignity or the dignity of your spouse.

A very special man I knew lost his wife to Alzheimer's disease. During the mourning period, the man reflected. "I can't say I was a good husband; but I can tell you that I never compromised her dignity." With your spouse, be on your best behavior, not your worst. This respect and dignity may be more important than kindness.

Then there is sanctity. Kindness and respect, the first two of our three pillars, are necessary in every relationship. They make a relationship real and lasting and true. Sanctity, however, is what makes a good relationship into a marriage.

There are few phenomena in the world that can be called sacred. Sanctity is something you cannot own or possess or buy. It is defined by the awareness that what you are engaging in is bigger than you and beyond you; and in the case of a relationship, it is bigger than the both of you.

Life is sacred. You cannot own life—not even *your* life is yours, and never will be yours. Hence, suicide is forbidden. (So stringently forbidden, it's punishable by death.) And the body too, contrary to the opinion of your average teenager, is sacred. It's not yours, and no, you can't just go and do whatever you want to it. It's on loan from God.

Similarly, to make a relationship into a marriage calls for a recognition of its sanctity. Imagine if a person were to believe, deeply and truly, that everything happens by divine plan, and that the reason this person is married to that person is because God chose them for each other. How would that belief affect their relationship? At the very least, it would eradicate all the squabbles and annoyances that would otherwise be so bothersome as to chronically impinge upon the quality of life. Knowing that a marriage is sacred, divinely orchestrated, makes the petty stuff completely negligible.

Marriage is holy because it is not our invention, but God's. It was a divine idea from the outset, one that demands of us that we become something more than inherently human. God is asking us to go beyond ourselves, to be able to hear another person without imposing our own prejudices, to consider and respect a perspective other than our own. To be divine is to rise above what human nature dictates. And because of the sanctity of marriage, when things are not going well, every effort to save the marriage is not just warranted, but morally necessary. If a marriage were simply an agreement between two people, and if it were simply a matter of poor judgment that got these two into this mess, then why perpetuate a mistake? Why not just call it off and go home?

We suggested earlier, in the chapter on dating, that if you're going out with someone and it's clearly a mismatch, call it off. Don't agonize, don't go for therapy. There are plenty of other fish in the sea. We would never say that concerning a married couple. You don't call it off; you *do* go for marriage counseling. "Yes," you say to yourself, "there certainly are other fish in the sea. But no other fish is *mine*."

When I was a young student I had a teacher, a respected rabbi of the community. One day while I was there a newly wedded couple came in and asked him to settle a disagreement. "Rabbi," the wife asked, "isn't it true that we're not allowed to ladle soup out of the pot on *Shabbos* while it's on the fire? Tell my husband. He doesn't know."

"Slow down, slow down," my teacher said. "What's the question again? Ladling soup from a hot pot? Over fire? On *Shabbos*?"

"Yes!" she exclaimed.

My teacher thought for a bit. "Hmm, that's complicated," he said. "Let me go home and look it up. Call me later and I'll tell you whether or not it's allowed."

As they walked away I stared at him, dumbfounded. "You're not allowed to cook on *Shabbos*," I said. "A pot standing over fire is cooking. If you ladle soup out of it, you're stirring the pot. Stirring is an act of cooking, which is forbidden on *Shabbos*. Every *yeshiva* kid knows that. What am I missing? Why didn't you tell her she was right?"

"And make the husband look bad in his wife's eyes?" he replied back. "We're not allowed to do that." I was completely in awe. He had done it just to preserve the wife's respect for her husband. Naturally and spontaneously, even exaggerating the question and playing dumb, he had disarmed the "he said/she said" emotional energy of the dispute so that together they would defer to divine judgment.

If we treat our own marriages with that kind of reverence, we will have established the third pillar of a relationship—the one that turns a roommate into a spouse, and respect into sanctity. That's the sanctity of marriage. Like the sanctity of the wedding canopy that transcends and envelops us, we can surrender ourselves to its embrace. In the presence of a married couple we are in the presence of something as holy as the holiest day of the year, *Yom Kippur*, the Day of Atonement.

The service of the High Priest on *Yom Kippur*, in the Holy Temple in Jerusalem, is the quintessence of sanctity. He enters the Holy of Holies, bringing in a fire pan upon which burns a specially compounded incense. He says a short prayer and backs out, bowing respectfully as he goes. In the time of second Temple, after the Babylonian exile, we are told that the High Priests were not of the same caliber as before, and that because they would have inappropriate thoughts they would die there in the Holy of Holies. It became such a frequent occurrence, the precaution was instituted of tying a rope around the High Priest so that if he died in the Holy of Holies someone would be able to drag his body out—since no one else was allowed to enter.

It's pretty hard to believe that a High Priest of any generation could be so reckless and irresponsible. The service in the Holy of Holies took a total of fifteen or twenty minutes. Most people, let alone High Priests, can concentrate on what they're doing for long enough and discipline themselves sufficiently to avoid indulging in inappropriate thoughts for twenty minutes—especially knowing that their predecessors had died last year and for years before. Even a High Priest with a lousy memory would realize that the rope around his waist was there for a reason. To say they were "not of the same caliber" is an understatement.

The key to understanding this remarkable bit of history is to realize that the "inappropriate thoughts" were more of a feeling of *entitlement*: no one may enter the Holy of Holies except *me*. Others may not, but I can! The High Priest's sense that it was his *right* to be there violated the sanctity of the Holy of Holies. The proper attitude would have been, *I am over my head, this is way too holy for me. I will do what God asked me to do, and I'll do it carefully, and back out. Because I don't belong here.*

The marriage relationship works the same way. When you start to feel entitled, you are compromising the privacy and the sanctity. This applies in all aspects of marriage, but it's particularly true in the realm of marital intimacy—as we'll explore more fully in the next chapter. Intimacy is not yours by right. But in the context of marital sanctity, God allows you to experience it. Like the High Priest in the Holy of Holies.

Many people report that the first time they go to the *Kotel*—the Western Wall of the Holy Temple—it's an overwhelming, awe-inspiring experience. They're not even sure whether they have the right to take a picture or if they're allowed to chew gum. The second time, it's not so awesome, and by the third time, they feel so at home there they'll sit down in the middle of the plaza and eat their lunch. They lose the sanctity; it's become familiar. The miracle of marriage is that with the appropriate attitude you'll never lose the sanctity.

And as with the third pillar, so it is with all three pillars of relationships, as well as with the unconditional commitment that is prerequisite to lasting emotional resonance. Having cultivated kindness, respect, and sanctity, what's not to love?

19

Sexuality and Intimacy

We don't need more pleasure.
We need more closeness.

A topic as delicate and as controversial as intimacy is rarely appropriate for public discussion. Unusual times, however, call for unusual measures. There is a great deal of unnecessary pain, confusion, and suffering going on in the world today, and it's precisely due to the fact that questions of intimacy are too often swept under the rug.

People say, "I don't need a rabbi to tell me how to have sex." It's true. If the birds and the bees can figure it out, so can you. If it's sex you're after, you don't need any help. But if what you are seeking is something higher, nobler, and longer lasting, you're going to need a little guidance and a whole lot of wisdom.

It was not so long ago that most, if not virtually all marital relationships, regardless of cultural differences or social strata, enjoyed at least some measure of that nobility and stability. Two people grew interested in each other, became connected to each other, deeply desired each other's company, and lived their lives intimately as one.

Marriages today are unlikely to exemplify that once-upon-a-time quality of meaningful connection and commitment. In fact marriage has become more the butt of jokes than a source of real and lasting satisfaction. It has become all about this convenience or that distraction, this fleeting attraction or that symbol of success; and if you no longer enjoy "this" or you don't think you need any more of "that," simple: you get a divorce. It's a tragedy. To begin to turn all this around, we need first to understand the distinction between intimacy and sex.

Sex is about a thing; intimacy is about a person. Intimacy means bonding with someone, merging and becoming one with another human being. Sex is about one body taking pleasure from another body. One feels like the cultivation of trust and the fulfillment of promise; the other feels like an obsession with the gratification of a desire.

They are two completely different kinds of pleasure. They look alike but have nothing in common. They produce different bodily responses, different hormones, different emotions, different sensations, and have a completely different impact on the people involved. When you become accustomed to the pursuit of one kind of pleasure, you'll find it almost impossible to shift your attention to the quest for the other.

Take for example that uncouth question often asked after sex: "How was it for you?" What are you really asking? *It?* What exactly was *it*? Or was one of *us* an *it*? And why would you have to ask? You were there, were you not? Don't you know?

It might sound as though the person asking was concerned, but in reality, he was lost in his own world. He knew what it was like for him. What it was like for her, he had no idea. They were two separate people, remaining very separate. Sex has become impersonal. It's become about a thing, not a person. Intimacy is never about an it or a thing. No *thing* should ever come between a couple in the bedroom.

When we strip all intimacy from sex and turn it into a recreational activity, we feel diminished. It takes a little something out of both partners, and neither is the same as they were a moment ago in each other's eyes. Even if married, if they're having sex without intimacy there is no real bond between them; the more recreational the sex, the further apart they become. Sex becomes free of attachment, free of commitment, and devoid of permanence. Intimacy, on the other hand, leads to mutual growth. It's expansive rather than dissipating.

Until the sexual revolution of the 1960s, when experimentation with the notion of free love took root, intimacy and sex were understood as a seamless unity. Since then, "experts" and their allies in the communications and entertainment media have promoted a doctrine that is destructive and degrading. A once-predominant culture went out of fashion, a culture that recognized the real human need for connection unobstructed by any extraneous *thing*, such as gratuitous sex. The idea that a man's deepest pleasure can reside in giving of himself, and that conversely a woman's innermost desire can be satisfied by surrendering herself, was suddenly antiquated and scorned. Sex has replaced intimacy, and we're paying a terrible price for it. People are confused, frustrated, bored, guilty, and just plain unhappy about their sexuality. It's true now more than ever. Even some experts are now admitting that putting all the emphasis on pleasure has been devastating. We don't need more pleasure; what we need is more closeness.

There's a still more disturbing byproduct of sex without intimacy. It's what happened to the ancient Greeks and Romans and other empires—once powerful and influential, now extinct: the separation of sex from reproduction. Many historians now concur that it's a form of decadence that leads to self-annihilation, to the end of a civilization. To rediscover intimacy, though by this point seemingly improbable, has become essential not only for our happiness, but for our survival.

A Plague in Every Bedroom

You can take a *bus* across town. At an all-you-can-eat buffet, you can take a *plate of food*. You're welcome to take a *seat* at the table. In other words, you can take an *object*. But to take something intrinsically human from another human being—to use a person for pleasure—is a violation, a trespass, a form of abuse.

Sex can destroy a marriage. Between husband and wife, there needs to be intimacy, not sex. If two people become one, that is intimacy. But marriage does not permit a couple to engage in sex. That's not what a marriage is. In a marriage, there can be no taking. Even when it's mutual and consensual, if it's just two people having a good time, sex in and of itself is about taking, not about sharing intimacy. At times, if there's a measure of coercion involved, it might border on violence, at least to some subtle extent. As such, we should not be all that surprised if it becomes actual violence. If it's completely involuntary on one person's part, it's called rape; if it's done with consent, it's called sex. In any event, two people taking from each other, with or without mutual consent, is what animals do.

"What should I do?" a gentleman once asked me. "Sex between me and my wife is not good." You're having sex with your wife? What are you? An animal?

Sex becomes a performance, a selfish and self-gratifying activity, in which both are on trial. Sexual pleasure is never enough; inevitably, after a while it fails to satisfy, and the couple is left to seek greater pleasure. Often they get so caught up in the pleasure of it, they are no longer conscious as to who the person is.

Since sex is about a thing, the person you have sex with becomes a part of that thing—an object. When people become "things" to one another, it's basically the end of decency, and it colors every aspect of what ought to be civilized society, the character of all relationships. If the "object" of your attention weighs one pound more than what you consider optimal, or if he or she is not exactly the right shape, the right height, or the right color, you're not interested. This is not the perfect *thing* you're looking for.

That's why no matter how good the sex is, a person can still feel alone in the world. A couple can be madly in love with each other, have great sex, and still never experience an intimate moment where they are bonded. Engaging in sex this way separates rather than unites. If your goal is good sex, you've stepped out of your marriage. Unchecked or unrectified, such a relationship is likely to end in divorce.

In an earlier, more polite time, sex was something that was shown only in movies that decent people did not seek out. The movies were sold in stores with boarded-up windows, because they were illegal to sell in public. It was considered pornography, a word whose definition can be distilled, again, to one body getting pleasure from another. When people are uncomfortable having sex face to face, it is pornography. We don't want to have a person-to-person connection. We just want to have *it*—i.e., sex. Let's keep our soul and personality out of it. This is one of the reasons why oral sex and other positions are often considered preferable. There's no need for eye contact, no need to connect with the person. You just mind your own business, which is your pleasure.

Today, what was once pornography is now the norm in the average home. It's no longer something that takes place in the movies or on the internet. It's a disease that has plagued bedrooms everywhere. What we hear and read about today—every magazine article, every talk show, every newspaper column, and every book—is basically advice on how to *get*, what to *get*, and how much more you can *get* from another human being. The advice from "experts" today is none other than instruction in pornography.

The sages of antiquity, however, bring us a very different sort of expertise and prescribe a very different mode of behavior. It's advice that is founded on the recognition that we are made in the image of divinity.

When entering the bedroom, a man should remind himself that to use her for his pleasure would be nothing less than abusive. This may sound melodramatic, but it's true. If you are seeking pleasure, you're not ready for intimacy. A man is not a taker. He is a giver, and giving means giving of himself, with no holding back, making himself completely available.

By the same token a woman should walk into the bedroom prepared to surrender unconditionally to her husband, rather than to get something she wants or expects. Surrendering means allowing him into her life, welcoming him into every fiber of her being. Provisional or conditional surrender is not surrender at all. Her surrender must be without reserve.

There is only giving and receiving, without constraint or vacillation. Both need to leave their respective default modes at the door and enter that childlike place inside where he lets go of any inclination to take from her, and she puts away all her judgments as to what he does or does not deserve.

Is this an impossible ideal?

Choose Your Pleasure

Make no mistake—intimacy is pleasurable. Pleasure is what creates life; it animates and motivates all our experiences. And we are empowered to choose our pleasures. There is pleasure from food, pleasure from shopping, pleasure from our children, pleasure from sex. There is the pleasure a couple enjoys from his body and her body, as *things*—and then there is the pleasure they experience in the intimacy between them as two whole human beings. That's the question: which is it?

The more she has of him and the more he has of her, the more pleasure they have. It's normal and natural that we should want it to be about bodies; but if it's *only* about bodies and we are not connecting with an actual complete person, the pleasure enjoyed by these two bodies will make them grow apart. It may not be immediately apparent, but we see it all the time, where two people have sex for a month or a year and then it's over.

Intimacy is a process of total giving and complete receptivity, in uniquely masculine and feminine ways. A man's essential nature is to give, absolutely and unequivocally, in response to a need. If he gives but 90 percent of himself, he'll be frustrated, because he is going against his true nature. A woman's essential nature is to receive, to invite and absorb another human being into her existence. If she can do so 100 percent, she will feel like a complete woman. As with a man, 90 percent won't be enough.

In order for a woman to achieve complete receptivity, she must have complete trust in a man. She needs to be assured of absolute security. If she is suspicious, if she feels a need to hold back, to protect herself, to keep her distance, she won't be able to embrace and envelop him entirely into her reality. In the traditional Torah definition of a man's masculinity, he not only senses his wife's hunger, he provides her with the safety she needs to feel like a woman. That's why it can scarcely happen outside of marriage. When a woman surrenders herself completely to a man, in her heart and soul they are as good as married; if the relationship were to end, her pain would be akin to a divorce.

The pleasure of true intimacy lies in the experience of losing oneself. A man loses himself in the giving, and a woman loses herself in the receiving. The result is two people dissolving into oneness. In yielding their separateness and individuality to their essential unity, their egos, opinions, personality quirks, self-centeredness, and self-consciousness—all their *schtick*—dissolve and disappear. They have become *one flesh,* as in God's command to Adam and Eve. What's left is the innocent state in which they were born. Having surrendered and become inseparable, to then part company would be unthinkable, like an amputation, as though their souls have been ripped out of them. Intimacy bonds a couple to one another; sex cannot.

The urge to be physical, to flirt and have fun chasing down sexual encounters, runs counter to progress toward mature masculinity and femininity, toward what it takes to make a marriage work. The more energy a man and a woman expend in this type of pursuit, the less likely they are to achieve the genuine pleasure of intimacy. Even when they marry, they won't become husband and wife; they'll remain a man and a woman seeking sexual gratification. It's a recipe for failure.

You've seen the magazine covers. There's the one that promises "Seven Secret Methods for Maximum Pleasure." Then the one on the next shelf insists there are actually "Seventeen Secrets." And here's a brand-new book on the market hyping "Fifty Ways to Please Your Lover!" Is there no end?

When it comes to pleasure there truly is no end. The question is, what sort of satisfaction do we seek?

Sexual Satisfaction 101

Let's turn to the tried and true metaphor of food. The reason junk food never satisfies is because it's a desire that doesn't stem from a real need, like hunger; it's a desire for instant pleasure—in other words, recreation. How much sugar does the body need? Not a lot. How much does it want? There's never enough. Where there's no need, there can be no satisfaction. But too much junk will make you sick. Maimonides tells us that the first sign of illness is the perversion of appetite, when you've come to the point where you've had so many potato chips, it's making you nauseous, but you cannot stop. A desire that is insatiable is not a real need. We are a junk-food nation.

If you give a starving person a sandwich and ask him how it tastes, he doesn't even understand the question. He's happy to be eating real food. Does it need a little salt? Does it need a little pepper? He couldn't care less. Only people who are so bored with eating they can't enjoy wholesome food need a little bit more salt, a little more spice.

Sex is the junk food of the social realm. You can always have more pleasure. But there's a difference between the pleasure one gets from what's necessary and pleasure derived from what's not. If your taste buds have already been corrupted, the extraneous pleasures can be difficult to resist. Like those guys who don't enjoy their wives anymore and "need" to be with other women. It's like saying, "I don't want a real meal. I just want potato chips." That's why people commit adultery. You can find another man or woman who's more attractive than your husband or wife any day of the week. To that sort of pleasure, there is no end.

The good news is that when you're satisfying a real need, you can ignore the unnecessary desire. The real need is to bond with a human being, and that's what provides the ultimate satisfaction. There are greater pleasures, it's true; but there is no more *satisfying* pleasure than intimacy. The pleasure attained in being a husband to your wife or a wife to your husband is a lasting pleasure that brings life-affirming satisfaction, not fleeting moments and destruction. Know which pleasure you are reaching for. Shallow people eat to entertain their taste buds at the expense of their stomachs. Are you feeding your mouth or are you feeding your stomach? Beware—the food your stomach wants is not the same as the food your mouth wants. If you let your mouth dictate what you eat, you are never going to be healthy. Should your stomach complain about the junk food, there are pills designed to silence your stomach, so that you can eat more junk. Are we doing the same with our sexuality?

This is what happens when you use a person as a tool. When you are getting pleasure from a tool, it means that intimacy is no longer interesting and you now need "very spicy food" to enliven it, so there is no end to pleasure.

Human sexuality that's about physical sensation is child's play. The real sexual urge is for oneness, not pleasure, and it comes not from any *thing* but in relationship with a person: your spouse. Pleasure will either bring you closer together or turn you away from each other. It will create either more respect for each other or less. It can diminish you or it can bring you into the presence of Godliness.

Three Levels of Pleasure

Human pleasure, a key aspect of our involvement with the world in which we live, can be experienced on any one of three distinct levels. The familiar pleasures we enjoy in our everyday lives are drawn from our various interactions on what we'll call the human plane. These can take place, for example, in the exercise of our intelligence, whether in communication with others or in our personal study and contemplation—in our appreciation of history or current events, science or philosophy, creative arts or practical invention. This is the *middle* level of the three. It's considered to be on the *human* plane, because its pleasures are derived from our quintessentially human character traits and sensibilities, be they intellectual, emotional, athletic, or aesthetic.

The *lower* level of pleasure stems from behavior and desires that draw us down to a level lower than ourselves—pleasures that are unworthy of the best of what it means to be a human being. The attraction to (or obsession with) food is an example of the sort of craving that offers fleeting pleasure but compromises our dignity and self-respect. This is because the foods we eat, whether belonging to the plant or animal or mineral kingdom, are created on an intrinsically lower level than a human being. This attraction pulls us from a higher status to a lower one. In essence we are asking a lowly substance to give us pleasure—*taking* from a material substance that is beneath us, which can only serve to diminish and weaken and drag us down.

On the other hand, it is true that eating foods that are in fact beneath us is, in a sense, distasteful. Eating like a *mensch* is to eat with the awareness that it is "not by bread alone" that man lives, but by the *word of God* that is bringing these foods into existence from moment to moment. Eating with the proper intention, understanding *why* we are eating, allows us to remain on the human plane and derive pleasure by being, in a sense, equal to ourselves.

Then there is a third dimension of pleasure, one that pulls us upward and beyond the inherent limitations of the human condition, toward something higher and greater than ourselves. Selfless kinds of pleasure, such as the pleasure of doing something right without thought of reward or the pleasure of seeing someone else happy. It's what we might call angelic behavior.

These three levels of pleasure are similarly available to us in the context of marriage, and we have the ability and the freedom of choice to decide in which direction we'd like to go. A successful, happy, fulfilling marriage is about becoming bigger than yourself. It raises you above the human realm, because the essential characteristic of marriage is oneness, and oneness is holy. Intimacy in marriage invokes that same ascendant movement, brings us up and beyond the human plane, and pulls us upward toward heaven.

Outside of marriage, on the human level, the physical and bodily pleasures of sex keep people apart, at the very least; they can also bring us further and further down to the lower plane, to that of the animal. Hence the need to call sex, "making love," to mask the fact that sex without intimacy always feels like degradation.

There are behaviors in the bedroom that can go in only one direction: down. For a marriage to thrive, there should be no such descent, only elevation.

Achieving oneness of soul and heart is easy compared to the challenge of transforming two bodies into one. "Therefore," the biblical passage in Genesis tells us, "a man shall leave his father and mother, and cleave to his wife, and they shall become one flesh." Become one flesh? How exactly do we do that? Every human being is a separate entity, with individuated tastes, styles, and opinions. When your wife is hungry, that doesn't make *you* hungry. How do two separate people defy the laws of nature and become one flesh? Only by rising above the human realm. Only through intimacy. It's the most sacred endeavor human beings are capable of—a divine gift, granted us because we are created in the image of God.

The Laws of Intimacy

The ultimate miracle of a relationship is in the bedroom. There is no other place where it is so supremely important to be sensitive, caring, and considerate. In this holy, private space, the intimacy between a husband and a wife becomes the key to their entire life together, to the exclusion of all other concerns. When the totality of their focus is on each other, mentally and emotionally as well as physically, every facet of their relationship—even the most casual interaction outside as well as inside the home—becomes imbued with that same quality of intimacy and deepest respect.

By definition, the bedroom environment must be preserved as sacred, free of diversion or disturbance. Mutual surrender cannot abide distractions, whatever they may be, that can come between a husband and a wife. The focus is entirely on the pleasure of intimacy, with nothing else there that might intervene: no television, no computer, not even music. You can have a phone in the room for emergencies, but it should be silenced. Walking into the bedroom, there must be a palpable aura of an intimate, perhaps even infinite, space.

This does not mean one ought to be uptight, overly serious, or conservative in the bedroom. Doing what is right is not the same as behaving like a prude. We shouldn't try to be more pious than the sages of old and the classical arbiters of proper conduct. The *Code of Jewish Law* clearly indicates that whatever a husband and a wife want to do together in the bedroom is fine. So yes, you have the freedom and the flexibility to do as you wish. Nonetheless we would be wise to consider what constitutes a truly suitable attitude and appropriate behavior in the context of that freedom. Certainly, we don't want to indulge every base, animalistic urge. We ought to be just as enthusiastic about making the most uplifting choices, as we are excited about the intimacy we are fortunate enough to share.

In every aspect of life there are life-supporting guidelines. We strive always to be a *mensch* outside the bedroom, so why not in the bedroom? When you know you are doing the right thing, with a clear conscience, with a refined sense of what is and what is not acceptable, you become a different person: you stand differently, speak differently, walk differently, and even sleep differently. Indeed, being conscientious about what is right and beneficial in the bedroom affects the rest of your life together. If everything in the bedroom is going well, any other problems that might arise in your relationship can be openly addressed and rectified. There is nothing richer and healthier than striving to be at your absolute best in every aspect of the marriage and giving it your all.

There's a core concept in Chassidic philosophy that explains how the lower the level to which something can descend in this world, the higher its source in a spiritual realm above. The metaphor used to illustrate this idea describes what happens when a tree falls: the fruit on the highest branches will inevitably land the farthest distance from the root of the tree. Sexual intimacy is well described by this imagery. The loftiest, most sublime qualities of marital intimacy are capable of descending into the depths of unhappiness and disconnect, if a couple should choose to disregard the wisdom traditions that guide us in rising above unbridled passion. In Jewish Law this is particularly emphasized in the cyclical rhythms of when intimacy is appropriate and optimal and when it is not. The specifics of how this is practiced are a bit too detailed for this discussion, but the guiding principle is easily understood. In the words of King Solomon, there is a "time to embrace, and a time to refrain from embracing." It creates an extraordinary quality of integrity and purity in marriage and family life.

How would one define *holiness* in the bedroom? What might that look like, given that we've never actually *seen* holiness? And more to the point, assuming we want to *create* an atmosphere of sanctity in the bedroom, where would we begin?

It begins with inner understanding and appreciation of the fact that people are not *things* to be objectified, and that treating a person like an object would be distasteful or abusive or may actually border on the pornographic. Nor should we allow anything extraneous to the relationship to come between us—whether it's visual stimuli or emotional blocks or even distracting thoughts. Those sorts of *things* will only serve to divert our attention from each other. The pleasure of intimacy lies in delighting in each other's company, in each other's exclusive presence, with no one and no *thing* to intervene, even in our minds.

Having said that, one aspect of environmental sanctity that becomes significant is the lighting—or rather the lack thereof. There's a big difference between *seeing* and *listening*. A visual experience of beauty can be provocative and compelling, but it's generally not conducive to a meaningful, personal connection, getting to know someone as he or she really is. *Listening* to a spouse, on the other hand, opens not only our ears, but our minds and hearts, so that we are able to *hear*, i.e., *understand*, deeply and without external distractions. That's why intimacy is best achieved under the veil of darkness, where concealment actually reveals something more important and pleasurable than can be experienced in brightness, and facilitates intimate connectivity. During the biblical revelation at Mount Sinai, when Moses and his people expressed a desire to *see* God, He insisted on *speaking* rather than revealing His face. "I don't want to impress you with My glory. I want you to listen to Me!"

Emotional and intellectual sanctity are also vital in marital relations. We're not permitted, for example, to be intimate while angry, upset, or resentful, and certainly not if one is planning to divorce. Proving a point in a heated argument may feel like a victory or a conquest, and that might in turn spark a certain volatile sexuality, but it won't create (or for that matter allow for) intimacy. It's simply not going to happen.

Similarly, if you're even moderately inebriated, it can ruin the intimacy, because you are not fully present. Even having relations in a somewhat public setting, where there's a risk of being seen, might add a measure of danger and excitement to the experience; but whatever pleasure that may bring, it is definitely not intimacy.

What about if you're with your spouse, but thinking about someone else, whom you imagine you would enjoy more? Is that adultery? Yes, mentally and emotionally without a doubt. Nonetheless some therapists actually suggest that such fantasies can enhance a marriage. While it might elicit some sort of highly charged sexual pleasure, it is an unspeakable violation of the intimacy in your marriage. Equally absurd is the notion that a "little pornography" will somehow enhance the experience.

You're probably asking, "Must it all be so choreographed? What about lighthearted spontaneity?" Spontaneity is not the same as recklessness. Sex with a stranger, for example, is reckless rather than spontaneous. Paradoxically, spontaneity within marriage is possible only when all these rules are in place, so that you can abandon yourself to the pleasure. Spontaneity lies in the safety and security of marriage and a mutual respect for intimacy. All these guidelines deeply enhance the special times in the bedroom—and moreover can bring healing and resonance to all aspects of our relationships.

It should come as no surprise to learn that according to the sages of Talmudic Law, intimacy is most appropriate on the Sabbath. It's the time when we turn away from all mundane distractions and extraneous concerns and connect with the most meaningful, uplifting aspects of our lives. Preparations for the Sabbath will often entail long and complicated to-do lists, along with plenty of hustle and bustle, but all those *things* vaporize into insignificance once the sun sets and *Shabbat* begins.

The great sage Maimonides cites the ancient mystical rabbinical literature, explaining how, when the final redemption arrives, it will usher in an epoch which will be celebrated as "the day that is wholly *Shabbat*," when all the things we need will be available in abundance. There will be no worries, nothing to disturb us, or intrude upon our most cherished, intimate pursuit—getting to know God. Nothing will be in the way, because everything pales in comparison with the holiness of God. Now *that's* intimacy.

20

Disharmony, Divorce, and Destiny

When a once-promising relationship appears to have broken a promise, rest assured that what's real is never random.

Let's begin here with a few fundamental questions people often ask: why do two people marry each other—the real reasons, not just the circumstantial stuff? And why do some people have two marriages? Or even three or more? Did these various couples have a relationship in a past life? Were there issues left unresolved that they needed to fix together? Or maybe one partner needed fixing and the other was the designated fixer? Perhaps the reason they married was only, or primarily, to bring children into the world? And was that just any children, or certain specific children?

The answers to such questions are *could be, maybe,* or *probably.* The truth is, there is no way of knowing. However, there's something more important than finding out the answers to these questions. It's for us to know that nothing happens in God's world that was not supposed to happen, even when it seems counterintuitive, contrary to common sense, or beyond our comprehension.

All that we need to know is that there is a reason, and whatever that reason may be it is not ours to figure out. We may even be better off not knowing, because even if we were to find out, it may not make much of a difference. Or worse, we might think we understood something we actually misunderstood, and then project those wrong assumptions into the "real" world.

Some years ago there was a popular documentary film, later expanded into a book, called *What the Bleep Do We Know!?* It's about the connection between some of the foundational ideas of quantum physics and our consciousness, explaining how little we actually know and yet how our perceptions have a profound effect on our reality. There is no way of knowing with any certainty the extent to which our experiences are simply an extension of our thinking, whether or not we're thinking straight. The only things we do know for certain, as taught by the great sages from antiquity right up to modern times, are that nothing in Creation is superfluous, and nothing is a mistake.

The principle of Divine Providence tells us that God Almighty not only creates but also oversees and involves Himself in every concern and every detail of human experience. Since God is infinite, His energetic supervision extends to even the slightest and most seemingly insignificant of events. Humans are limited and therefore cannot be aware of, nor can they be bothered with, the fine details of life. God can and does. Moreover, He takes into account the ways our own perception influences our relationship with what we refer to as "reality," so as to be able to present *His* reality in ways we're more likely to understand. He puts on our plate precisely what belongs there, then gives us what we need in order to triumph over the external obstacles in our way and the inner limitations that hold us back. We may not think we can get it right and do the job, but God believes in us and makes sure that we are neither hindered nor ill-equipped. It's actually a great compliment that He has such faith in us.

If some choose instead to believe that life is just a random game that people play, that the world is an unruly and arbitrary place where nothing makes any sense, and that, given all the terrible things that happen, our existence is just one big blunder, they are setting themselves up for a life of utter misery.

It's Happening to Me; It Must Be Mine

During one of my speaking engagements in Argentina I had an unforgettable experience. It was a particularly long and miserable trip from Minneapolis to New York, then to Miami and on to Buenos Aires. Needless to say I was not in a very good mood when I arrived. I was eagerly looking forward to finally getting some rest. However, when the colleague who had invited me there picked me up from the airport, the first thing he said to me was, "Oh, by the way, we made you an appointment with a woman who has had a terrible tragedy. She is severely depressed and hasn't left her apartment in six months. Although she hasn't spoken with anyone, she agreed to meet with you. So we'll stop there on the way to the hotel and you will talk to her."

I was not pleased, to say the least. I thought, first of all, what do you say to someone who has experienced a serious tragedy and is severely depressed? Moreover, you went ahead and made this arrangement without asking me? Don't you think you might have first discussed it with me when the meeting should take place? I was quite upset. But the woman was waiting for us, so we kept the appointment.

Anyway, we arrived at her apartment, and I met the woman, who was practically catatonic. There was no color in her cheeks, there was no life in her eyes, there was no energy in her voice. When we sat down, she painstakingly described how her special, precious, beloved son had been killed in a car accident, at nineteen years of age. When she finally finished describing how amazing he was, I said, "Well, you've got to be grateful that you had him for nineteen years." She did not appreciate that comment. I added, "I understand the shock of it all . . . it was so sudden and unexpected. But imagine if you had known upfront that he was only going to be here for nineteen years. Imagine if God had come to you and said, 'I'm looking for a mother for an extraordinary boy. But he's only going to be in this world for nineteen years.' And He asked you to be his mother. What would you have answered?"

To my surprise, she said, "absolutely not."

I replied, "Well, then, it's a good thing He didn't ask you."

With that statement, a floodgate of tears opened up. I saw the unimaginable grief of a devastated mother dissolve before my eyes. She came back to life. It was probably one of the most moving and dramatic moments I have ever experienced. It was simply astounding. On the way back to the hotel, I thought, *Here I was, so upset that my host had made the appointment without asking me.* But I then realized that had he asked, my reply would have been, "absolutely not." And that would have been the wrong answer.

God does us a great kindness in not asking us what sort of lives we want to live. Were He to ask, we would no doubt embarrass ourselves with the wrong answers. What kind of pathetic creatures would we be if we were given the option to refuse every challenge? We would reject them all! If anything sounded a little off the beaten path or remotely difficult, we would bail out. "Oh no, I can't handle that!" And we will have missed out on the purpose and the mission for which we were created.

So great is God's confidence in us, there ought to be a special blessing to recite, thanking God for believing in us, for not asking for our approval of His plan, for sparing us the humiliation of shortchanging ourselves. By not leaving us to our own devices, He has done us a wonderful favor.

When contemplating, therefore, such questions as whether an unhappy couple *should* have married or whether it was just a big mistake, it's important to consider how the match was made, and by Whom. As we discussed in the chapter titled "The Jungle of Dating," human beings (who by nature make mistakes) have no say in the matter. In reality there are absolutely no mistakes. God does not allow that to happen. It's all His decision, so you simply cannot marry the wrong person.

Children raised in dysfunctional families often wonder whether their parents made the right choice. Had it been their parents' decision, it could indeed have been a mistake. Given the choice, based on the information they had, they said yes. Then when it didn't work out, all they had to do was apologize. "I'm so sorry, my mistake. I'll be more careful the next time." But that was not the case. *God* married them, so they were married to the right person. And that's the tragedy of it: these two were the exact two people God chose to be married to each other, and they couldn't hack it. But a tragedy is not a mistake.

Marriage is not about two people who are attracted to each other trying to make a go of it and then, realizing they had married for all the wrong reasons, getting divorced. If you think your parents' marriage, or your marriage, or your great-grandparents' marriage was a mistake, your whole concept of marriage is flawed. It's not a human endeavor. It's actually a miracle—a common and familiar one, perhaps, and therefore we might take it for granted, but nonetheless a miracle.

Sometimes it takes incredible, earth-shattering, or catastrophic events just for two people to meet. As in a world war, for example, where everyone is displaced. People from Russia find themselves in Hungary. People from Hungary find themselves in America. Through Divine Providence, unseen and unforeseen, they meet. There's a lyrical passage in the Talmud that says God stays up all night making marriage matches; and even for Him, it's more difficult than splitting the Red Sea. It's nothing short of a miracle, because marriage is a reunion of two parts of the same soul. There is no way for us to know, nor are we expected to know, who our predestined soulmate will turn out to be. The only thing we can do when we meet someone who appeals to us is hope that he or she is the one; and if you end up marrying each other, then you know for sure this is the one God has selected for you.

Let's say you entertain the possibility that you can marry the wrong person. Does that also mean you can have the wrong children? If your parents' marriage was a mistake, then that would mean *you* were a mistake. That's ludicrous thinking. If they should never have been married, you should never have been born.

I was once introduced before giving a speech as the father of eleven children. At the end of the speech, about an hour later, a woman raised her hand and said, "Eleven children?" She hadn't heard a word I had said after that. When I assured her it was true, she said, "Are you aware that some people don't have any?" Her comment caught me off guard, and for a moment I felt really guilty. I was taught to share. How could you take eleven children for yourself, leaving others with none? But then I quickly realized that you cannot have someone else's children. They are yours by divine selection. Therefore, the marriage that produces them cannot be a mistake.

There was a woman in our community who tried every form of birth control. She was desperately trying to not get pregnant, but nothing worked. She was always pregnant. Then one day she referred to her children as "unwanted." It gave me pause for a moment; then I told her, "Your children are the *most* wanted—by the Creator. You tried everything to prevent them from being born, but nothing stopped them. Obviously according to God's plan they are extremely necessary."

There are three partners in the creation of a child. God is the third partner and a very active one at that. In fact He has veto power. It's His responsibility to make sure nothing happens that is not supposed to happen. He is not going to allow two foolish young people to mess up the coming generations. The future of the human race is not something with which God will allow frail and fallible human beings to interfere.

The freedom you *do* have lies in deciding how to make the marriage (and the parenting) work. You could be thoughtful and kind, or you could be nasty and cruel. You can choose to be generous or you can remain selfish. God would not interfere with that, because He does not take away your freedom of choice. However, knowing that you have free choice and knowing that we are all capable of wrecking a marriage, God puts certain padding and protection around the child, so that the child won't suffer difficulties he is not meant to experience.

This is important to know for parents who worry that they're responsible (read guilty) for their children's unhappiness or psychological issues. Everything that happens to your children is in accordance with God's plan, for they are His children first. It's not always as pleasant as we hope; it may not even be God's first plan. Even God may sometimes have a plan B. Still, He remains an active partner. At no time does He step out of the picture or abandon His children, contrary to however we may think or feel.

As vital as this information is to a married couple considering divorce, it's equally valuable for children (including adult children) who have been raised in a broken family. Like everything that happens, divorce too would not happen if it weren't meant to be. Whatever difficulties you now face are *your* challenges, meant for you. Since God is giving you this set of challenges, He also gives you the tools and abilities to handle them. People who don't have these challenges have no idea what it takes to do what you need to do. Only you know.

Hence, the first rule in life is no regrets, no second thoughts. "If only I could turn back the clock" or "If I only knew then what

I know now" are absolute heresy. Take comfort in knowing that what is, is exactly as God meant for it to be.

This is your life. And it is the only one you have. Is your story about how you were traumatized by your dysfunctional family of origin? No matter what your parents might have done, you'd still end up with the same issues and the same challenges. These are your challenges, not your parents' or your siblings' or your friends'.

The life you have is right for you. It belongs to you, and it was given to you for an awesome divine purpose, even if it sometimes seems bleak. It's not as though someone made a wrong turn and your life has been derailed. That can't happen. Align your thinking correctly, stop wondering about what might have been, and it will make a huge difference in how you handle it all.

There are three ways in which the child of a divorced couple tends to react. The first is a combination of rejection and denial: "I didn't have a say in this. I don't agree with it, and I don't want to deal with it. I don't care what you're telling me. I didn't ask for this and it's not what I want at all. My life is ruined." This is obviously not the wisest way to respond.

Alternatively, a person can be obstinate and adamant: "I'm tough. I will push ahead no matter what happens. I'm not a quitter." This sounds a little healthier than the first, but it's still not a wise response, because what you're saying is, "Everything got messed up, but I'm strong enough to handle it."

The third way of handling it is acceptance: "My life has not been torn asunder or derailed." This may be difficult, but it is the calmest, truest, and most positive of attitudes, not to mention the most wholesome and sensible way of coping with any and all challenges in life. "If this has happened to me, then it must be my life. I accept all of it, even though I don't know the reasons. I will do my best, and I will live my life without regrets or anguish."

Shoes or No Shoes, Life Is Good

We had a friend in Minnesota who epitomized what it means to fully embrace life. One summer, when he was sixteen, Larry went diving together with a close friend. Larry dove off a cliff, unaware that the tide had gone out and the water at the bottom was only five feet deep.

He remembers floating on the water with his face up. All he saw was blue sky, but he felt nothing—because his spine was broken. He was sure he had died and gone to heaven. Instinctively, he heard himself saying *Sh'ma Yisrael,* the traditional Hebrew prayer. Eventually he realized that he was alive and paralyzed from his neck down.

He lived in a wheelchair for forty-six years, which probably broke some sort of record; it's almost unheard of to survive that long as a quadriplegic.

Yet Larry made it, against all odds, because his spirit and approach toward life were simply astounding. Every now and then he would say, "I know why God did this to me. I was a wild animal! I was out of control. God had to slow me down." People who met him would look upon him with pity and ask, "How are you?" He would reply with a robust, "I'm fine! How are you?" One time he saw someone in obvious pain, and he asked, "Are you okay? Are your shoes hurting? Are they comfortable? I don't need shoes, so I wouldn't know."

He had this larger-than-life attitude. He actually became a counselor, helping veterans coming back from Vietnam who were broken and traumatized by the war. I knew him for a number of years before he died, and I used to visit with him often. Each time I saw him I was more amazed than the previous time.

One year, his kidneys began to fail, and he had to be on dialysis every morning, a three-hour ordeal. As it was, it took him three hours just to get out of bed *before* the dialysis. It was excruciating. During one of my visits, he said, "I think I'm done. There is only so much you can push, you know? How much can I push?" I thought that was it; he was finally giving up. It was heartbreaking.

Two weeks later I returned for a visit, and to my surprise he was back to himself, upbeat and cheery as if nothing had happened. I said to him, bewildered, "What? What did you discover? What did you come up with this time?" He said simply, "Life is good."

What's so good about life for a quadriplegic? I don't know. But he knew. Because when God gives you your challenge, He gives you exactly what you need to go with it, to make it work, to fulfill your mission.

As an interesting aside, the buddy with whom Larry had gone swimming that fateful day remained his best friend for many years. A musical performer, he traveled a lot, and whenever he'd come to town he would invite his old friend up on stage and they would sing together. Larry sang pretty well! Those duets were the highlight of his life.

Larry's friend bought him a van equipped with all sorts of special gadgets and facilitative technology, and hired a driver for him. Larry was so proud of his childhood pal, just about every conversation I had with him somehow ended up reminiscing about those times they had spent together.

One year we took Larry to New York, wheelchair and all, to meet with the Rebbe at one of his public addresses. When we arrived we brought him up to the dais to get a blessing from the Rebbe. A Rebbe, of course, is full of surprises; you never knew what to expect. The Rebbe poured him a small cup of wine, looked him in the eyes, and said, "*l'chaim,*" to life. Then he leaned in further so no one else could hear and said, "Don't be dependent on anyone."

I later asked Larry, "What did the Rebbe say?" He said, "I don't know who he was talking to. 'Don't be dependent on anyone?' I can't do anything by myself. I even need someone to help me *cough*. What did the Rebbe mean?" We were all stumped. What could he have meant? How do you tell a guy who's been a quadriplegic in a wheelchair for forty years not to depend on anyone?

A few months later, Larry's old buddy broke up their longstanding friendship. No more singing at the concerts, no new upgrade that he had previously scheduled for the van. Just like that. He was devastated. But it was then that he remembered what the Rebbe had said: "Don't be dependent on anyone." He realized he had been relying on his friend for his happiness and well-being. So for a while he was down, but then bounced right back—as if the Rebbe had given him the strength he needed just with this simple instruction. "Don't be dependent on anyone." Is that not amazing advice?

When a person adopts this attitude, he rescues himself from unnecessary anguish, pain, and the struggles that come inevitably with existence. *This is my life, it is mine, it belongs to me. Life is good, I am grateful, I love my life.* Now he is empowered to proceed with his life—if not with ease, then at least with the strength and the satisfaction that he is exactly where he is meant to be. Now he is able to fulfill the mission for which he was created.

Dysfunction and divorce are family tragedies. Each family member—child or adult or adult child—suffers and is called upon to cope in his or her own unique way. Every effort invested in trying to heal the disharmony and save the marriage is worthy of admiration and bestows great merit, merit that lasts forever. But there is no blame to be assigned, no guilty party, even when it may seem so. Again, there are no mistakes, there's no cause for shame. Life has not been derailed; its path has taken an unexpected, maybe undesirable turn. But nothing happened that was never supposed to happen. Whatever form the challenges take, they are there for reasons that have been there, hidden, since birth. One's perspective broadens, and one's power immediately shifts into high gear, the moment one says, "If this is my challenge, bring it on!"

• • •

The following section is not so much a single chapter, as it is a compendium of frequently asked questions that have arisen in the course of decades of marital and relationship counseling. Some of the most poignant and pressing demands on the capabilities of a counselor or mentor are the issues that come up in the midst of dealing with family disharmonies. But the questions and challenges don't begin or end there. They span the whole spectrum of the joys and trials and tribulations of marriage. We've arranged these question-and-answer topics into four general segments. The first three correspond to these previous chapters: "The Jungle of Dating," "Sexuality and Intimacy," and "Disharmony, Divorce, and Destiny." And then, finally, a collection of questions and answers that will shed still more light on the real-life details and the many mysteries that make marriage matter. We'll call that segment "Happily Ever After."

Marriage Matters

Frequently Asked Questions

Q & A: *The Jungle of Dating*

When is a person ready to date?

If you say, "I'll be ready to get married when I'm good enough," you'll never get married. It's not about how well you've taken care of yourself.

If you can actually put a wedding date on your calendar, you know you're ready to get married. "I want to be married by June of next year. It's time. The only reason I'm waiting until June is because of the caterer." But if the wedding date is not real in your mind, you're not ready.

There's nothing wrong with marrying young. In fact it's a good idea. The Talmud says you're as ready as you're going to be by age eighteen, and it says nothing about why or how that is, or what it means to be ready. Are you concerned about maturity? We often see that in trying circumstances—in wartime, for example, or when life leaves no other choice—people can mature in an instant. When a teenager becomes a mother, she grows up overnight, with priorities that shift so quickly you can hardly believe she's the same irresponsible kid you once knew. How is that possible? The truth is, we become mature only when we need to. That's why today there are some thirty year olds who still behave like teenagers.

When will we know each other well enough to make a commitment? Don't people change over time?

A human being is always evolving, changing, and growing. You'll no doubt realize after having been married for ten years, you don't know all there is to know about your spouse. Then after twenty years you'll find out there's even more to learn, and as your lives unfold together, you will discover more and more. It's a good thing. You don't come into a relationship as a finished product and then try to blend with your other half; you grow together, you get to know each other, you discover life together. There is nothing better.

What should I be looking for in a potential mate?

Practically speaking, the first thing you want to know is whether he is hungry for marriage, or just wants to date. If you say, "I'd like to be married by Passover," and he says, "Wow! So soon?" forget him. If he's looking ahead with trepidation toward some distant future, there's nothing to talk about. He doesn't really want to be married. But if his intention is to marry this year, he's for real. What you want to look at is not what he thinks of you, which is guaranteed to change, but what he thinks of marriage.

Look for a healthy person who enjoys healthy relationships. Someone who is still hung up, whether positively or negatively, on his or her relationship with a parent, is probably not all that emotionally available. If he's angry with or distant from his father, if she's still caught up in an intense battle with her mother, that's likely to follow one or both of them into their marriage. Someone who hasn't made peace with immediate family may not be ready to move on to the next. Only when issues are resolved, or at least well on the way to resolution, will it be possible to be fully present with a new family.

Unreasonable perfectionism can be another red flag. A guy who says I'm only going to marry a *very special woman* may not be ready to allow another person into his life. Which woman will be good enough for him? Let's say he finds this very special girl, and it turns out she's just a girl. Now he's disappointed, and the marriage fails.

How much of my personality should I show on a date?

You often hear that an outgoing or overly confident girl can intimidate a boy. It's true. Therefore, don't marry a boy. Marry a man. A man won't be intimidated by your self-assurance. Or if he is, he won't marry you. But don't hide your qualities or minimize yourself.

There are those who advise a man or a woman to be a little more talkative, or a little less, or to say something funny. No, don't try. You are not there to win a contest or entertain or prepare a speech that needs rehearsing. Just be yourself, and whether the conversation is light or serious, that will be fine. Just refrain from speaking about anything overly personal. The reason for that is because neither of you is ready to be so intimately involved. You are strangers until you marry, at which point you then become deeply important to each other. Until then you don't owe yourselves an account of your respective lives, and you certainly don't want to turn your date into your therapist.

How much of your life experience should you be sharing, then? If it's interesting, share it. If it is personal, don't—particularly in view of the fact that the more one opens up, the greater the risk of getting hurt, if the dating should yield no lasting result. Don't tell your date anything about yourself that your mother doesn't know. Remember, you are talking to a stranger. Don't discuss shortcomings or help solve each other's problems. That's not your job. If you see faults that bother you, just say goodbye. Eventually, of course, you are going to find out all of each other's flaws and idiosyncrasies. But during the dating process, he or she should appear perfect in your eyes.

How much should I disclose about myself?

Honesty is important; but when it comes to disclosure, always consider what it is you're trying to accomplish in sharing the information. If you have had embarrassing or regrettable experiences that don't need to be known, or may prove disturbing, refrain from sharing. Why burden your date with feelings or personal issues that neither of you is in a position to help?

If you're uncertain, ask yourself if it's about something in the past, or ongoing. You once had pneumonia? It's none of his business. If you have pneumonia now, that is his business. If it's a current condition, you ought to tell him. But whatever took place in the past, for either of you, if you're over it, forget about it. Don't bring it up. This is true not only in dating but in marriage. Consideration is more important than honesty.

Before you disclose anything, think about whether it's going to make it harder for him or her to respect you. Don't be so righteous that you have to tell the truth at another's expense. There's no need for confession of any kind. It's more important to be kind and considerate than to say anything negative or questionable about yourself, even if you imagine it'll make you feel better.

Should I be cautious before agreeing to go on a date?

When consulting with a matchmaker (and you should always use a matchmaker), if a potential mate suggested to you sounds interesting, by all means check it out. It's best if your parents, as well as his or her parents, are also comfortable with the prospect. Try not to be too particular at this point; be open, especially if you've heard good things about the person.

Once you meet, however, every detail becomes critical. A major purpose of the date is to find out if there's anything about this person that bothers you. When you see something, don't think, *Hmm, that's no big deal. I can overlook it,* or try to tell yourself you really shouldn't be feeling this way. What *should* or *shouldn't* trouble you is not a good question. If anything disturbs you, even a little bit, you ought not ignore it. You don't need to be able to explain what bothers you. If it rubs you the wrong way, that's reason enough to move on.

When meeting, you're doing so to see how it really feels, not how it *should* feel. Be true to who you are and resist the temptation to be philosophical about how you feel. It doesn't have to make sense.

Your parents and siblings are generally good barometers as well. Consider their opinions seriously; they're usually able to gauge if a person is a good match for you. Ultimately it's your decision whether to marry or not, but if something worries them, don't ignore it. Still, from the parents' side, once the children have made up their minds, the family should not remain involved, either positively or negatively.

It's also helpful to hear what others think about the person before you meet for the first time. What do those longtime friends say? They won't have been easily fooled, and their insights may end up being more reliable than what you're going to see early on.

How can I tell if we really have good chemistry?

First dates are usually so awkward, you can hardly tell what you're feeling. Is it you who is nervous, or is it he who is making you nervous? You feel like you have to make a good impression and can't quite be yourself. It's rare that a couple will experience a great deal of comfort at first. By the second or third meeting, however, you ought to be able to discern whether or not it feels okay. Some people make you uneasy just being in the same room or sitting across the table. That's not good chemistry.

Sometimes a bit of tension or discomfort can be exciting. You feel this urge to argue or to show how smart and knowledgeable you are, how witty and interesting you can be. There might be a slightly competitive edge or a need to demonstrate how much you have in common. That's fine if you are trying out for the debating team, but not appropriate if you're looking for a husband or a wife. You don't want to spend the rest of your life reacting to a sense of being judged or criticized, however subtly.

With a spouse, you want to feel comfortable, at ease, accepted just the way you are. No worries about the way you look, as there would be with someone else. If a few minutes go by and no one says a word, that's okay. Good chemistry makes even silence feel good.

Before you start wondering what it'd be like to spend the rest of your life with this person, just look at whether being in his or her presence makes you feel good. Good about *yourself*. If the answer to that is positive, now check out whether being with you has the same effect on him or her. If so, you have great chemistry, and you are ready to move on to the next stage of your relationship.

What about romance?

The sort of passionate romance that belongs in a marriage is frequently sought too soon. First there's romance, then (maybe) you'll get married. It doesn't work. When the romance comes first, it complicates the relationship with an enchantment that is neither real nor sustainable. We've been brainwashed by media that have hammered us with the idea that once you get married the romance will inevitably fade away. The opposite is true.

Real romance happens within the married relationship. Outside of marriage, what people call romance is just the thrill of the hunt. There is the predator, and there is the prey. It's not only not romance, it's not even pleasant—just a nasty, competitive, adrenaline-driven game. If you find that challenging, fine, but don't call it romance.

A young woman once complained to the Rebbe that she had gone out with many men, but none had swept her off her feet. He asked her if she had been reading romance novels, to which she replied, "Yes." He suggested that she select more edifying reading material. A short while later she met and married Mr. Right.

I'm going out with the sweetest guy in the world, but I don't know why I'm hesitating.

Every woman needs to be able to look up to a husband. If a guy seems really nice, it may be that your maternal instinct is drawing you toward him, in which case you may want to adopt him. But don't marry him.

Let's try to keep gender roles appropriate. A husband is supposed to be someone you can lean on and depend on to provide the certainty and the security you need, who will be reliable, trustworthy, and confident. She should feel free of worry, comfortable enough to surrender herself to his care. If that's not present, then he's not the one.

The wisdom of Chassidus sees virtually all interactions as a dynamic exchange between a *mashpia*, a giver, and a *mekabel*, a receiver. In marital relationships, being a *mekabel* calls for the ability to be disarmed, vulnerable, and receptive; and it is the responsibility of the *mashpia* to proactively provide. It's not necessarily a clear-cut division of labor, in such a way that he will invariably be the active, masculine *mashpia,* and she will always be the accepting, feminine *mekabel.* It takes a certain strength to be a *mekabel* and empower a *mashpia*, just as being an effective *mashpia* requires a measure of sensitivity and deference that enables the *mekabel* to be *mekabel.*

A woman generally needs and seeks in a mate something that she is not, or does not have. Something about him needs to inspire her trust and admiration. It may be that he's sharper, braver, more mature, more talented, or even just more socially adept. It could be that he is more capable of handling a crisis, or that he is simply street smart. On the other hand, a wife might excel and outshine him in any of these various virtues. She's often smarter, especially in the realm of social intelligence. Sometimes on the surface it appears the woman is the stronger of the two, "wears the pants," and makes the decisions; and he's comfortable letting her run the show, because he's secure, confident, strong, and silent. Nevertheless, in a crisis she needs to know and feel that she can depend on him.

This could simply be a matter of taste. If you are the carefree type who trusts everything will turn out fine, if you can respect a guy without a job or who is uncertain as to what he wants to do with his life, then by all means marry him. But if this is who he is and ironclad practicality is nonnegotiable for you, don't go there. If you can't look up to him, sooner or later you won't be able to stand him. The bottom line: be true to yourself. If he makes you feel like you want to follow him to the ends of the earth, then marry him. Not just because he's a nice guy.

What do I need to know about men before I get married? Should I make a list of what I'm looking for?

It's not helpful at all to "know what men are like." You're not going to marry a man; you are going to marry a husband. Your husband. And husbands are not like men. Men are self-centered and animalistic, and husbands are exactly the opposite. When a man becomes a husband, he becomes an entirely different creature.

Since your husband is already who he is, you cannot redesign or change him. If he's tall, he's tall. If he's not, he's not. You cannot stretch or alter him. To worry about his looks or his personality would be a waste of energy. So instead of making a list of the qualities you're looking for in a husband, make a list—or better, a picture—of the kind of a life you envision for yourself and intend to live.

In the olden days, things weren't complicated. A woman might tell a matchmaker, "I want to have lots of children. I want to teach them the right values, send them to a good school, and raise them to be God-fearing. Find me a husband who can help me with that."

Today it's not so simple. What kind of life do you want? You might say, "I am not sure if I want to have children." Okay, that takes a certain kind of husband. What else? "I want to have a career; I'm not about to stay at home." Okay, that takes a different kind of husband. You may need to ask yourself what kind of life you want to lead before deciding on a husband.

More important, think about the kind of home you wish to build, how you want your home to look and feel. What kind of atmosphere do you want to create? What kind of mother would you like to be? How will you raise your children? You could base it on the home you came from. What did you like that you wish to replicate, and what would you do differently? As an example, you might make a decision never to criticize your husband in front of the children because you remember how painful that felt for you as a child. Think twice, however, before thinking you don't want to be anything like your mother. Chances are you'd be just overreacting.

Above all else, you need to contemplate the kind of relationship you want to cultivate with your husband. How are you going to treat him? Will you be kind and forgiving when he crosses a line or makes a mistake? Do you see yourselves supporting one another, making life easier and more rewarding? Will your lives be richer and more noble by being together? It goes both ways: will you build each other up, or criticize each other to smithereens? Once you're married, your life is together. Having a hard day? Tell him. Share it with him. But never blame him or use it as an excuse to be surly. As a spouse, you need to be kind, respectful, and considerate at all times.

If I'm going to give this matchmaker thing a try, what questions should I be asking as we proceed?

The thing you need to ask *yourself,* after the first date, is whether you want to spend another hour with this person. You will report this to the matchmaker, who in turn will tell you whether the other party is feeling the same way.

If you come home to your mom and she asks whether he or she is someone you could marry, or for that matter if you're wondering the same thing yourself, tell her *and* yourself that it's too soon to know. Again, the only valid question is, "Do I want to spend an hour with him next Tuesday?" Or "Is she interesting or impressive or nice enough to see again?" If the answer is yes, go right ahead. You simply take it one meeting at a time. After the second date the question remains the same. Only after three dates, at the very least, should you begin to consider whether this is someone you could marry. Once you both establish that you'd like to continue seeing each other beyond this, then you can start thinking in a direction that might lead to an engagement. But continue to involve the matchmaker every step along the way, until the wedding day.

I really like this guy, but he hasn't suggested marriage. Should I bring it up to him?

Never tell a man you are ready to marry him if he doesn't ask. It's bound to make him feel at least a little awkward. How do you imagine he'll be able to bring himself to propose, if you've already given him an answer before he "popped the question"? The marriage proposal is his job. Don't take it away from him. He has to ask you, he has to lead you to the canopy, he has to place the ring on your finger. If you push forward first, it just confuses everything. How did you make up your mind so quickly, he may wonder, when he's still in the throes of figuring out who you are (or maybe who *he* is).

In any event, a proposal is always best when the ground has been prepared with the assistance of a matchmaker—a *shadchan*. When the *shadchan* ascertains that each of you is ready, your young man won't propose prematurely, so you'll never have to reject him. No pain, no foul, no one gets hurt. Don't think this makes it a mere formality; the excitement is in no way diminished by the refinement in the way it unfolds.

How do I prepare for marriage? What do I need to do?

To prepare yourself for marriage, practice giving. Give to friends, give to community projects, give at the office. Then take an hour a day to forget about yourself, about who you think you are, about what your needs may be.

Next, notice when you find yourself judging other people—your family, your coworkers, your friends. Try turning that around and practice seeing only the good in others.

Once you are married, you'll need to become completely selfless. Oftentimes a man and a woman get married, but they remain a man and a woman and do not become a husband and a wife. They've grown so accustomed to being man and woman, as two separate selves, when it comes time to make the switch to the dynamics of husband and wife, they have no idea how. They are courting disaster. Within three months of marriage they'll very likely begin to fight.

When two people get married, they become inextricably joined together as one. They will never be alone again. A husband and a wife are nothing without each other. There is a feeling of complete connection; there is someone who was once an *other* and is now a permanent part of your life. It's not about how much fun you have together or how much you love each other. That's all fine, and you will have both. But marriage is intended to give you so much more—something you cannot get from any other relationship.

Once married, you will have to transform what had been an understandably selfish attitude to one of complete selflessness. People too often forget or neglect to make that switch. Don't let that happen to you. It's the most important change you will ever make.

Q & A: *Sexuality and Intimacy*

What's the difference between intimacy and "making love"?

When we see people attempting to sugarcoat intimacy by referring to it as "making love," we can assume they have no idea what intimacy is. They are thinking of sex, and they're trying to make it nice. Sex is not nice. Sex is taking. Taking is abuse. When you're just having sex, why not call it what it is, having sex? But "having sex" sounds crude, so we need to embellish it, as if calling it love somehow adds value to it.

But if you're making love, you're still not experiencing intimacy. Intimacy is truer, infinitely holier, and more important than love. We do not have to justify intimacy by calling it love. Intimacy doesn't need justification. To restore normalcy to the act of sex and bring back our natural sexuality, love alone won't get it done. We need to regain our understanding and respect for intimacy.

Love is personal, and intimacy is interpersonal. What you do personally with your love is your business. What you do interpersonally can bring holiness, value, and growth to a relationship. Or it can be destructive, even criminal. When intimacy is violated, there is no redemption.

What do you say to a teenager who's not allowed to have sex and not ready for intimacy?

There are legitimate needs and illegitimate needs. What teenagers experience with such urgency is not the desire for sex; it's desire for the pleasure of sex, for which they have *no actual need.*

Ask yourself—are you responding to a need or are you indulging a pleasure? Say you are responding to the need for nutrition: true nourishment can wait until supper. If you are reacting to the pleasure of your taste buds, however, it's all impulse. *Why wait? Why not now?*

The need for intimacy is not urgent. There is no such thing as immediate intimacy. The satisfaction of intimacy stems from the true and genuine need to bond with another human being. To become one. Not to have sex. Eating to entertain your mouth, when the actual hunger is for nourishment, is like sex without intimacy.

Sexually hyperactive teenagers know they've had enough. But teens who have had excessive sex will never admit to it in public, at the risk of being called different or weird. The mere thought of sex has become sickening and nauseating, but they can't stop. And it's not just teens; anyone who has been sexually active can attest to the fact that sex without intimacy takes away a piece of your soul. You lose respect for yourself and for the person you are with.

We also need to dispense with the jokes about sexual conquests, and shatter this myth that sex is all everybody wants—that it's the only thing even married couples care about. It is simply not true. People are ready to move on to permanent relationships.

Why is it that men are so easily sexually satisfied but women are so often not?

First of all, if that were true, then men would never be on the lookout for an extramarital affair. So to say that a man is easily satisfied, or to suggest that male sexual satisfaction is something purely physical, is incorrect. Men also yearn for intimacy and bonding with their soulmates. It's human nature, whether male or female.

What *is* true is that the respective anatomies of men and women are not created equal. Their sensitivities differ, and the key is for him to be sensitive to her. For both husband and wife, however, if the focus is on performance, or achievement, both will experience frustration—he in his way and she in hers. Such disappointments will not arise if you care deeply for one another, focus on your partner, and let go of concerns about performance or peak experience. You have each other, and there's nothing better than that.

All these absurd mythologies about performance and satisfaction that have accumulated in our culture and captured our minds are ruining marriage. "If you can get your wife to a certain place, you're a good husband; and if you don't, you're not." Get her where? This is both mechanical and impersonal. A man will be satisfied when he knows he is being a husband to his wife, giving all of himself without holding back. A woman will be satisfied when she feels safe enough to surrender all of herself with no reservations. If the husband is looking for some sort of predetermined satisfaction, he is not being a husband. He is simply acting like an animal. It's all part of the same cultural brainwashing.

Sadly, unfortunately, there are couples whose attention is solely on the enjoyment of doing all sorts of things with each other and *to* each other, but when it comes to true intimacy they're not interested. How did this happen? How did *doing things* come to take the place of intimacy? The answer: *things* are easy; becoming one with another human being is hard. When *things* replace intimacy, what you end up with is a feeling of being used and of being alone. You become an object, not a person. Sometimes the *things* you're doing become more important than the person you are with. If this continues, you will eventually stop being human beings with real human needs, and the marriage is not likely to survive.

What if my husband's desires in the bedroom are outside my comfort zone?

As newlyweds we begin a new phase in life, starting out at ground level and climbing higher and higher up the ladder of growth, maturity, and responsibility. As we advance, sometimes a husband and a wife find themselves on different rungs of the ladder. One may have risen a rung or two that the other hasn't taken; and voilà, they're out of sync. It's at that point that we have to remind ourselves that what's important is not the issue at hand. It's really about each other. It's a challenge that comes up in every area of our lives. Why not also in the bedroom?

The sexual experience can be so powerful, either partner can become distracted, even by the experience itself. If she is concerned only with the pleasure of climax, she can lose the pleasure of *him*. The same is true for him. If *she* is not his pleasure, no matter how much enjoyment he's having, he's not enjoying *her*. Then it's no longer about each other; it's about *it*, whatever *it* may be, and it has come between them.

If a husband and a wife can make each other happy in the bedroom, they should do what it takes, as long as the focus remains on each other and not on something else. However, if pleasure or performance or *it* becomes the *thing*, the relationship ceases to grow, at best. They might even fall off the ladder. We cannot let this become the norm. We want to go from sex to intimacy, not the other way around. As exciting as it may be, it's the wrong direction and can jeopardize a relationship.

There's this funny parable about a couple going through a divorce. As the settlement proceeds, the woman is told she can take only one thing from her marriage. So she chooses to take her husband. When a couple sees each other as indispensable, they'll climb the ladder together. "Every *thing* is negotiable. *You*, I have to have."

What does intimacy have to do with procreation?

There are certain scientific (though wildly erroneous) articles promoting the idea that the attraction between men and women is all for the sake of the survival of the species. This is, needless to say, far from romantic—but it's also not even true. The allure of the opposite sex is not about making babies. It is the desire for oneness. True intimacy not only unites a wife and a husband; it makes their as-yet-unborn child feel a part of that same oneness. It makes a child feel welcome, invited in.

That's what we mean when we say there are three partners in the birth of a child. This means that intimacy is sacred, and as such makes room in the relationship for God. God becomes an active partner—not a casual presence, but engaged, invested, a stakeholder in the enterprise of ensuring the continuity of human life.

If a husband and a wife are not deeply into each other, however, but rather are only into *it*, the child will feel like an intruder. When two parents are not one, not fully united, the child will not feel related. We see this often today, where children feel no sense of connection to their parents. Ask a teenager, "How's your mother?"

The reply might be, "I don't know. She has her life. I have mine." It's also not uncommon to hear from children who are depressed: "I didn't ask to be born. Anyway, you didn't have me for me. You were just doing your thing."

Science is only beginning to discover that a fetus knows and hears everything that's going on. Imagine the conversation of a couple, after discovering they're pregnant: "Should we have this baby or get rid of it?" No wonder this generation of parents produces so many children who are reckless with their lives.

But when a man is deeply, irrevocably attracted to a woman, and vice versa, their union stimulates uniquely different sorts of hormones, eggs, seeds, and genetic makeup. The child born of this union is born of intimacy. Becoming one, dissolving the *otherness* that separates them, the three are absorbed into oneness. That's a family.

How do we achieve oneness?

God created the first human as male and female, together as one: one being with two sides. Then He separated us into Adam and Eve. Immediately thereafter He asked us to become one again through marriage. Why then did God separate us in the first place? Because oneness is such a holy state of being, God wanted us to achieve it on our own, as a matter of choice. The other reason we were separated and then told to become one is because we were originally one—but back to back. Through marriage we can become one again—but face to face.

But what is it that's keeping us apart? It's not that we are two and we need some sort of glue to reunite us. Oneness is our true and natural default condition, our reality. Clearly, however, something is separating us. It could be said that it's our bodies that keep us apart, and of course there's truth to that. But the interference is also more subtle; it's rather like two drops of water next to each other on a table, and all that's keeping them apart is surface tension. One needs only to breathe on the drops, breaking the surface tension, and the two become one naturally. In the moment of intimacy, you transcend the distance and the differences. You dissolve.

In the Jewish Laws of intimacy, married couples are not to wear anything at all when intimate—not for erotic purposes, but because no physical, emotional, mental, or spiritual *thing* should come between them. For the same reason, husband and wife are forbidden to attempt intimacy if they are angry at each other, since a wall has come between them.

We tear down the walls by a process of elimination, ridding ourselves of every thought, feeling, awareness, distraction, or desire that has even the potential of separating us. It's a capability that's not easy to obtain or maintain. So many things pull at us, distract us, demand our attention. Intimacy is delicate. It's very focused. Anything that causes us to lose that focus can ruin it, and we're likely to find ourselves doing all the right things, yet still feeling painfully disconnected and alone. How did that happen? Things got in the way. What sort of things? Ego? Opinions? Personality quirks? Anxieties? Trauma? Yes, all of the above.

But in truth what keeps us apart is *everything*. To separate ourselves from the things that come between us, we need to think past *things* and get past every*thing*. Part of the solution is that intimacy must be in the dark where you *see* nothing, without television or radio or music so you *hear* nothing, and without conversation so you *say* nothing. When we do that, we're focused and aware of each other. As long as we're focused on the *who*, we're on the right track. The minute it becomes about the *what,* we've lost it.

Even in the best of marriages, husbands and wives do not always achieve intimacy. But at least you're both reaching for a common, worthwhile goal. If from time to time you manage to achieve intimacy and be fully connected—for let's say, twenty minutes—your relationship will become immensely powerful, nothing short of miraculous. If you can attain this holy state once in a while, you're rich; and if you're united every time you're together, you are wealthy beyond imagination.

Q & A: *Disharmony, Divorce, and Destiny*

What—if anything—do I owe my dysfunctional parents?

You owe them their child. You have to be their son or daughter. You may feel that you're not getting much from them other than pain, or disappointment after disappointment. Still, even if your relationship is less than positive, they are your parents and you'll never have others. You can't wish them away.

It's to your own benefit to be at peace with your parents. If you're not, it will inevitably compromise your ability to be available to others. If you marry, for example, it's imperative to first resolve issues you may still have with your parents. How free can you be to build a family while preoccupied with your family of origin?

Imagine that your parents truly are strange, maybe downright impossible, a source of unspeakable embarrassment. If you're able to bring home your best friend, or your soon-to-be-bride, and present them—"Allow me to introduce my parents. They're really weird—but hey, they're my parents. Say hi!"—it's a sign that you're getting healthier. You don't need to move back in to rebuild a relationship from scratch. You just need to make peace with them.

Everyone is entitled to a certain amount of failure. This includes them. So if in your mind your parents failed, entitle them. They're entitled to make mistakes, and you still owe them. They failed at being parents, but you don't have to fail at being their child. If you choose to remain angry and reject the reality that you're your parents' child, then who are you? And what are you? The commandment is to honor your parents, even when you don't admire them.

I acquired bad habits in my unhappy home. Am I doomed?

Traumatic experiences leave scars, which can seem permanent, but they are not. If you have the desire to change, you're already more than halfway there. The mind, the sages say, rules the heart. Wishful thinking? Not at all. It is how humans are made.

"My wife got me angry," says this guy, "so I hit her. I couldn't help it, I lost control."

"You lost control?" I asked.

"Yeah!" he replied.

So I said, "Did you hit her with a baseball bat?"

He said, "What are you, crazy?"

"Why didn't you hit her with a bat?"

"Do you think *I'm* crazy?"

"You said you lost control. When you lose control, you're crazy. So don't say you lost control."

He didn't lose control; he gave himself permission to let go of *just so much* control and no more. To his mind, it was acceptable to hit her with his hands, but not with a bat. When the mind decides something is crazy, the heart won't go there, so he never allowed himself to even *feel* like hitting her with a bat.

There was a cannibal in Wisconsin years ago. He killed somebody, cut her up, and ate some parts of her. They caught him and, of course, when it came to trial, he pleaded insanity. Most people said, "Sure, this guy is obviously nuts." But one rabbi in Wisconsin said, "No, he's not insane. If he's really insane, why didn't he chew off his own arm?" And the rabbi was right. He was evil, but he wasn't totally insane. He had given himself permission to eat other people, but eat himself? *That* crazy, he was not.

If someone is convinced that some action is truly evil, yet doesn't hold himself back, now *that's* crazy. You never go where your mind doesn't allow you to go, unless you're truly insane, which means your mind has lost all control. And once you've done that so many times, it becomes a habit.

Maimonides, in his discussion of the development of character traits, offers sound, practical advice as to how to break a negative habit: whatever the habit is, go to the opposite extreme. To break extreme attachments, you can't be sensible or moderate. You have to use extreme measures. Are you a tightwad or a thief or a kleptomaniac? Give and give and give some more. Do you tend to speak excessively? It'd be a good idea to take a "speech fast" from time to time. Going to the opposite extreme for a while neutralizes the intensity of a bad habit, after which you can gradually adopt a more moderate approach.

If you want to conquer extreme evil, you need to be extremely good. You can't fight terrorism with gentlemanly moderation. You can't eradicate deeply entrenched bad habits by small incremental steps. Certainly, there are areas where this does not apply, such as when a person is an overeater—if he were to go to the opposite extreme, he could die. But with most negative habits, you can't fight extremism with moderation. You need to know when and in which situations the method applies. For that you have to use your head *and* your heart.

How can I gain the self-confidence I never learned in a broken home?

Confidence is an important trait, but only up to a point. Too much self-confidence can become arrogance, which can destroy any relationship. Humility is the opposite of arrogance. It is a rare and valuable character trait that not everyone has, and it's not easy to come by.

Confidence is often superficial, and therefore temporary. Sooner or later, many apparently confident people are likely to run up against something they're not good at, or someone whose confidence is less vulnerable. Humility, on the other hand, is real and lasting and in many ways is much greater and stronger than confidence. A humble person doesn't get offended or offend others or get discouraged so easily. He'll tend to endear himself to others rather than turning people off. Humility is an extremely positive, virtuous character trait worthy of emulation and praise. Better to be exceedingly humble than extremely confident.

The key is not to dwell on what you're missing, but to focus instead on the qualities you do have. Children of divorced parents are generally rendered humble by their experience. It's not necessarily a weakness, but a strength that others may not have. Coming from a divorced family doesn't take away self-confidence; it can make you humble enough to acquire an inner confidence that comes from beyond yourself, rather than being all about yourself.

I'm often asked, "How do I nullify my ego?" People who come from divorced families don't usually have ego problems, except when it's a disguise for what they think is a humility problem. Some may try to compensate for a lack of ego by becoming *macho* or *overconfident*. This is insecurity, not ego. If you feel you need to be tough, it's because you are not.

So don't be fooled or discouraged. You're already ahead of the game. Life has given you plenty of reasons to be humble, and it's a gift, a powerful and useful tool. Use it wisely.

My siblings are having a rough time since our parents split up.

Your parents are divorced, and now your siblings are having a hard time too. This can't be good news for you either; once things go wrong, they can only keep on getting worse—right? And you're next.

Divorce is not hereditary. It's not genetically transferable, and you are not doomed. Neither are your siblings. Yet you're expecting to suffer. In fact you welcome the suffering, because somewhere inside you believe you deserve it.

If you walk into any situation expecting to be disappointed, you will be disappointed. Likewise, if you're expecting disaster, you will invite disaster. This is an attitude problem, and it cries out to be rectified. Imagine instead (you might suggest this to your siblings) that your marriage is perfect, as you had hoped and envisioned it would be. Your husband or your wife is exactly what you need in a spouse. How would you treat him or her, if this were the case? If your spouse were absolutely flawless, how would you behave? Picture it that way and behave accordingly. You'll be amazed at how things will turn around.

Tell your sibling who's having marital problems (in other words, tell yourself) never to walk into the house at the end of the day expecting to pick a fight. And don't jump back into that argument that began this morning where you left off. Break the cycle. As you're turning the doorknob, try thinking, *My wife is perfect for me. I'm totally happy with her.* Fake it, if you must. See what happens.

We're often so convinced that things are bad, we unconsciously surrender to the intimidation of our own expectations, kicking and screaming as we pretend to protest. Your parents are divorced and miserable? Obviously your marriage doesn't stand a chance. You might as well give up now. If you should decide, however, to act as though everything were picture perfect, how would that feel? You will quickly discover that it feels pretty good. The key to a good marriage is to expect nothing and appreciate everything. A grateful attitude will have a positive influence not only on your mind but on your communication skills. What would that sound like? How would you speak to your spouse?

If you want global redemption, we're told, start behaving as though it's already here; everything you are hoping for will begin to transpire between the lines. The same with your marriage. If you want your marriage to be healthy, happy, and pleasurable, don't wait till the last minute. Start now and keep acting "as if" until it becomes a reality.

I'm terrified of marriage. Is there a self-help technique you'd recommend?

Personal growth, self-development, or self-help are all positive pursuits; the problem is, how do you know when you're finally developed enough? Those bodybuilders who pump iron? They don't know when to quit. People hell-bent on improving themselves rarely feel "I'm good enough." A person can become so self-focused and self-absorbed, there's no room for anything or anyone else. It can be a lifelong obsession.

There's a very different approach to the commitment for growth and development: turn your attention outward. "What can I do for *you*?" Working on yourself means cultivating the ability to see the beauty and the importance of others, then developing the desire and the will to serve them. That's true personal growth. It's consistent with the Torah's mandate: "Love your neighbor as you love yourself."

Similarly, serving God doesn't mean becoming a holy person. It's not about hoarding wisdom or knowledge or even spiritual sensibilities. What looks like righteousness can be self-righteousness in disguise. Genuine self-development means stepping out of and beyond yourself, not getting more into yourself. Self-care is often essential in small doses, but it's a slippery slope. If it distracts you from the question "What can I do for God?," consider it poison.

When it comes to knowing whether you're ready to get married, there is only one relevant question to ask yourself: are you generous enough to take care of another person? Or does the responsibility of caring for someone else's feelings and well-being seem like too big a burden? If you feel magnanimous and sensitive enough to actually devote yourself to making someone else happy, go for it. You've grown enough. Don't let a little thing like fear of failure get in your way.

We're miserable in our marriage. Should we stay together for the sake of the children?

There are unhappy couples who stay together because they are somehow comfortable making each other miserable. As a result, they make their children's lives miserable as well, though that's not their conscious intention.

Far more egregious are those couples who manipulate their children and wield them as a weapon to punish their spouse. That is out and out evil.

Most people, however, who choose to remain married for the sake of the children, are genuinely committed to their children's well-being. They probably won't mess up their children's lives by staying together, even if they find themselves arguing from time to time in front of the kids. It's a matter of degree; unless there is some ugliness that has to be stopped, there's no reason parents shouldn't stay together for their children's sake. And if that intention is genuine, the kids will most likely bring them closer together.

Parents who feel responsible for their children and opt to stay married for the sake of the children are simply being dependable and conscientious. It can be the most noble way to go.

The Rebbe once asked a couple who wanted to divorce, "Who's going to walk your children down the aisle to the wedding canopy. A stranger?" What he meant was, once you've taken care of your children and married them off, then you can focus on yourselves and get a divorce. Until then, stay married. It's the responsible thing to do. This couple had seven children. There was a pretty good chance that after the seventh child was married, they'd have become accustomed enough to the marriage not to want a divorce anyway.

By the way, many divorced couples look back at their marriage after a number of years and say, "You know, we weren't that far off. With a few adjustments, it might have turned out okay." If it's too late now, well, perhaps this will give them the courage to remarry and start over again.

Why does God allow divorce?

When someone asks me, "Do you think I should get divorced? I have this problem…" the answer is a definite no. However, if a person says, "I can't take it anymore. I'm done," the answer is, "What can I do to help?" When married people are at the end of their rope, desperate to divorce, they're not asking. It's a done deal. This is when we need to do whatever we can to help them part ways as amicably as possible.

Divorce is a spiritual amputation, not at all God's desire. Still, God, in His mercy, provides a dignified way out for married couples who can no longer stay together. It is actually a testimony to God's kindness that He has established a path to divorce. It was He who made the marriage in the first place; His intention was that they stay married. "This is your soulmate," He tells us. "Get married, become one, raise your children together." But when we can no longer fulfill His will, it's, "Okay, let Me help you out." It's as though He is saying, "My plan failed. But let's move on."

For a Jewish couple there's a specific procedure according to Jewish Law. He shows us how to write the *gett*, the bill of divorcement; He explains how it should be given and how it should be received. Having done so, the couple is no longer responsible or connected to each other, neither spiritually nor physically. Divorce is actually considered a *mitzvah*—unlike when an as-yet-unmarried couple breaks off an engagement. In that case, all we're left with is two very devastated people. Divorce, however, is different, in that some good can come out of it. What was once toxic can now effect a healing.

A marital relationship very closely reflects our relationship with God. Both call for faith, trust, and love. There's also humility, reverence, and respect, not to mention responsibility and accountability. All the qualities required in a healthy relationship with God are precisely those you need in your marriage. Our relationship with God is spiritual, paralleled by the earthly bond between husband and wife. Every marriage can benefit greatly from a healthy relationship with God.

But though they mirror each other and balance each other, we should not attempt to mix the two. Some may try to turn their marriage into a religion. When marriage becomes a sort of replacement or outlet for the soul's need for devotion, this will add unnecessary heaviness to the relationship. The reverse can also happen. Religion can become an obsessive, fanatical preoccupation, going so far out of control as to transform what may have seemed heavenly into a living hell.

It's interesting to see how people who would never think of harboring unreasonable expectations of God can expect a husband or a wife to act as God's understudy. When a person says, "My wife is not giving me everything I need," he's forgetting that only God can give him everything he needs. No human being is capable of fulfilling all the needs of another human being.

It's a confusion that lies at the root of many a divorce. But God has provided us with the opportunity, when all other options have failed, to cut our losses—and His—and move on.

Raised by my divorced mom, I've been missing a male father figure all my life.

Suppose you call a repairman to fix the air conditioner in your house. This guy pulls up with a truck full of tools. He comes in strapped like a soldier on the battlefield with all kinds of equipment hanging from all sides. He's carrying on his body every single tool imaginable. You know right away he can't be very competent, because the last time this happened another guy walked in with nothing but a screwdriver. "You need your air conditioner fixed?" he asked— and proceeded to get it done. Now *that's* talent. He can fix anything with a screwdriver.

Everyone has a purpose in life. To fulfill your purpose, you need certain talents, abilities, and strengths. God never gives you a job without providing you with the tools to do it. If you don't have it, you don't need it.

It's important to know that if you don't have a father, challenging though that certainly must be, you can manage to live your life and fulfill your purpose, with flying colors, without a father. If you couldn't do without one, God would have made sure you had one. You have been given every possible tool necessary to succeed in life. In that sense you are no different from the next guy who comes from an intact family, lives on the right side of the tracks, and was born with a silver spoon in his mouth. In some ways, you may be even better prepared to succeed. That guy needs a truckload of tools. You don't. He has what he needs and so do you.

Logically, if you only have a mother figure and she's lacking the partnership and the balance a father figure provides, it will inevitably be difficult for both of you. First of all, it might be a good idea to tell your mom that you don't need her to be your father; she can relax about that. She really can't be a male role model for you anyway, and if she tried, all she'd probably be doing would be overmothering. That'd be just as frustrating for her as for you. So let her be as soft and as feminine as she inherently is, and you look for a male role model who is an actual male.

Optimally, when a person doesn't have a father he can look to a grandfather or an uncle, if he's fortunate enough to have one. If you do have such a relative but he's distant, whether emotionally or geographically (as frequently happens in this scattered world we live in), find out as much as you can about him and if possible connect.

There is still another, greater option. You can trace your lineage all the way back to God, Adam's father, who has been known throughout the ages as a father to the fatherless. God comes through in many ways for those who make room for him. Children from divorced families often know this intuitively, even if their environment or education doesn't support conscious awareness of His presence. We frequently see that the fatherless are better able to develop their faith and connection with God, and at an earlier age than most.

Once a group of wounded war heroes in wheelchairs came to meet with the Rebbe in the central Chabad synagogue in Brooklyn. Among other words of insight and encouragement, the Rebbe told them that they shouldn't refer to themselves as *crippled*. He suggested instead that they call themselves *special*. What exactly is it that makes them special? Think about a person who can no longer walk. Does this mean he's not going to fulfill his purpose in life? Of course he will—without the use of his legs and feet. Special indeed.

We need all sorts of things to fulfill our purpose, and each of us has limitations of one type or another. We can allow our limitations either to get the better of us, or to bring out our specialness and talents. Use your apparent handicap to your advantage, and you can succeed as well as anyone who doesn't happen to have that disadvantage. Or even more so.

Q & A: *Happily Ever After*

Do I have to work on myself before getting married?

There's nothing intrinsically wrong with working on yourself, but that's not what marriage is about. Working on your *marriage* is the more noble endeavor. It means finding ways to make your spouse happier, more comfortable, and more secure. You've already given yourself plenty of attention. You've no doubt given yourself the best years of your life. Time to bring someone else into your life. If you're still preoccupied with the quest to find yourself, you probably have no room for anyone else.

Marriage works when you no longer care about being perfect. To make room for another person in your life, you don't need to be perfect; you need to be perfectly content with yourself yet dissatisfied with being *by* yourself. Perfecting yourself has nothing to do with it. God was already perfect when He created the world—so why did He bother? Purely to have us with Him, so that we'd be together with Him and become one with Him. Your motivation in working on your marriage ought to be the same. You don't need anything from each other, you just need to have each other. Even if only one spouse is working on the marriage, it's bound to get better for both. And you can do that even while wrestling with your own personal demons. Each person might have personal issues to deal with, but there's something much bigger than that: the marriage. It's sacred ground.

Is marriage about compromise?

We hear all the time that marriage is about compromise and sacrifice. That may be true from time to time, for an hour, even a day or two, but not for a lifetime. If you can't shake the attitude and the perception that you're living a compromised life, the marriage won't last very long.

Compromise is not consistent with life, whether we're talking about your marriage or your relationship with God. When a person strives to serve God, it has to be an expression of a valued and cherished relationship of love, appreciation, and awe, not a sense of compromising one's own feelings or personal values. If a relationship feels like a compromise, then something is wrong.

Whatever husbands and wives do for each other should never seem like a compromise or a sacrifice. If you've done what makes your spouse happy, and you've achieved the desired result, you haven't compromised; you've perfected your life. Because your marriage *is* your life.

The only thing you might have sacrificed is your ego. You're no longer focusing on yourself. You've traded in your ego for goodness. When a mother attends to her infant's every need, is she being taken advantage of? Does she feel like she's being controlled? No, she's just being a good mother.

In a marriage, *goodness* means the husband feels that his wife's *petty* problems are more important than his own *serious* issues. And likewise, to her, his apparently small problems take precedence in her mind and heart over her own difficulties, however troubling they may be. If a marriage is a matter of mutual benefit—I'll be good to her, she'll be good to me; I'll take care of my appointed tasks, he'll cover his part of the bargain—that's not a marriage, it's a business transaction. It may be practical, maybe even realistic, but it's not goodness.

Putting someone other than yourself before yourself lifts you above the merely human realm toward something higher, not to mention infinitely more pleasurable. That's humanity at its best.

Is honesty the best policy?

Honesty is absolutely imperative in just about every situation in life, whether at work or play. But when it comes to intimate relationships, kindness and thoughtfulness take precedence. The adage "Honesty is the best policy" does not apply. In a marriage, it is far more important to be considerate than to be honest.

There are occasions when lying actually becomes an important part of being married. If she asks her husband, "Do I look fat in this?" and he says, "No!" she knows he's lying, but they both know that's how you make a marriage work. If she feels a need to be perfect in his eyes, he needs to make her feel that she is. For the sake of *shalom bayit*, peace in the home, you are allowed to lie. It's perhaps the only time this permission is granted, but here it's *demanded.*

In the same vein, dignity is essential in marriage. It means you don't invade your spouse's private inner places if he or she is not willing to share that space. Don't impose yourself in areas where your spouse is likely to be made emotionally uncomfortable. Before telling something upsetting to her husband, a wife should ask herself if he really needs to hear it. Before a husband unloads his anxieties on his wife, he needs to consider whether it's going to help make things easier for her. If the answer is no, then lie. Even if it's pretty obvious that you're covering something up, that small measure of consideration will be appreciated and reciprocated.

When I was growing up my father had a store on Kings Highway in Brooklyn. Ten years after he gave up the store, we happened to be sitting around talking about armed robberies and similar kinds of dangers in the local neighborhoods. At that point my father revealed that a guy once came into the store with a gun, and my father had to fight him off. We were shocked by the story, not to mention the fact he'd waited ten years to tell us about it! Why did he hide it? It was out of kindness for his wife, my dear mother, because he imagined what knowing about it would have done to her. She would have worried every time he went to work. Would he have felt more relieved if he had shared the story right after it happened? Most certainly. But he chose to be considerate to his wife instead. We ought to aspire to that level of thoughtfulness.

My spouse and I are on different pages.

To some degree, a husband and a wife will always have differences of opinions and perspectives. They're two different people with two different personalities. This is how God created us; and being different is not a red flag.

In marriage, we accommodate each other and our differences. This is not the same as compromising. With time, we grow toward each other, become a little more like each other. This is not something you can impose artificially. It takes time, and it calls for respect. Ideally, a couple can learn more about each other and grow together by staying in touch with each other's progress, maturation, and change. Even when that's not the case, if one spouse becomes healthier, the relationship as a whole becomes healthier. It may be far from complete, and you might still argue occasionally, but it's definitely healthier. Never underestimate how powerful this can be.

For a marriage to work, we have to maintain the utmost respect and never lower our standards of dignity. This includes never judging your spouse's significance by their acts. You may have different standards than your spouse regarding everything from religion to social issues to child raising, but even if your opinions do not match up, you must still protect and cherish the respect you have for each other. You must be able to disagree about things without it becoming a reflection on the person.

The story of Noah and his sons exemplifies this. Noah had gotten drunk and was found naked by his sons. The Torah says that two of his sons covered him with a blanket, but "their father's nakedness they did not see." They saw a need for a blanket; they did not see a fault in their father. There was no loss of respect.

You may disagree with whatever your spouse does, thinks, or believes, without losing respect in the process. When you love someone, don't let your differences diminish your view of the person. You must separate the person from the flaw. That's the positive side of "love is blind."

Isn't marriage supposed to make me happy?

It's not uncommon for people to end a marriage because they've found someone else who makes them happier. That's a conditional marriage, and the condition is happiness. Do we define a good marriage by the level of happiness? What actually validates a marriage?

People think they should stay married as long as it makes them happy or provides love and security. When a person marries for love, but the love is unrequited, every minute they stay married is torture. But marriage and love are not the same thing. If marriage isn't about love, security, or happiness, what then is it good for? The answer is that it's not good for a single thing. Because, as I'm so fond of saying, it's not about a *thing*. If life were about getting things, we wouldn't need marriage to get them.

To use a somewhat melodramatic example, if a man were in a coma for several years before passing away, and during those years his wife got nothing from him, she would still grieve when he died—because she had *him* all those years, and now she lost him.

If you want to have a happy life, marriage will not do that. Instead, be happy for the sake of the marriage. Do not expect the marriage to do it for you.

Why is marriage so hard?

Marriage is not hard. People are hard. Difficult people have difficult marriages. If you're not a difficult person, why would your marriage be difficult? Marriage, by nature, doesn't make people worse. On the contrary, it should elevate them.

Marriage is a challenge, but if it's a *daily* challenge, something is amiss. If you always have to be on alert and on your best behavior, that's misery. You need help. In any marriage more than two weeks old there could be grounds for divorce, based on our personality idiosyncrasies alone. The trick is to find reasons to stay married. Sometimes it comes down to a couple developing a clear and strong recognition of each other's roles and the built-in difficulties they face—in which case they can reframe their differences as good news. For example, men tend to thrive on change, while women thrive on stability. Understanding that, with some effort they can each find ways to complement the other.

Let's say a man notices that his wife is unhappy. Theoretically he'd do everything he could to make her happy, even go to therapy. But if she's still stubbornly unhappy, he might begin to question why he even needs the aggravation at all. It'd be easy to say, "I've done my best. It's no longer my problem."

A *man* might say that, but that's not what a *husband* does. A husband takes full responsibility for his wife's happiness and never steps out of his marriage, nor separates himself from her. If his wife is having a hard time, he feels obliged to come up with a solution and help her. He never says, "I've done my part, now she has to do her share." Even if he thinks she's not pulling her weight, it's still his job to make sure she's happy. It's not his fault, but it's still his responsibility.

By the same token a wife must absolutely commit to making her husband's life easier. She's not there to correct, educate, or raise him; she's not even there to please him. She's there to hear what's hard for him and what he needs to make it easier (not what she perceives he needs).

The good news is that every husband and every wife already possess the natural talent for hearing and understanding what their respective spouses need, even (or especially!) when it's hard.

Is friendship the key to a good marriage?

There is a commonly held but mistaken impression that spouses are not as close as friends. The fact is that the closeness between a husband and a wife is far greater than that between friends. When you don't want to be friends with someone, you don't need to get a divorce, you just stop taking their calls. You can't do that with a spouse.

Picture two friends on a sinking ship. One manages to save himself, but in the midst of the panic forgets about the other. To most people, he would not be chastised or even considered necessarily wrong, because he panicked. However, if these two were a married couple, even if married for a week, no one would forgive the husband for "forgetting" to rescue his wife.

When a friendship ceases to be mutually beneficial, it's usually over. Marriage is incomparably stronger than that.

Does familiarity breed contempt?

It's not unusual to see a couple turn cruel toward each other when their marriage ceases to work. The husband might have been known as the nicest guy in the community; suddenly he's behaving viciously with her. Or vice versa—an otherwise kind and gentle woman becomes shrill and insufferable. This happens because they've come to know each other so well, inside and out, that they imagine they know everything there is to know. The result is either boredom (a minor problem) or hatred (a serious problem) or worst of all, contempt.

There's a faulty assumption that with strangers we need to be careful about how we look, act, and talk, but with our own spouses we can behave however we want. No, we can't. In fact we must be more dignified, more considerate, and even better behaved with our loved ones than with strangers. If a stranger loses respect for you, you can move on and go learn some relationship skills. If your spouse loses respect for you, your life is ruined.

Dignity and respect go hand in hand. If you lose your own dignity, it becomes hard for someone else to respect you. In the same way, when you disrespect another person, you strip that person of dignity.

Do you ever yell things to each other from another room across the house? Growing up, we never knew what our mother's name was, because whenever my father wanted to speak to my mother, he would walk over to where she was. He never yelled or called for her.

Imagine a guy at a restaurant with his wife. He accidentally spills wine all over the table and his clothing. The wife turns to the other people at a nearby table and rolls her eyes. In that moment, she has stepped out of the marriage and severed the intimacy with her husband, all because she thinks she knows him so well it's okay to conspire with the other diners in the room.

It's immature for people to think that once they get married, they get to act however they want, because their significant other will still love them. It doesn't work that way. With your spouse, you must have absolute consideration, respect, and dignity. You cannot afford to lower your standards—and it's more important at home than on the street, because a home is holy. Whether or not the mail carrier respects you is not going to affect your life. Unlike your spouse.

Just as there's an appropriate tone of voice for every occasion, there's only one tone that's appropriate between husband and wife. Children are particularly sensitive to it. When your children hear you speak to each other in the right tone, it sets them on the right path for life. If they hear the wrong tone, it disturbs their entire foundation.

What actually constitutes abuse? Are there gray areas? And how can we help?

If you're being physically abused, put down this book immediately and call the police. There is no tolerance for physical abuse. Abuse in any form has no place in any relationship, let alone a healthy one.

In cases of emotionally abusive spouses, people tend to assume that the problem is a lack of respect. In actuality, the issue of abuse is at least three steps removed from respect. The core problem is that one person is not making room for the other. It's no wonder therefore that the marriage never took off. When a husband is constantly criticizing and correcting his wife, the problem is not that he doesn't respect her, it's that there's no room for her in his world. He doesn't want another person in his life. He may want the comfort and benefits that accrue from having her, but what he essentially wants is not another human being but a clone. Loss of respect is only a minor detail. And it's not just "him"; the same can be true of a wife vis-à-vis her husband.

If a husband and a wife aren't civil to each other and we want to help, the first thing we must do to help restore respect between them is to feel compassion for them. Certainly, we can assume that they want a good marriage; but maybe they never saw one when growing up. Maybe they have a blind spot and can't even see what they're doing to each other. Perhaps the constant criticism is their way of being helpful, or so they think: *I'm the smart one.*

I know a better way of doing things. Why not do it my way? They don't see the hurt, the dismissal, and the distance they're creating.

With compassion, one might ask, "What do you think the problem is in your life that leads you behave in thus and such a way? Surely you have no intention of destroying your marriage or hurting your spouse. Would it help to know that your spouse deserves better treatment? Is there maybe something happening here that you're not seeing? How did you both get so out of touch with each other?"

None of this advice applies, however, if there is evil intent. You can't make a good marriage with a person who's out to hurt you. We're talking here about the average dysfunctional couple, where the dysfunction is not malicious, yet they hurt each other to the extent that they're risking the destruction of the marriage. In these cases, assuming both parties are decent human beings, we can help the suffering spouse view the more obviously offending partner with compassion—enough to see that the other partner is also clearly in trouble. As such, both can come to the realization that it may well be a two-way street. Without compassion, there's no place to go.

My marriage is what you might call functional. But I can't help feeling alone.

We live in a very lonely society. Some go so far as to say that loneliness is one of the most serious health issues of this generation, at the root of all sorts of illnesses and autoimmune disorders.

But there is loneliness, and then there's being alone. They are very different. *Loneliness* can actually be a sign of selfishness, as in, "I don't like this feeling of emptiness, so I'm going to use another person for company." The feeling of being *alone*, however, is a quest not just for company, but for meaning. It's a sense that "by myself, I am not enough." And it's the opposite of being selfish; it's selfless. When you're ready to make room for another person, the self has to move aside.

The remedy for aloneness is only found in marriage—in principle—but in these times, not necessarily in practice. Marriage is supposed to be a permanent cure for your sense of aloneness. There's another half to you, and the bond is immutable. Your spouse may be on the other side of the planet, but though you may feel pangs of loneliness, you know you are not alone. Yet this is barely true—perhaps even *rarely* true—today. It's because marriage is no longer intimate, and husband and wife are no longer one. What prevails today is a lack of understanding of the perfection, the awesomeness of marriage. God has brought us together, given us a home, and established our marriage as a reality in our own world. Yet we take it lightly. And as a result, today's marriages are lacking in quality.

For example, it is not uncommon for couples to speak to each other in a condescending tone. "Get over here!" they yell, or "Leave me alone!" It's grating to the ear, and to the heart, to hear couples calling each other from the other side of the house as though summoning a dog. It's a tone of impatience and annoyance that is not only inappropriate and vulgar, but disrespectful and presumptuous. It's just not the way one talks to a spouse. Married couples ought to be expressing themselves to each other with elegance, grace, and good taste.

A couple in a store arrive at the checkout counter with their purchases. The wife looks into her purse and can't find her credit card. The husband turns to the cashier with a crooked smile and says, "Par for the course. Happens all the time." He thinks it's a joke, but the way his wife feels, it might as well have been infidelity. She's uncomfortable and embarrassed, but instead of helping her, her husband throws up his hands and steps away, as if to say,

"Not my problem, don't get me involved in this. I know where I keep *my* credit cards."

In such a moment, she is alone. These seemingly insignificant behaviors are ruinous to a marriage—not because someone is going to complain, but because the marriage *itself* will complain.

Marriage is sacred, deserving of our utmost care and absolute respect. It is the most precious and delicate aspect of our life, and it should feel that way. We really must get back to the original plan.

Our grandparents and great-grandparents were possessed of a wisdom that wasn't articulated much, because their relationships were very private and understated. But to the sharp observer it could be seen in their behavior, and often in the smallest ways. For example, it was an accepted tradition that a husband would sit at the head of the table. It was one way in which a wife would establish, ever so subtly, that her husband was the head of the family. It was neither sexist nor chauvinistic, because it was at her respectful insistence, communicated with an air of dignity and strength. She would continue to demonstrate her respect by serving him first, treating him as the head of the household. And at the same time, the husband at the head of the table was equally gracious and courteous, if not more so, never starting his meal until his wife was comfortably seated and ready to eat as well. Their mutual recognition and respect were palpable. Even if she were to say, "Please, start without me," he would wait. In previous generations we were expected to understand this, instinctively, as though knowing it through osmosis.

We keep looking for love, thinking it will be the solution to all our issues. Instead, more often than not, it has brought only confusion and frustration. Even otherwise thoughtful, responsible, and dignified human beings, who do everything right, need to distinguish their marital lives from all their other relationships. If we fail to do so we will be, eventually and inevitably, inwardly and essentially, alone.

What do people mean by "heaven on earth"?

On July 4, 1976, Israeli commandos broke into the Entebbe airport, eliminated the terrorists who had hijacked an Air France Airbus, and rescued 102 Israeli hostages. What was the first thing they said to those who had been so tormented with uncertainty, so frozen in fear for their lives? In the heat of that awesome moment, they might have said, "We love you! We've come to rescue you! You are safe!" Instead, intuitively and instinctively, they said, "Let's go home."

There is nothing more powerful or significant than the feelings generated by the word *home*. When we come home, we are where we belong. "Home" evokes the most comforting, pleasurable, and rewarding feeling. The promise of going home from a place of unspeakable terror is nothing less than a moment of perfection.

Usually, wherever we are, we have doubts. "What am I actually doing here?" we wonder. "Is this where I really need to be?" We're not referring to the big cosmic question of *Why are we here?* Rather, this is just one of those nagging questions that lurk in the corners of our minds: *Hmm, where else could I be? Is this place working for me?*

When you're home, there is no other place in the world you'd rather be. No other place can compare or compete. You shut out the busy, noisy, cacophonous world outside and feel at peace. Is it like that for you? When was the last time you walked into your home and it felt like you were in heaven? That's what home should feel like. Heaven on earth. It means you are where you belong, with the person with whom you belong, and you're doing exactly what you're meant to do, with confidence and in comfort. If you were to walk through the front door and feel like you *didn't* belong, that would be the opposite of heaven. Heaven forbid.

What happens at work, at school, or in your place of worship are all important. But they're not everything, and they're not *home*. Even if you spend more hours out and about, pursuing a livelihood or an education or a social life, all that is extraneous by comparison. Home is your marriage, your family, your most cherished personal domain, your life.

The reverence and respect with which we approach our marriages define and refine our lives. There are moments in a marriage in which if time were to stop, if we were to remain right there forever, we would be perfectly content. Those moments represent a perfection that is beyond the changes and the challenges of life's ups and downs; and they bring that heavenly contentment into our homes, into our nights and days, to see us through the trials and tribulations.

There was a wonderful woman who worked for many years as a housekeeper in the home of the Lubavitcher Rebbe. When the Rebbe's wife, the Rebbetzin Chaya Mushka, passed away, this woman was discovered by one of the Rebbe's Chassidim in an upstairs room, crying bitterly. She was not crying for the Rebbetzin, she said; she was crying for the Rebbe. And she explained: often, when the Rebbe would come home late at night bringing an enormous load of work with him to prepare for the next day, she would see how the weight of the world was on his shoulders. Then when he saw his wife, his eyes lit up, and all his burdens slipped away. And now, she cried—what will the Rebbe do without her?

That's what a home should be like. When you return home from the world and its uncertainties, you should feel such profound relief that all those worries vanish into thin air. You are without a care because you are home, with her or with him. What is it all for, what is wealth or health, if not to experience the heavenly life of home, spouse, and children? For that, it's worth doing whatever it takes to have this divine blessing in our lives.

PART THREE

Fathers & Mothers & Daughters & Sons

21

Fearless Parenting

Climb the ladder safely, securely, confidently, enjoyably. And don't forget to bring the kids.

Raising children means giving them a firm, strong, and clear understanding that life is about making a difference. Raising them means elevating them, lifting them up from being primarily concerned with their own needs to focusing on how and why they are needed.

Thousands of books have been written about parenting. It's an essential skill, one that unfortunately has met with a great deal of confusion in contemporary society. But there's no need to reinvent the wheel. We can avail ourselves of the wisdom that our forebears have been gathering, practicing, and refining for more than five thousand years.

Simply stated, effective parenting means living a life that will inspire your children by example. The repository of all this wisdom is the Torah. Internalize it, adhere to it, and your children will admire and emulate the way you live. That's the natural way of raising children. They will hope to be like you and want to have what you have. You won't need to coerce them or try to convince them, much less argue with them, about how to behave.

In the past, parents would take their children out into the fields to work with them. It's not that they were of much help plowing the fields or baling the hay; it was just the way life was. Children learned about life by living it with their mothers and fathers. Contemporary parents pay homage to this practice on Take Your Daughters and Sons to Work Day; but one day a year is not enough. Your children need to see and participate in activities that constitute your life—in an age-appropriate manner, of course.

With the invention of schools, children stopped spending so much time with their parents. They began sitting in classrooms, a new and unnatural world. Once school became the major environment in which children lived, they began to live according to books and theories. Children no longer knew the life of their parents, and in some ways became estranged from them.

In an effort to be good parents, many devoted and well-intentioned parents began to live according to their children's lives rather than allowing the children to follow their lead. They would plan their days around a child's activities, lowering themselves to the child's level. Children were no longer seeing and experiencing how their parents lived.

Raising children is not a project you need to take time out to work on. You're parenting all the time, in the way you live your life. There is no need to carve out quality time with children. You don't even have to be a great communicator, or contrive ways to lecture your children about life. If you're living a purposeful life, you needn't even be conscious of the fact that you're raising children. It's a part of life. It *is* life. As parents, you ought to be busy living a life that isn't just good and moral, but also so compelling and meaningful that your children run to keep up and emulate you. Show them the life they should desire.

Too many parents don't trust themselves, always wondering whether they're getting it right or ruining their children's lives forever. They're so afraid of making a mistake, they don't parent with confidence, and therefore hardly parent at all. They cater to their children's whims, hoping they'll be appreciated for all they do.

Parenting requires no profound or deep insights, just the simple trust that God is giving you what you need to raise your children, to elevate them above their natural instincts. You've probably been working on that in yourself for years anyway. God knows what He's doing. If He gave you children without waiting for you to be perfect, then don't be afraid. Raise them fearlessly, notwithstanding all your imperfections, faults, and gaffes.

When you worry too much and try too hard, you almost guarantee your own failure. Be confident. You're the adult. You know right from wrong, and you know what your child needs. With this knowledge alone, you're already well-positioned. Parenting works when children see that their parents are confident. If a parent is absolutely sure of what he's saying, he can trust that his children will understand and follow suit—if not right away, then they'll get the message tomorrow. Without confidence, however, everything you say to your children sounds hollow and often desperate. And they tune it out. If you don't have confidence, why should they?

Parenting requires patience, with yourself as well as with the kids. Once you recognize that you're engaged in a long-term enterprise, you can remain calm, even when you make a mistake (mistakes are rarely catastrophic) or when you're not seeing immediate results. With a well-defined destination, even if you take a wrong turn, you can feel secure and still find your way, because you know where you're headed.

Imagine a frog being shocked that its tadpoles don't look anything like it. If the kids aren't living up to your expectations, remain calm and optimistic, and they'll no doubt turn out the way they were taught to be. All the frog has to do is wait a few weeks and the tadpoles will become frogs too.

Psychology versus the Test of Time

There was once a time when we relied solely on the teachings of our sacred traditions to guide us in all matters of childrearing. Parents had but two questions: "What do the sages and the prophets of old have to say? And how have these principles, guidelines, and laws been applied in real life down through the generations?" It was obvious to the children too that these were—and long had been—the rules. Naturally, therefore, enforcing the rules was easy, because children knew what was expected of them, and knew when an instruction was nonnegotiable.

Today, such issues have become open-ended, because parents aren't sure anymore what to follow. We read books and articles on childrearing and question our own intuition. We listen and subscribe to the latest psychological research, while forgoing time-tested wisdom traditions. It is noteworthy that most of psychology deals with the troubled or the disturbed, rather than with healthy children engaged in the normative processes of life.

As parents began putting their trust elsewhere, they also started to wonder if they were actually any smarter than their kids. There's a lot of modern advice out there suggesting that children are just as wise as adults, if not wiser. Are the old rules psychologically damaging, as some psychologists want to say? Or rather, does tradition reveal the toxic tenets of psychology?

When minds and hearts are grappling with two conflicting agendas, they both become weaker. And as soon as a child senses that Mom and Dad are unsure of themselves, poof—there goes the respect. Parents of past generations didn't have this problem. Instead of offering the kids their opinions, they quoted a higher authority. "God says you're not allowed to do that," they'd say. Or "My father taught me to . . ." It was credible and effective, because the child was presented with a firm and unimpeachable source for what is right and wrong. There is nothing to fear but fickleness itself.

One the most crucial moral lessons embedded in the Ten Commandments is to honor our father and our mother—in Hebrew, the *mitzvah* of *Kibbud Av v'Eim*. It applies equally whether a child is seven or seventy. It's a concept we would do well to learn, practice, and teach. Once this is understood, everything else becomes easier. Without *Kibbud Av v'Eim* parenting is a never-ending battle. We almost have to give up and let someone else take over, because our kids have tuned us out.

The beauty of the *mitzvah* is that we don't have to agree with our father or like our mother to honor them. There's no need to be psychologically uncomfortable or emotionally entangled. We can honor them just by doing the right thing; that alone will make the relationship better. If we want to make serious improvements in our lives and in our children's lives, honoring parents is a logical place to start.

The basis of the *mitzvah* is clear: you're a child, and I'm a parent, and as such we are light-years apart. When a child says, "You're not the boss of me," or "If you don't give me, I'm not gonna give you," the backbone of the relationship is lacking. The thought that child and parent are equal, and they have to negotiate, means that the whole foundation is amiss. A father is a father, and a mother is a mother—not a friend, or a buddy, and certainly not a servant. The mere awareness that *I'm the child, and I have to honor my parents* is a huge moral accomplishment. Parents must have the clarity and conviction to wear the mantle of authority. If a child doesn't have that firmly embedded in his consciousness, he's missing the groundwork, and there's nothing to build on. And it's a principle that doesn't change with age.

In practical terms, honoring one's parents means doing menial tasks for them, so that they won't have to. If they're carrying something, carry it for them. Help Dad with his coat if he's having a hard time putting it on. When they're sitting at the table, bring them what they need. Anticipate their needs and do for them the things you know they usually do themselves, like boiling water for tea. You should always be looking for opportunities to serve and properly respect your parents.

According to Jewish tradition, a child, no matter how old he is, is not allowed to sit in his mother's or his father's chair. It's a powerful visual, a constant reminder. A child must also speak to parents in a respectful manner at all times. Refrain from contradicting or criticizing them in public. Don't call them by their first names. A child should stand up to acknowledge his parents when they walk into the room, if he hasn't seen them all day. Children ought to put their parents on a pedestal; and if they step off, put them back up. Parents who humbly reject such gestures are not doing the kids any favors.

I had a great uncle who was an extremely humble and simple man—*Feter* (Uncle) Chaim. He managed to escape Poland before the Nazi invasion. He led an exceedingly modest life, supporting himself by collecting donations for various *yeshivas*. He was a truly humble and gentle soul. For many years, he would come to eat dinner at our house. He was so quiet and soft-spoken, I almost never heard him speak.

Once, when I was about eleven years old, we were sitting together at the kitchen table. Our kitchen was very small, so there was very little room to move around. It happened that my mother was right by the sink washing dishes, so I asked her for a spoon.

My gentle *Feter* Chaim became suddenly indignant, red in the face. *"Banutzen di Mameh?!"* he cried in Yiddish. ("What? You're using your mother?") Uncle Chaim had been raised in a Torah-observant home, where asking your parents to do something you could do yourself was unthinkable. His reaction had such a powerful effect on me that to this day I'm afraid to ask my mother for anything, lest Uncle Chaim will come back from the grave and yell at me again. And had my mother said, "Get your own spoon," it wouldn't have had the same effect at all.

We tend to be casual about this *mitzvah*. "Ma, can you bring down my sweater from upstairs, as long as you're coming down anyway?" "Dad, can you bring me a glass of water, since you're standing by the fridge?" This may seem silly by today's standards, but neither of these are acceptable behavior. Children are supposed to make their parents' lives easier. The only time they ought to ask a parent to do anything is if it's something they can't do on their own, such as drive them to school.

Once when I was giving this idea over to schoolchildren in Brazil, a boy protested, saying that his mother *loves* doing things for him. "That means she's a very good mother," I said. "She deserves a good son. Stop asking her to do things for you. Do for her instead."

What if a child *does* ask his parents to do something for him—what should they do? Do it. But later that day, sit the child down and explain how it was inappropriate. For example, a mother might say, "If you ask me to do something, of course I will, because I love you. But you're not supposed to ask." It would be even better if the other parent were to say it; or if they happen to have an Uncle Chaim in the house. The message is always more powerful when delivered by a third party.

Obviously, if we haven't cultivated this awareness from a young age, we can't suddenly demand it. We could say, "I can't tell you what to do. But you're supposed to honor your parents, so do the right thing." If we've already discussed this with our child a number of times, the next time it happens, we could say, "You know better than that."

Sometimes we tell our children to do the right thing "for your own benefit." Really? Who says *mitzvahs* are for their benefit? We want our child to do good because it's the right thing to do, not for his own benefit. Should everything be for his benefit? Can he steal for his benefit? Not to mention the fact that saying it's "for your own benefit" smacks a little of manipulation or apology. Why not say, "Just be a *mensch* and do the *mitzvah*"? Is that not sufficiently compelling?

When we measure core values by the yardstick of contemporary psychology, our values easily become muddied. This is not the case with clear allegiance to the commandments. For example, Jewish people who keep kosher don't mix milk with meat. There's no psychology there. What do we do to get our kids to keep kosher? Nothing. Milk and meat together are simply out of the question. When it comes to the *mitzvah* of honoring parents, however, we suddenly feel a little shaky. *Am I demanding too much? Will my high expectations damage my kid?*

So how do we teach our children the positive commandment of honoring parents? The real question is, why is that even a question? When we teach them to keep kosher, we don't sit them down, explain it to them, give them samples of kosher food, and delve into the purpose and benefits of the *mitzvah*. No; at this point, it needs no explanation. They'll figure all that out for themselves eventually. It works the same way with *Kibbud Av v'Eim*.

The Mommas and the Poppas

Parenting is based on certain nonnegotiable principles that establish the foundation of a child's life. That foundation needs to be stable and strong.

Why did yesterday's children accept discipline from their parents, even spanking, while nowadays kids won't even go to their rooms without putting up a fight? Today's children don't believe their parents have authority over them. They are missing the concept of honor.

In the past, mothers used to say, "Wait till your father comes home!" Why does it take the father? What does he do that she can't? Unlike a mother, a father's disappointment is devastating. A father is like a principal, while a mother is like a teacher. The teacher works with the students, and the principal checks their progress. If they don't make progress, the principal steps in. Similarly, the father sets the standard and evaluates pass or fail. This doesn't mean the father can't help the mother out in her role, but he must maintain the primary role of the father, a step or two removed. He also needs to have confidence in the way his wife raises their children, and demonstrate that in their presence. Today, men are more aware and involved in the family than ever before, sometimes acting as an assistant mother. That's fine, but a child needs to have a father. If the father gets too involved in the more empathic process of mothering, the child may become confused.

Children need to know their father has authority. That doesn't mean "my way or the highway." No one can establish authority by demanding or bullying. But he must be firm, even if that makes some people uncomfortable. Authority should be an unquestioned fact of life. Young children need facts, not rationalizations or justifications. They're counting on their parents to teach them right from wrong.

While the mother reinforces the father's authority, her role is to nurture and support. Because she was so intimately involved in the child's creation, she can express only a limited degree of negative discipline. Her role is more of a coach, training and guiding her child; and for that she needs to trust herself. Though she's not perfect, she is the mother her children were destined to have, and by that merit she usually knows what's best. Unfortunately, many mothers and fathers today don't trust their respective maternal and paternal instincts. Then they run to the psychologist for parenting advice—a risky choice that can lead to chaos.

Most parents harbor a noble and idealistic desire to give their children everything they themselves never had. Can that actually be done? It's unrealistic at best. You can't give what you haven't got. "I want you to go to school and get good grades," they say, "so you don't end up like me." Translation: "I don't want you to be like me." It's not a good message; children seek continuity and long to remain faithful to their parents.

In fact the attachment of children to their parents is phenomenal—and sometimes dysfunctional. Often, children who could have had a better life than their parents subconsciously refuse to be more accomplished than they were, out of a sense of loyalty. They may be more capable, more talented, or have better business sense than their parents, but they sabotage their own success.

To tell your child, "Don't end up like me" is neither useful nor inspiring. Telling them to find their own world and live life their own way is tantamount to throwing them out of the house. Effective parenting means making the bold statement, "This is how I am. You should be like this too." Raising children means striving to ensure that the life you're living is good for you, and that they will want to follow in your footsteps.

Your children don't welcome conversations about your mistakes, not even in your misguided youth. You don't need to tell them how human you are; they'll figure it out eventually. By trying to convince them not to do something by cataloguing your own failures, you're encouraging them to make the same mistakes. It worked out for you, and everything's okay now, so why not?

They know nobody's perfect, and that includes you, though they have no idea what their parents' imperfections are. Let it stay that way. They don't want to hear about your misbehavior. It's not possible to shield them from all of life's disappointments. It isn't even healthy. Instead of trying to give them what you never had, give them what you have in abundance. Give them the best of you. Go with your strengths, not your weaknesses.

How many talents or strengths does it take to make a lasting impression on a child? It only takes one. Think about what adult children remember their parents for after they pass away.

"My father never lost his temper."

"My mother was always generous to the poor."

In essence, it doesn't really matter *what* you are to your child. What really matters is that you are there at all. All children need to know is that they have a mother and a father. That's it. It makes them feel normal, that life is good. How exactly does your mother convey her presence in your life? It almost doesn't matter.

"She always has food for us when we come home."

"She always buys me something for my birthday."

It's not about the birthday, and it's not about the food. It's the plain fact that she's Mom, and she's here. When it comes to your children's education, of course, the details make a difference; but in terms of their security, sanity, or self-esteem, the fact that they have a mother at all is enough. Just by being there, you're giving them a vision of what life should be, where they're headed, and what their future holds. Through your example they can picture themselves as adults, and they won't be afraid to grow up.

One of the problems in the world today, including in the religious world, is that the people worthy of esteem are mostly in the past. There were "greats" back in the day; now, not so much. For your children, that's a real issue. Your nostalgia is not their nostalgia. There has to be someone alive and real today, whom they can look upon with great respect. If there is a person you admire or revere, let your children know it. Tell them what it is that you appreciate about that particular person. It's a powerful message to give them, a tangible example of what respect means and what it means to look up to someone. And it will pay off in enhancing their respect for you.

22

Love, Selfishness, and Self-Esteem

A need is a weakness. Our strengths are to be found in a sense of purpose.

It's widely believed that the answers to all childrearing problems lie in demonstrating more love and building self-esteem. Experts claim that if children have issues, they need more love, regardless of how much love they have already received.

Are parents more loving now than ever before? Yes. But are children happier, healthier, or smarter as a result? No.

Telling children they are special might build their self-esteem, but when life gets tough and they can't get what they want, they're presented with a huge contradiction. They feel they deserve everything. Yet life isn't fair. It's terrible, tragic: they're not getting what they think they deserve. It's a classic case of high self-esteem making life worse, not better.

Saying, "I'll love you unconditionally" is akin to saying "You don't actually matter. What you do doesn't matter. How you behave doesn't matter. I'm going to love you whether you like it or not." How can someone be lovable when they're being awful? It's not okay when no matter what the child does, his parents' reaction is the same. Is that a relationship? It actually breeds resentment. When told they're loved unconditionally, kids will often feel a need to act out just to prove that it's *not* unconditional. They want to be noticed and responded to appropriately.

Children need to be needed. If they don't feel needed, no amount of love or self-esteem will make up for it. If a child feels unnecessary, all the love in the world will come across as foolish and meaningless, because there's no one there to receive the love.

When we say a child is needed, we're not talking about performing everyday functions or doing the chores. Sure, the dishes need to be washed and the books need to be put away. Somebody's got to do it; and if the kid is capable and available, great. But that's not what you need her for. The message she has to hear is that you need her to be in your life. Her very existence, her presence, is necessary. She gives your life its meaning, its definition.

Of course, she can be needed and useful too. "Go ahead and clean your room if you have some time." But if the message she's getting is that you *need* her to clean her room, she's going to resent you and rebel. What she really wants you to say is, "Without you, I am not me. Without me, you're not you." The parent is defined by the child, and the child by the parent. Make sure *that's* the message, and that it comes across clearly.

Every time you tell a child, "Go take a shower" or "We're going out now" or "It's time for dinner," you're introducing a reality that supersedes the child's five senses. Generally speaking, children are governed by what they feel, see, hear, taste, and touch. What you're saying is, "Regardless of how you feel, it's time to do this." If you come along and say, "It's eight o'clock. Bedtime," that's an objective reality. Instead of asking the child whether he's tired, simply say, "It's bedtime." It's a nonthreatening, educational message, stating a reality.

Chassidus, the Jewish spiritual movement whose modern resurgence began in the eighteenth century, emphasizes that it's what we think, say, and do that matters. It's not whether we are important, smart, talented, or well-positioned that makes a difference; it's what we *do* that counts. For children, it's a path to self-esteem. Their behavior matters. It matters to their parents, it matters to society, and it matters to God. Telling them they're "the best" won't help them live a healthy, balanced life. (They won't believe you anyway.)

Judaism is full of opportunities to put this idea to work. According to Jewish Law, we make a blessing before eating anything. There are different blessings for different types of foods, and of course this comes up all the time. It's among the first things a child learns and is expected to internalize in Jewish education. Let's say a child is reciting the appropriate blessing before a meal, but imperfectly. The parent tells her, "You made the blessing, but you didn't get it right." This parent is not judging or destroying the child. In fact it's actually a compliment. The parent is saying, "There's a right way and a wrong way, and then there's the proper and perfect way. From you, my child, I expect the perfect way." Why? "Because your blessing is important enough to do it right." The focus is on the significance of the task at hand, not on the worthiness of the child. Self-esteem doesn't come from generic flattery. It comes from knowing who one is and where one belongs. Just being the smartest or prettiest child in class is not an identity.

If a child does something wrong, you'd never call him stupid, evil, or rotten. Instead, you simply tell him that what he did was wrong. Conversely, when a child does something good, don't change the focus and shower him with compliments. Stick to the issue: "What you did was good!"

Parents need to be consistent and conscious of the language they use. Saying, "You're such a good boy, I love you!" can serve only to confuse the child. What happens if tomorrow he does something wrong? Now he's unsure whether he's still good, or even whether his parents still love him.

Sometimes when parents catch a child doing something he's not supposed to, they'll say, "I hate it when you do that." They're not teaching right and wrong; they're changing the subject, voicing what they like or dislike. Or when a parent says, "How many times have I told you..." What difference does the frequency make? When training a child to tell right from wrong, stick to the good or bad deed itself, not personal preferences or scorecards.

A better time to tell your child what you think of him and how much you love him is when you're just sitting around or tucking him into bed. Then you can call him an angel or a *tzaddik* or any words of praise you wish, because you're not confusing the issues. But when he's doing a good deed, the subject is the good deed. A *mitzvah* is a *mitzvah*. The same is true when he does something wrong, it's about the action, not the child. Don't confuse him.

Understanding boundaries fosters another sort of self-esteem. When a child knows that she can't eat a candy because it's not kosher, or that he needs to go home in time to get ready for *Shabbat*, that's true self-esteem, and it far surpasses random, indiscriminate accolades.

We met once with a Catholic priest in Brooklyn, New York, a very elegant, educated, and charismatic young man, to talk about what's going on with the children in his parish these days. It seems the issues are the same regardless of the culture or religion. The teens in his community hang around the streets of Crown Heights—a very diverse neighborhood—where there's a great deal of adolescent crime, because there are no planned activities or supervision. He's making a real difference by creating programs for these kids, and, as important, helping them develop a balanced, healthy self-image.

An elevated self-image and a low self-image are two sides of the same counterfeit coin. What they have in common is the word *self*—and it's toxic.

How low can you go? When a person is overly focused on his bad fortune, it's always about himself: the loser, the failure, the dropout, the victim. A person with an inflated self-image isn't much different; it's always about what he or she needs, wants, and (especially) deserves. There's a growing consensus in America that crime doesn't come from poverty or being underprivileged; it's more associated with having a distorted sense of self-importance and personal entitlement. These people feel they can take what they want, and no act of violence is too extreme.

And so our children need to learn that it is not as important to fulfill their own needs as it is to know they're fulfilling someone else's needs. A human being is essentially a purposeful creature. We are driven by purpose, not by our need. Our needs are our weaknesses. Our purpose is our strength.

Another thing we discussed with the priest was the realization that telling children that God loves them, which used to be a very appealing and effective message, doesn't help anymore. When children don't feel needed, love is not going to make up for that. In the old days, you were needed and necessary to the people around you. If you were loved, that would make it so much the sweeter, but primarily, what was essential was to know you were needed.

Today, children may feel loved, but they don't think they're necessary or needed. So to tell them "God loves you" only begets resentment. If I'm not necessary, but you love me, something is wrong with *you*. What are you loving? You can't make something important by loving it.

What we need to teach children is that "God needs you. He created you for a reason and a purpose as part of His eternal plan. Whether He loves you or not, well, that will depend on how you behave. If you're lovable, He'll love you. If not, He still needs you."

Of course, children need to be loved, and know they're being loved. They need to see, feel, and hear it. But that's just the icing on the cake. If life is the cake, love is the icing. What we hunger for is the cake, not the icing. In other words, what we hunger for is nutrition, not the look, or the crunch, or even the sweetness of it. Like the sizzle of the steak, it does not satisfy. Love makes life sweet, if you have a life. And if you have a life, but you're missing the sweetness, you still have a life. It'd be great if it were also sweet and pleasant. The icing enhances the cake, but it can't replace life.

Maturation, Step by Step

We are disappointed when our children get upset over silly things. We wish they'd be more mature. Is that fair? Is it helpful? We evaluate a child's growth by age, intelligence, maturity, and behavior, not by a birth certificate. There is no objective standard as to how behavior lines up with developmental phases and milestones. Children today tend to be way ahead of themselves. They clearly have access to information they were never meant to have and have absorbed opinions they're too young to understand in context. How, then, are we to determine what is age appropriate as they grow?

If your child is seven years old and still gets upset about trivialities, first of all remember that he's only seven. Refrain from getting angry at him. What you can do is tell him, maybe even explain to him, how some things aren't worth getting upset about. "Stop crying" is *not* a message. "You're crying over a toy?" is a lesson.

Appealing to your child's intelligence is always helpful. To that same seven-year-old, try, "Have you ever noticed what three-year-olds cry about? When they're hungry or tired, they cry. Isn't that babyish? Seven-year-olds don't cry when they're hungry. That's for babies."

Paint the picture and set it up so it's not a battle. While you want to raise them to value maturity, remember that children will be children. Don't expect too much from a three-year-old. You are engaged in the monumental task of building values. It takes time.

Let's roll back to the beginning. What about a baby? Of course, love is wonderful, but that's not what a newborn needs or expects. His need at this stage is absolute security. And because that sense of security is his foundation, we should never let a baby "cry it out."

Modern methods recommend letting babies cry, suggesting that it's good for a baby's lungs, and it prevents them from expecting always to be picked up. Ignoring a baby who is panicking and desperate is inhumane. Sometimes, if you listen attentively to a baby's cry, you can hear that he's actually worried whether anyone is there, or if he's on his own. Crying it out doesn't teach independence. It makes a human being desperately dependent.

Of course, not all cries are desperate. There are differences in the sounds of a baby's cry, and a parent needs only to pay attention and learn. Sometimes, a baby is just fussy. That's not the same as a cry for help. Listen to the cry to hear what he's saying. But the general rule of thumb is when your baby cries, comfort him. Can you feel the child's fear and desperation? Even in a car, it's better to pull over and calm the baby down.

What does it mean when babies cry themselves to sleep? When eventually they begin to sleep without crying, it means they've given up in despair. They've learned that crying is not going to help. What kind of message is that? Never give them the impression that this world is distant, cruel, or painful. Respond to their call. When a desperate cry becomes a shriek, it's like going numb. You can't let that happen. It teaches that there is no security, that no one will respond. That's terrible. It undermines a child's whole connection with life.

Whereas with older children, it's important to help them learn to control their emotions, it's not so with infants. To an infant, having his need met quickly is a matter of survival. It affects his outlook on the world. Life will be a lot harder on both of you in the long run if your child is insecure.

When people used to live with extended family, someone was usually around to care for a baby, even if not the parent. Letting a baby cry was unheard of. During the first year of a child's life, it's imperative to instill the feeling of absolute security.

In their second year, children need predictability more than anything. It's another form of security, but now it's no longer about survival alone; it's about forming habits, establishing routines and certainty. But it begins in the first year as well. The reason babies love playing peek-a-boo is predictability. Knowing the parent comes back each time is reassuring.

A certain researcher who is also a psychologist discovered that there's a specific hormone babies need that isn't present naturally at birth. It develops in response to the mother's attention. Hence, every look, every touch, and every moment of contact a mother has with her baby strengthens the baby's immune system. This researcher was criticized and condemned for supposedly "setting women back fifty years," as though pointing out the importance of a mother's role was sexist. Her research further suggested that any consistent female caregiver also helps to produce that hormone. It was common in an earlier time for people to engage wet nurses. It helped, because it wasn't a different babysitter every week. These findings, however, didn't help change those critics' opinions.

Chanah, one of seven biblical female prophets, waited until her son Shmuel was three years old before leaving him with a babysitter to make her yearly pilgrimage to the Holy Temple in Jerusalem. Until then, her priority was being present. Later, she took him to the High Priest to train him. She pledged his life to the service of God; but not before completing the birthing process during the child's first three years.

For children under the age of three, reality is based on taste and touch. From three to four years old, they should learn to like being clean and not to be too picky about food. Start moving them away from the narrow world of taste and touch. Introduce it as a value, rather than as a correction of a personal weakness, so that the child will become less finicky in other aspects of life as well. If a child understands there's a difference between clean and unclean, then he or she will eventually be able to understand that certain thoughts are clean, and certain thoughts are not. Begin by introducing these concepts in the purely physical realm, and it will be easier to make those distinctions in their behaviors and thoughts as they mature.

When a child turns three, you can't expect him or her to suddenly become nice. You have to guide them away from not being nice. It's also not too early to teach obedience. Start by asking them to do things you know they'll do. Then use affirmation, such as, "You listened to Mommy. That's good! And it's the right thing to do." Positive, affirmative, and *specific* language is encouraging. "You just listened," is a lot more productive than saying, "Good job."

By five years of age, children should be neat and able to obey their parents and teachers. A child at six years of age should know that time is precious. He or she should also appreciate learning.

How do you get a ten-year-old to do a task? In general, how do you get children to do anything? For example, no child knows instinctively how to clean a room. To clean a room, children have to see how the room ought to look, and where things go. Help them do that. Even an older child can't necessarily be expected to clean up without guidance. Most children don't know where to begin. At first, all they see is that after moving things around, the room still looks messy. Instead of asking why the room's not clean, get in there and help. Do it ten times, and on the eleventh time slip out. The child will finish the job on his own.

Learning and Levitating

When the Lubavitcher Rebbe was a child, he'd come home from school and his father would ask him, "What did you remember?" Not, as most parents would ask, "What did you learn today?" His father's intention was to stimulate memory. And he'd reinforce the boy's power of memory in many ways—anchoring it, for example, by identifying it with a name, either by topic or by chapter and verse. It was a method that paid off not only the next day in school, of course, but throughout the years to come. The Rebbe's phenomenal memory was only one of his remarkable qualities, but it was key.

Although this astute sort of mental training, along with other such advice offered in these pages, is intrinsic to Jewish modes of learning, it's by no means exclusive to Judaism.

As a child gets a little older, you have to introduce the idea that everything you've taught him is between him and *God*, not you. Otherwise, once he becomes a teenager, he might misconstrue Judaism as *his parents'* rules, *his parents'* practice, and *his parents'* God. And he might abandon it.

Before that can happen, start to cultivate your child's personal relationship with God by instilling the concept that it is her personal path. Once a child turns twelve or thirteen, she's already acquired some learning tools. If she asks, for example, why something ought to be done, your answer should be on the order of, "Go find out. It's your God, your *mitzvah*, and your *neshama*."

Furthermore, as teens get older, you ought to be able to pose questions to *them*. When your daughter come homes from school, you might ask her age-appropriate questions, pertaining to Jewish Law perhaps, or the biblical source of the law. "How come you're not allowed to do this . . . ?" Ask as if you expect her to know the answer. If she doesn't, she needs to find out.

The Torah guides us in the paths and the processes of educating our children. When the child is old enough to speak, we're told to teach him his first prayer. It should be a prayer that you yourself say every morning, not something fabricated and abridged for children. At what age do you take your child with you to synagogue to pray together? When would you take a child with you on a pilgrimage to Jerusalem? In other words, how do we gradually introduce our kids and involve them in our lives? Gradually, we raise our children through these stages until they begin to acquire on their own the qualities that are worthy of pursuit.

Education and upbringing entails helping children in elevating their sense of pleasure. Pleasure is synonymous with life itself. Young children only experience the pleasures of life through what they see, taste, and touch. The role of a parent is to uplift those pleasures to a higher level. The many levels of pleasure are like a ladder that stands on earth and reaches to heaven. Raising children means accompanying them on that ladder and up through the rungs of life's delights.

For example, the pleasure we derive from music is higher than that of taste and other physical sensations. Music appreciation is certainly a pleasure worth cultivating. Ever wonder why Jews sing at the *Shabbos* table? It enhances and deepens not only the deliciousness, but also the holiness of eating the Sabbath meal.

Another step up elevates the child's aesthetic experience from auditory pleasure to visual pleasure. Children can be encouraged to appreciate beauty, whether in nature, photography, fine arts, architecture, or a flower arrangement in the living room. After which we can rise further with the child toward an appreciation of the pleasure of learning. We can see how a child lights up when he or she knows the answer to a question. It's a pure, unadulterated pleasure, one immeasurably greater than cookies or candy.

The pleasure of acquiring good character is nourished by the pleasure of hearing about it and seeing it in others. When we read stories to children about someone doing something virtuous, it warms their hearts. They will love, learn to appreciate, and begin to emulate kindness and good deeds—another significant step in the developmental process.

Ultimately, of course, we want to cultivate the pleasure of serving God. They must realize that we are all here to serve God, and especially that serving God by being joyful is the highest form of pleasure. What we want for our children is to bring them, and ourselves, beyond the *obligatory* performance of *mitzvahs*, and discover the delight of living Godly, holy lives with *joy*.

It's a good idea to try to rise through these levels incrementally and not be tempted to skip a step. A parent might make the mistake of cultivating a child's pleasure in intellectual pursuits and academic excellence without taking the time to foster an appreciation of generosity, compassion, or honesty. The result may be a child who is bright, but callous, who is clever enough to find more ways of getting into trouble than a child who is not so sharp.

Clearly, we can't expect to refine any aspect of a child's experience by demanding compliance and barking commands. It's a process. We have to find ways of bringing out the pleasures that each child needs to develop. Ultimately, the character of your children is shaped by *your* character, by the quality of your own experience. Whatever you're enthusiastic about is what defines your life and influences theirs. It's not about the activities, but the *life* expressed in those activities. You give value to whatever you do with zest and energy.

Children appreciate refinement. If they grow up witnessing the respect their parents have for each other, hearing the special tone they use when speaking to each other, they will want to emulate that as they grow. There is an irresistible, contagious level of pleasure in gracious behavior from which the child will never walk away.

The Baal Shem Tov, the eighteenth-century founder of the modern Chassidic movement, blazed a trail that made enthusiasm for Godliness—*excitement* about what God needs and wants from us—accessible to everyone. Kids are particularly sensitive and open to the pleasure, the joy, the sheer delight of connecting with God. As you introduce them to age-appropriate *mitzvahs*, pay attention to making sure it's fun. Gradually, step by step, knowing how much they love doing the *mitzvah* now, you'll see them climbing higher and higher up the ladder. Because they know intuitively that a *mitzvah* is not only about how good it makes *them* feel; it's about making *God* happy. It's like when a wife asks her husband to bring home flowers. He walks in with a nice bouquet, and she goes on and on about how beautiful they are. And he says, "I didn't buy them because they're beautiful. I brought them for *you*, because I knew you'd like them."

23

Teaching Morality

When an immovable objective meets an irresistible force, someone's got to give.

An infant is a human being with a unique destiny. Every child is his own person and not an extension of his parents. While his parents can contribute to his development, they can't control him. He's already a person, an individual, albeit with a long way to go.

So where do parents fit in? It is every parent's responsibility to teach moral issues. Although you can't change a child's destiny, you can have an impact on whether he's going to be good or bad. Each individual has freedom of will, and where there's freedom of choice, children can't be expected to choose correctly. They have to be trained to rise to the challenge of morality and choose the good. Even if you happen to be blessed with a child who has a good heart by nature, morality is not automatic by any means, nor spontaneous; it has to be taught. Morality requires choice, and that requires commitment.

Having a good character doesn't necessarily mean having good morals. A nice person who has nevertheless never made a commitment to do the right thing can commit acts of horror when provoked.

We are often surprised to find that people who commit heinous crimes were not monsters all their lives. A good nature will incline a person toward morality, but beyond that, there's no guarantee.

This is also why it's so important to teach moral issues early in life. You have to let children know that you are aware that they have free choice, that they have the capacity to behave properly or badly. They must also know that you're willing to work with them.

It's equally important that a parent get comfortable with the fact that a child has free will, and that a child with free will is capable of doing just about anything when put to the test. Expressing shock or surprise—"How could you do this?!"— is a counterproductive reaction that will only evoke rebellion.

Lying, though commonplace (what child doesn't lie?), is one of the moral concerns we need to watch out for. That includes half-truths, such as conveniently leaving out certain details. It may not be a blatant lie, but it's still dishonest. By the age of five, a child ought to be made aware of the value, the necessity, of truthfulness.

Training your child also calls for a measure of equanimity. It's not something that should be taken personally. Your role is to educate, not to get angry. If you allow it to become a battle of wills, you're setting yourself up for failure.

If your child doesn't want to make the appropriate blessing before eating, for example, it's best to respond by saying something like, "Okay, I'll make the blessing for you." You haven't set it up as a win-or-lose situation, so nobody loses.

If you say, "Go to bed now," or "Stop playing with the iPad," and you know your child is not going to comply, it doesn't mean you're failing. You just need to refrain from making absolute statements. Even when threatening punishment, avoid absolute ultimatums like, "Stop, or we're never going out ever again," or, "Go to your room and never come out." You're not there to enforce. You're there to educate. Likewise, drop the *you cannot* and replace it with *you ought not*—unless you're looking for a declaration of war. It's better to simply tell them they "shouldn't do that," and honor the fact that it's their choice.

On the other hand, when teaching morality, you cannot be wishy-washy. The simpler and more direct the statement, the better; otherwise you give the impression that morality is negotiable. For example, you shouldn't say, "If you want to be good, make a blessing." She can easily respond, "I don't want to be good," or attempt to engage you in a debate about the value of the instruction itself. What if you've told your child to do something, but you catch him violating the rule? If you let it go, you're not being consistent. If you intervene, you'll likely start a fight. You can't dismiss it, and it would be unwise to try to enforce it against resistance. One option is to choose not to see it for the moment. You don't have to notice everything right away. Then later on, possibly the next day, you could take him aside and say something like, "I noticed that sometimes you make the blessing before you eat and sometimes you don't. What's that about?" Be firm and consistent, without being a tyrant. He may well see through his own excuses and reassess his behavior, or give you another chance to convince him to comply.

Flexibility and Rigidity

"Spare the rod," we read in the Book of Proverbs, "and spoil the child." (It's an imprecise translation of King Solomon's words, but it'll do for our purposes here.) A rod or a staff is an inflexible, rigid, unbending piece of wood. The proverb means that if you're flexible about everything, your child will be spoiled. When conveying right and wrong, you have to be as rigid as a stick. If not, you're giving him a flimsy rather than a solid foundation in life.

As an example, when you tell a child she can't lie, it should be said firmly, unembellished by any additional nuances that might invite possibilities of doubt. If she hears that something is bad, but isn't convinced that it's always true, the doubt will weaken her, leave her vulnerable, and undermine her life.

The Lubavitcher Rebbe has often been described as presenting two very contradictory qualities. On the one hand, he was gentle and flexible; on the other hand, he would seem as immovable as an autocrat. How can one person be both? Simple. When it comes to Torah principles, the Rebbe wouldn't budge. Yet he was extremely sensitive to the human condition. He understood people's weaknesses, loved them, and made room for them despite their frailties.

To have moral influence calls for espousing an inflexible standard, while remaining a flexible person in real-life relationships. The same applies to parenting. You need to be gentle, flexible, and forgiving, while being unyielding when it comes to moral teachings. Contrary to popular belief, knowing that a teaching cannot be compromised stokes children's enthusiasm, rather than the opposite. Doubts only serve to drain their interest and excitement. If a leader is not unbending, he'll be useless and ineffective. Yet we also need to be very flexible in our judgment of our children. With house rules, for example, exceptions abound. You're not supposed to eat on the couch—unless you're really careful.

But in matters regarding right and wrong, we must remain resolute. *Halacha*—Torah law—is not like house rules. These are God's rules. A sin is a sin. It's flat-out wrong, and it's simply not allowed.

Once the Rebbe was asked about certain Jews who get up early on *Shabbat* to attend morning prayers, so they can go to work immediately afterward. Of course, going to work is prohibited on the Sabbath. The Rebbe said, "Yes, it is indeed an issue that they rush off to work. Wrong is wrong. But the fact that they are waking up early to attend synagogue services is precious in the eyes of God."

In some communities, such a person might be considered a hypocrite. He may even be denied entrance or not given certain honors during the prayer services. The Rebbe had a whole different attitude. Even if he works on *Shabbos*, which is unconscionable, the fact that he enthusiastically comes to *shul* early is wonderful.

Had this person gone to the Rebbe and asked if it was okay to go to work after prayers on *Shabbos*, the Rebbe might have replied, "It's your responsibility to make sure that other Jews don't go to work." Not only was he inflexible on principle, he was demanding as well.

That's how we have to be in parenting: flexible, inflexible, and expressing high expectations. We have no right to be compromising about God's laws and concerns. When it comes to *mitzvahs* and moral issues, the Law is the Law. But when considering a child's shortcomings, limitations, handicaps, or failures, we need to be totally flexible and understanding. A child is wonderful in every bit of good he does. We must accept and not overreact to our children's faults and character flaws. When it comes to a Jewish tradition or commandment, however, again, who are we to bend the rules?

So if a child is eating without saying a blessing, he should tremble. But if he doesn't, he's still a great kid. Help him channel his energy. If one of his hands hits, punches, or steals, we don't cut off this hand. On the contrary, we talk about the virtues of the other hand, and about how great this hand could be as well. A hand can give charity. It can massage a sibling's sore muscles. It can light the *Shabbos* candles. Use it well.

Battles and Strategies

Imagine your house is falling apart. The children have run amok and are climbing the walls. You don't know how to regain control. A stranger walks in, sits down, and strikes up a conversation with the kids. Now he's got their attention, they're behaving well, and you're feeling completely useless. A total stranger shows up and suddenly the children are engaged and listening? It's because you've been all about the chaos, and the stranger doesn't care about the chaos. He's addressing *them*.

Parental approval may be the most important thing to a child, and, conversely, our disapproval can be the strongest and most effective form of criticism. That's assuming they're listening, which in turn may be affected by how well we're listening to them. How our children respond to us—or sometimes whether or not they respond at all—may depend on something as simple as our tone of voice. It's also important that we weigh each situation appropriately before taking the risk of turning the home into a battleground.

Every home has its own style and flavor. In some homes, parents are uncompromising about cleanliness and order. Others are very meticulous when it comes to table manners. Still others focus more intensely on healthy food. Although cleanliness is next to Godliness, it's not a moral issue. A little chaos means a child is allowed to be a child. Just as it's not a realistic expectation for a two-year-old to eat with a fork and a knife, it's perfectly understandable that older children will also make an age-appropriate mess.

The only thing we need to be inflexible about is morality. Cheating, lying, stealing—these are never acceptable. You can, and ought to, be flexible with your own rules. For example, if you know a daily room cleanup is unrealistic to expect, relax a little rather than pick a fight. When you tell your children to brush their teeth, it's not a cardinal principle, and needn't become a crisis. Asking your child to recite a blessing before and after eating, however, is a matter of a *mitzvah*. A child should know immediately from your tone whether you're talking about a nonnegotiable commandment or training them to develop a healthy habit.

Ideally, that kind of conversation should go something like this: "Did you brush your teeth? No? So, go brush your teeth."

A half hour later: "You still didn't brush your teeth? Okay, you'll brush your teeth later."

Or "If you want to be able to find your shoes in the morning, put them next to the door." Maybe he doesn't want to find them in the morning. Fine. It's not a sin. Tailor your tone to the reality. Of course, you want him to do whatever you tell him to do. But not everything is of equal importance to everyone. Some might consider brushing teeth more important than saying a blessing. "If he doesn't brush his teeth, he'll get cavities. That's more serious." On the other hand, it's common in kosher-observant families that a child won't listen when told not to eat candy because it will ruin his teeth or his appetite, but tell the same kid it's not kosher and it's out of the question.

We can be lax with our own rules; that can get a little slippery with God's laws. Still, the key is to help them, not force them, to grow. You're cultivating a habit and a taste for what's right. If they balk, is there some information they're lacking? Remind them that God wants and needs them to make a blessing over food, and that it's so easy to do. "Why wouldn't you?" you might say. That's called teaching. They may or may not be ready to get it.

Once a child is over the age of about six, you can begin a conversation about the sort of inner conflict we all face—the ever-present duel between our best intentions and our natural tendencies toward selfishness or negativity. If that goes over well, it might be the green light to introduce the idea of the evil inclination, the *yetzer hara*, and the challenges God gives us to help us grow stronger and smarter and better.

Trial lawyers say never to ask a witness a question to which you don't already know the answer. Don't start an argument with your child, if you don't know where it's going to go. If you can't win, don't argue. You'll just be setting everyone up for failure, and the resulting confusion will be far worse than the bruised egos.

Every time a child wins a battle with a parent, it actually makes him angry, because it goes against the parent-child dynamic: inwardly, he knows that parents make the rules. He'll feel good for the moment, until he realizes the rug has been pulled out from under him.

If you hear a lot of "I don't care," that's probably a sign that a bad habit has already taken hold. It may be the result of some prior damage, whether in school or at home. Anger may well have been the issue. It's certainly not a natural response for a child. Under normal circumstances, kids have energy and enthusiasm to spare. They're not subject to burnout like some adults. They care.

Anger has no place in matters of principle or values. Anger is generally reactive, therefore a sign of insecurity, a futile posture of self-defense. God does not need us to defend his laws. Whatever you do, don't make it confrontational or personal. And refrain from invoking the sacrosanct authority of the *Code of Jewish Law,* if you'd rather your children didn't come to hate Judaism.

Teaching Obedience

Reality is not obvious to children. We have to make reality real for them. It's a key to teaching obedience, and it begins with modeling our own behavior in accordance with reality.

We often model pettiness without realizing that's what we're doing. It could be about something as simple as food, or grumbling at the fact that it's raining. That's when we have to push ourselves. Is the food too salty, or not salty enough, for your taste? Eat it anyway without making a big deal about it; make sure your child notices. You'll have taught her that even though the food is not exactly the way you like it, you'll eat it anyway, imparting to the child the importance of getting over pettiness.

When dishes are piled in the sink, you could say to your child, "Ugh, I washed the dishes already once today. Do I really have to do this again? I am *so* not in the mood." Then proceed to roll up your sleeves and get it done. You've shown him that your mood doesn't dictate how you behave.

The best way to begin training children to obey is by asking them to do things you already know they'll do. Then tell them how good it was that they obeyed. By helping them practice obedience when it's easy for them, you're reinforcing the habit of obedience. For example, you can tell them to come and sit down for dessert. When they do it right—of course they'll cooperate, it's dessert—tell them, specifically praising the action, not the child. It's not just obedience to you, it's also obedience to reality: the idea that when it's time for something to happen, it happens. It's good exercise, and it lays down a precedent for future expectations as they grow.

You can use a time frame to extend the habit. When a child does not want to do something, try saying, "Well, okay, I understand, but after your birthday you won't be able to say no to that anymore."

Let's say you tell your child to go to bed, she refuses, and you start to get angry. Don't change the subject and spout warnings, like, "I am going to count to three! If you are not in bed by..." All of a sudden, you've changed the subject. Instead, say, "I know you don't want to go to bed. But you are supposed to listen to your mother." Your goal is to get her to obey, not to threaten her. But don't let her change the subject either. When your child asks, "Why do I have to?" don't start explaining why. Stick to the subject and say, "You're going to bed because you have to listen to your mother." If you're firm, and mean what you say, she'll learn.

And don't feed the "me monster." Feed the objective bigger-than-us truth. If you try to make it personal by making it about them, as in, "You love this, so eat it," or "We know you care about your books, so put them away in a safe place," such ploys are too easy for them to resist or deny. But if you say something like, "I'm going to light candles now, because it's time for *Shabbos*," rather than pressuring them, you're showing them reality, and modeling the correct thing to do. The same principle applies when you tell them a candy isn't kosher. Each time they see the candy and don't eat it, their ability to do the right thing is strengthened. If something is wrong, they don't do it, not because they think or feel something is wrong, but because they know it's objectively wrong. They're learning that there's a reality bigger than themselves, an objective truth that calls for the right response without any sensorial or selfish incentive.

The ability to obey is a fundamental and empowering art, not a necessary evil. To obey means to be capable of doing what needs to be done at the time when it needs to be done. Children who can obey have a much easier, smoother, and steadier life than those who can't. One who fails to acquire this art is not a fully developed human being.

Although if your child tunes you out, you can no longer be the solution, don't aspire to forced compliance. It's demeaning, even oppressive, to tell a child, "You don't know half as much as I do, so do as I say." Obedience does not mean obeying a boss, but rather it is obedience to reality. A child listens to his mother. It's just the right thing to do. It's the way it should be, the way reality works.

Lack of obedience is an inability to take instruction. Developing obedience is a natural, learned process. When a child is born, there is nothing outside of him. There is only the self. Gradually, he discovers the reality beyond himself. How long will it take before he realizes that when he's tired, he should rest, and when he's hungry, he should eat? The rate of growth will vary.

Obedience is an empowering art, because it is cultivated in the awareness and acknowledgment that everyone has his own particular temperament, sensitivities, and weaknesses. If you tell a child to do something and he says no, it's probably just too hard for him right now.

How do you teach a child to do as she is told? Imagine telling your child to put something away on the shelf where it belongs, and she won't. If you try to pull the old *How many times do I have to I tell you?* routine, what have you conveyed? That you get frustrated easily? Or that you're bigger, stronger, and can intimidate her? She wouldn't say it, but she might think, *If you really need the book on the shelf, put it there yourself.*

What you want is for the child to obey you. So don't give her a whole lecture about a place for everything and everything in its place. The child is in no mood at the moment. Obedience is the issue, not the thing or the shelf. Just be clear and say, "You're supposed to obey me."

When you tell a child, "You should be going to sleep," what dictates this? Reality: it's that time. Likewise, if you say, "This book belongs on the shelf, not on the floor," you're making an objective statement. Can children obey reality's signals? They're tired, but they don't want to go to sleep. They're hungry, but they don't want to eat. Why? They're busy or distracted. In other words, they're functioning according to whim, not according to what needs to happen. Our job is to help them overcome through obedience, to grow comfortable with reality dictating their behavior.

When Listening Happens

We've discovered, beyond a shadow of a doubt, that children are allergic to adults. When an adult speaks to a child, the immediate reaction is to shut down. How, then, are we supposed to communicate with our children? By sounding not like an adult, but like a parent.

There are different tones of voice we use when speaking to a customer, or a manager, or a friend, or an elderly person, or our parents. The words might be exactly the same, but the tune is different. You can tell who a person is speaking to based on the tone, even if you hear only one side of the conversation. Your children know when you're talking to your mother on the telephone, even without hearing her voice.

There is one tone that an adult uses when speaking to children, and then another unique voice that belongs only to a parent. When you sound like a parent, your children will love everything you say, even when you're reprimanding them. If you sound like an adult, your children will tune you out, even when you are giving them a blessing. In fact they will even resent it.

There is a famous story about the Alter Rebbe, the eighteenth-century founder of the Chabad movement. The Alter Rebbe customarily read the Torah at the synagogue. Once, while he was out of the country, someone else read that week's portion. It happened to be about the biblical curses, a gut-wrenching rebuke. The Rebbe's son, about nine years old at the time, listened to the reading and fainted. He was so traumatized that a month later, there was doubt as to whether he'd be well enough to fast on *Yom Kippur.* They asked him why, having heard these curses read many times before, he became so ill due to this reading? "When my father reads them, they sound like blessings," he answered. But when someone else read the portion, the curses sounded to him exactly as they are: curses. He was horrified.

Why did *only* the Rebbe's son faint? Because a father's voice has an irreplaceable impact on a child. When you sound like a parent, your child loves it. Even if you're reprimanding him, it will sound like a blessing.

What does it mean to sound like a parent as opposed to an adult? Let's say a child is making noise inappropriately in a public place. The adult wants quiet, and makes his need known. When an adult corrects or criticizes a child, it's out of annoyance and agitation. The tone of voice is reactive, rather than proactive. It says, "*I* am disturbed."

A parent, however, tells a child to behave because the *child* needs to hear it, not because the parent is annoyed. Of course, a parent can also be annoyed; but it'd be a waste of time to say anything, even something loving and wise, when the child is not listening. So, as a parent, he chooses his tone and the substance of his words carefully, effectively. He delivers an intentional, *premeditated* message, to teach the child what he needs to learn.

A premeditated message is one that the parents have been weighing, preparing to say perhaps for many days or more, waiting for the right time. When a child senses that you've been thinking deeply into what to say and how to say it, it's powerful. You may never need to repeat it.

If you want your discipline to be effective, wait. A day or two after the event in question, when everyone is in a great mood and there's no more tension, sit down with your child. "Remember what you said on Wednesday? That was not right. You don't talk like that." The child will be so amazed, so pleasantly surprised, your message is guaranteed to meet the mark. He knows that you've been thinking about him for days, and that you have sensed that his heart and mind are now open. When you sound like a parent, your child will be receptive and retain your words.

When the Rebbe Rayatz was four years old, he came home from school one day and asked his father, the Rebbe Rashab, "Why do we have two eyes, but only one mouth and one nose?"

His father thought about it for a few moments. "Do you know the difference between the letters Shinn and Sinn?" the Rebbe asked his son.

The boy had just been learning the difference between the two nearly identical Hebrew letters. "Yes," he answered. "I know! The Shinn has a dot on the right, and the Sinn has a dot on the left."

"Those are the two eyes," his father explained. "There's a right eye and a left eye. The right eye, which is stronger, is like the Shinn.

It even has a stronger sound. The left eye, which is weaker, is like the softer-sounding Sinn. You use the strong right eye to look at a person with warmth and affection. Your left eye is for silly things, like toys and candy.

The Rebbe Rayatz later wrote in his diary that from that moment on, he had an endless reservoir of love for the people in his life. He also lost interest in candy.

His father had a message, a principle to impart to his son. He was simply waiting for the right moment. He didn't respond to the question with a merely factual answer or dismiss it as inconsequential. He saw it as a ripe opportunity to teach an essential lesson: that some things are profound, while others are just silly. All things are not created equal. Some should be taken seriously, and others do not deserve our wholehearted attention. Physiologically, two eyes afford us three-dimensional vision, so we can tell the difference between things that are shallow and things that are deep.

The answer sounded like it came from a father, not an adult, nor even a teacher. It was a conscious, deliberate, and premeditated message, delivered as only a parent can, in that unique, powerfully effective parental tone.

Reprimand and Reinforce

Consider the difference between a police officer and a sergeant in the Army. A police officer swings into action when people misbehave. If they're law-abiding and upright, he has nothing to say.

A sergeant is precisely the opposite. When a sergeant tells a soldier what to do, and the soldier won't do it, the sergeant's work is done. He calls the military police and has the soldier whisked away. A sergeant doesn't waste time with the grunts who don't comply. Still, he disciplines his troops.

How so? When a soldier does as he's told, the sergeant's disciplinary strategy is to tell him that whatever he's done until now is not good enough. He can do better. If a sergeant says to stand at attention and a soldier doesn't listen, he simply calls the military police. But if another soldier straightens up and does as he's told, the sergeant will walk over, gets in his face, and say, "This is what you call standing at attention? Shoulders back. Tuck in that chin. Stand the way you were taught to stand." Or say he tells you to polish your boots. You polish your boots. He takes one look at them and growls, "This is polished? Do it again. Get it right. I want to see my face in that shine."

The sergeant disciplines good behavior. The police officer disciplines bad behavior. The same is true in the realm of parenting. Raising and educating a child is primarily achieved not by focusing attention on a child's misbehavior, but by the disciplinary art of making the child's good behavior better, and better, and better.

What's worth noting is the fact that people don't generally develop close relationships with police officers. Yet they remember that tough, gruff drill sergeant with great fondness. Most people think a good soldier is an obedient soldier who always follows orders. It's a shallow definition. A soldier who does nothing but what he's commanded to do is not very useful at all. Wars cannot be won with a bunch of soldiers who need to be told what to do at every turn. Obedience is necessary, but not sufficient.

You can tell an enlisted man that the enemy is way up on top of that hill, and he has to climb the hill and take them out. Now the hill is very steep and slippery, and the day is particularly hot and humid. Maybe he didn't sleep very well the night before; and he certainly hasn't had his morning coffee. A normal human being would say, "Climb up there in that mud? On a muggy day like this when I'm falling asleep on my feet and the bullets are flying? I'm hungry. I'm tired. No way."

A real soldier is *not* someone who merely does what he's told. A soldier with a *can-do* attitude gets done whatever needs to be done, and then some. Such a soldier is empowered. If he has to carry sixty pounds up the hill on his back, he'll do it. It doesn't matter if it's the middle of the night in a thunderstorm, or in the blazing heat of the afternoon sun, or if he hasn't eaten or slept for days. He is capable not only of obeying, but of going beyond minimal expectations in ways that an average person would not.

Good parenting empowers a child in the same way. The Rebbe Rayatz's father once said to him, "I saw you share your candy with your friend. But it wasn't with your whole heart." Most of us, upon seeing a child of ours sharing candy, would simply be thrilled and proud. But what the Rebbe's father saw was that although his son had shared, he hadn't done so in the optimal manner. And he let him know it.

When you tell your daughter to make a blessing, and she does so, what's not to be happy about? At least you didn't get into a fight, right? No. That's not education. Suppose she slurred or skipped over a couple of words. Isn't that better than nothing? No, not better enough. This is an opportunity for a teaching moment, to lift her up from her default behavior toward an empowered mode. Encourage her to get it right—not just technically, but "once more with feeling." There's a chance that she might resent the extra push, temporarily; but she will grow up to love it, if in pushing her you are consistently expressing your confidence and trust in her ability to grow beyond her limitations. By cultivating the art of disciplining good behavior, you will reinforce that growth. Like the sergeant, and unlike the police officer, you won't have to discipline bad behavior.

But when you do need to do some policing in the face of rough-edged disobedience, learn at least how to be a good police officer. We often assume that a child disobeys because he's invested in being defiant. It's probably truer to say that he *can't yet* obey, not that he doesn't want to. It can be very difficult for a child to think straight. In a way, it may be an actual disability. Many children don't have the focus or concentration skills to complete a task. Sometimes they just can't get themselves to do what they want to do, because they haven't yet acquired *self-obedience*.

Suppose you tell your son to put his toys away, and he says, "I don't want to. I hate doing that." Instead of being upset with the child for insisting he doesn't want to do something, we want to raise him up from focusing only on what he wants to do toward what he should do. Again, when a child says no, it's a perfect time for education. If you say to the child, "I understand that you don't want to do it. But you've got to do as you're told. You hate it, and you're not in the mood, I get it. But when you have to do something, you do it." What you're accomplishing is guiding the child away from his natural habits—liberating him, giving him the ability to do whatever has to be done. As with the example we mentioned earlier about washing the dishes, it's a very good idea to model for your child, as often as possible, how there are things you don't want to do, but you do them.

In general terms, there are two types of concentration problems. One is when a child can't stay focused on even a single thing; the other is when there are so many things to focus on, he can't ignore any of them and is overwhelmed. Obedience, especially *self-obedience*, requires learning to eliminate the little things that prevent us from doing what needs to be done. Adults too encounter such difficulties; we frequently can't function under certain conditions. We need to be understanding and sensitive to our children's limitations, as we are to our own. There may be a hundred reasons behind every act of defiance. We simply need to help the child sail beyond them all, to see obedience not as a necessary evil, but as true freedom, affording him the power to do just about anything.

It is also important to consider the reasons and motivations that may lie behind the urge to reprimand your child. They are usually one or the other of two: either you want to be a good parent, or you wish to discharge your responsibility so that others will think you are a good parent.

Imagine you're sitting in a restaurant and your kids start having a food fight in public. You're mortified, of course, at how it must reflect on your parenting skills. Uncomfortable, embarrassed, you yell at them, "Stop it, now!" Needless to say, they don't. Feeling the pressure of the other diners' judgment, you divert attention and put pressure on your children instead. Even in the unlikely event that they were to listen, they will resent the pressure and the deflection. You've lost an opportunity.

Or maybe rather than being worried about what others will think, you are just concerned that your little ones should grow up to be decent people. So you try this (not from a distance; eye to eye): "Be a *mensch*. Don't throw food around. Grow up."

You're not asking them to change at that moment. You are asking them to grow up, which cannot happen immediately. It happens over time. You want to say things that will have an impact and produce results in a week, a month, or a year. You are cultivating the child, not making demands. It's called planting seeds. You just need to wait till next season to see any growth.

I once asked a group of young *yeshiva* students to do an experiment. "When you wake up tomorrow morning," I said, "tell yourself this: *Just for today, I can do anything that needs to be done. Tell me what to do. I can do it. Go ahead, test me. Tell me to learn* Gemara. *I can do it. Tell me to say all the words of the prayers and actually* think *about them. I'll do it. I am capable today.*

"See how that feels. Do you feel like a wimp because you did what you were told instead of what you wanted to do? Or do you feel like you're fully empowered, maybe for the first time in your life?"

The resounding feedback was: *I am a mensch.*

24

Independence and Identity

Raise them their way.
They're not about to cut and run.

Parenting is a balancing act between cultivating independence and instilling obedience. There are various schools of thought as to how to foster a child's independence. With older children, we might encourage them to make their own decisions, then let them reap the natural consequences of their actions. That may or may not prove to be wise, or even effective, depending on the maturity of the child and the nature of the question at hand.

In earlier stages of development, some say that independence grows when we let the kids do simple things, like getting dressed, on their own. But is that actually independence, or just a practical way of getting things moving that make little or no difference? "Do you want to wear the blue dress or the pink dress? Do you want to eat pizza or hot dogs? Do you want to go to sleep now or in five minutes?" Yes, sometimes you let the child choose. It's no big deal if he insists on putting on the yellow T-shirt. But let him, and then forget about it. In doing so, you're demonstrating that it's not important. We want to avoid raising children who revel in our overreaction when they say, "Eww, the peas are touching the ketchup." So we respond, "You don't want to eat it? You don't have to. It's not a *mitzvah*."

Many children today grow up thinking that life is a like a fast-food menu. These are nonessential, unimportant questions. So why pretend to make them an issue? Psychologists agree that giving children too many options can drive them mad—like the sensory overload that happens when a child walks into a toy store and his brain practically blows a fuse from the confusion. Don't create significance around issues that are of no consequence. Giving children a false sense of freedom by presenting them with choices about things that are not essential is not helpful. There are times for choices and times to obey.

Learning and experiencing independence early in life begins not so much with what we do or what the children do, but with the attitude and the desire we want to impart. The default mode for every child is independence—unless parents block it. If you want your children to be independent, you don't have to do anything. Nor should you, other than just that: to *want* your children to absorb your heartfelt intention that they become more and more independent as they grow. That's all it takes.

Some parents are reluctant to let a child develop his own ability to make decisions, perhaps for fear of losing control, and as a result those fears will very likely come to pass. Parental interference is in fact not only an impediment to the growth of healthy autonomy; it can also erode the child's ability to respectfully defer to authority. The delicate balance of humility and individuality we want for our kids is best achieved by beginning at a very young age.

And it begins first thing in the morning.

The *Modeh Ani* prayer is an expression of gratitude recited upon rising every day, thanking God for the new day and the restoration of our souls after a night's sleep. When the Rebbe Rayatz was about six years old, his father taught him the proper way of saying the prayer. At that point in his life, the boy had already been saying the short prayer for a few years, his own way, with no particular protocol. Now, however, his father recognized that he was ready to learn the details: that upon awakening, he should sit up, put his hands together, bow his head, and then recite the words.

The young future Rebbe asked why. His father didn't answer him directly. Instead, he called in his household worker, a man in his eighties. "How do you say *Modeh Ani*?" the Rebbe Rashab asked the man.

"I sit up, put my hands together, and bow my head."

"Why do you do it that way?" the Rebbe inquired further.

"That's how my father taught me."

The Rebbe then turned to his son. "Here's a man who has lived through so much, for so many years, and even for him it's enough to remember that his father told him how it should be done. He's been doing it that way for over eighty years. You're six years old. Is it not enough that your father tells you that this is the way to say it?"

Why didn't the Rebbe just answer his son's question? He could have easily explained the reason (or one reason among many) by telling him, for example, that sitting up is a sign of respect, which includes self-respect; and that bowing is an act of humility. Both are important when we're about to get up and begin the day. These are not difficult concepts to explain.

When his son asked why he had to say *Modeh Ani* in a certain way, the Rebbe chose not to answer the question, because the more significant lesson was not about *reasons* for the custom. He considered the tradition itself more important than its explanation. The message he wished to convey to his child was that truth is true, whether we understand it or not. This was the real lesson: if you know the right way, do it that way; and whatever else you need to know, the whys and the wherefores and the therefores, you'll figure out in due time. The Rebbe Rashab wanted to nurture in his son an appreciation for the idea that if you know what's fundamentally right, you'll eventually learn everything that's important—not just in general, but specifically for you.

Childlike, Not Childish

Once again we refer to the Book of Proverbs: "Teach the child according to his own way; even as he grows older, he won't depart from it." The question arises, what's so good about that? Is "his own way" the true way? Wouldn't it be more appropriate to adapt a child's education according to his level of understanding and maturity as he grows?

There is a certain precious quality that children have, of openness and innocence and wonder, that can get lost with time. Of course, we want our children to outgrow their childish behaviors; but we never want them to stop being childlike. It's a very subtle distinction.

A child has the ability to accept and appreciate simple facts. Walk down the street with a very young child, and he might ask, "Why is this tree here, and that other kind of tree is over there?" You can answer that God made them and put them there. And he'll be perfectly happy, because he now knows, in a matter-of-fact sort of way, what is. But as the same child grows older, he starts to develop theories and opinions. Which is great, because it leads to more knowledge and understanding; in this case, perhaps, about why certain trees thrive in certain environments, or why some trees do or do not bear fruit. Now he's a scientist. Then, before long, he's a philosopher. And he may be running the risk of losing a little bit of his childlike quality; and then his curiosity might turn into a temptation to complain. "How come I have to do this, and that other kid doesn't?" Until now it would have been fine to say, "Well, you have to do it, so you do it." Now all of a sudden he's an attorney.

There was a family we knew in Minnesota who was becoming more and more interested and involved in Judaism. Sadly, toward the end of the year during which we were getting to know them, the father passed away. Naturally, the family wanted to arrange the funeral properly, according to Jewish Law.

One of their daughters had been living away from home for some time. She came home for the funeral and barely recognized her family. She was shocked to find rabbis running around, organizing the services and prayers, making all sorts of traditional arrangements for those mourning their departed loved one. She did not understand what was happening, felt extremely uncomfortable, and let everyone know.

One day during the *shiva*, the seven-day mourning period after a person passes away, she opened up a little with me and felt comfortable enough to explain her behavior.

"I know I was very difficult during the funeral. But you understand, this is all new to me. I didn't know what was going on. What I want to tell you is, it feels good to know that my father was buried the right way."

What she was really saying was, "I have no idea why this is the right way, but I'm really glad that my father was buried the right way." Now, I could have said to her, "Let's sit down and we'll go through the *Halacha*, the relevant Jewish Law, and see why this is the right way." But she didn't care about that. She wasn't interested in the philosophy of it. She was simply comforted by the fact that it was done correctly. Living the ordeal of her loss, she rediscovered her childlike innocence.

We should nurture an appreciation in our children for the simple fact that what's right is right, that truth is truth, and that we must do what we must do. At the heart of educating a child lies the art of instilling in them an appreciation for what is true, important, gracious, and good.

Starting Over

Once, a wise and well-respected educator was asked by a group of mothers, "What do we do if our child is out of control?" He responded to the question with a question.

"When you walk into the room, do your children stand up?" Everyone thought he was joking. The idea that their children would stand up when they walked in a room was unimaginable. "Then you get what you deserve," the educator said. "Your relationship has been derailed." How did we come to abandon such a basic teaching? If your children can't even stand, take notice, and offer a simple gesture of respect when you enter the room (it happens to be stated explicitly in the *Code of Jewish Law*), what do you expect? Yet most of us think it's a ridiculous, outmoded, and unrealistic notion.

There are certain fundamental rules that are designed to keep familial relationships on track. Another—also written in the *Code of Jewish Law*—is that according to the principle of honoring your parents, to sit in your father's chair is a violation of boundaries. It means you have no idea who you are or who your father is. You have failed to recognize that you are his child. You don't know where you end and where your father begins.

We have to make it clear from a young age: "You're the child; I'm the parent. We love each other to the moon and back, but we're light-years apart." It's not for the parent's sake; it's for the child. The parent needs to sit the child down and straighten it out. It'll save everyone a lot of pain later on. It's often best when one parent steps up on behalf of the other parent: "That's Daddy's chair; don't sit there," says Mom. Conversely, Dad might take the child aside (when she's in a good mood) and say (in that affectionate tone only a parent can convey), "Yesterday, when Mommy asked you to do something and you said, 'soon'—that wasn't right."

If a parent tells a child that something she's doing bothers him, and the child says, "So?"—that's a relationship in need of repair. I once told an eighteen-year-old girl that what she was doing was hurting her mother. "So?"

"Why do you hate your mother?" I said.

"I don't hate her."

"But what you're doing is killing her."

"Too bad."

Is that not hate? Is this acceptable? Is it really that unthinkable for a child to do something solely for her mother's sake? How can children become so indifferent to anything other than their own appetites? There is a glue between humans that has gone missing.

On another occasion I gave a mother and her child a ride home from school. The seven-year-old was standing up on the back seat gyrating this way and that. His mother turned to him and said, rather sternly, "Sit down." He said no. She waited a few minutes, and once again turned around and told him to sit down. Again, he said no. Finally, she said, "Wait until you get home."

"Wait until *you* get home," the boy replied, chillingly. "I'm going to take a knife and stab you!" The mother turned to me with a shrug of the shoulders. "What am I going to do with him?"

The core of the problem was not his threat of violence. It was his utter lack of respect for a parent. The entire relationship was off.

One time during a counseling session with a mother and her daughter in their home, in the midst of explaining the situation, pleading for advice, the mother began to cry. Her daughter rolled her eyes, as if to say, "Here she goes again." I got up and left.

The mother called me later to ask why I left. I told her the honest truth. "I couldn't take it. She is not acting like your daughter, and you are not acting like her mother. A daughter doesn't roll her eyes at her mother. And you've gotten so used to it, it doesn't even bother you anymore."

When a five-year-old is told to do something, and he says he'll get to it later but keeps on playing his game, the relationship is threadbare. You have to start all over again.

When you call a child by name once, twice, three times, and he finally replies without looking up, in a voice dripping with irritation, "*What???*" the tone has grown intolerable. You have to start all over again.

When a child mocks a parent, sneers at a parent, or threatens violence toward a parent, it's simply unacceptable, if not dangerous. You have to start all over again.

We have to stop such behavior while it's still minimal. By redefining and reestablishing the proper roles of parent and child, we can save ourselves from a world of grief. You might experiment with a role play. Sit down with your child and say, "Let's play house. I'll be the mother and you'll be the son. You know how a son behaves with a mother, right? Let's try that."

There are basic modes of decency, essential standards of normal behavior. Without them, what's left is not a relationship. If we forget them altogether, no one in the family will know anymore what is down and what is up.

Being One of the Good Guys

Helping your child develop a strong identity is all about giving him the respect he deserves; and that respect generates a reciprocal, positive quality of life for the entire family. It's particularly true of his relationships with his parents, because their influence and their responses to his behavior can help make the difference between a confident or a pessimistic sense of himself.

A solid or a weak identity can make or break a person. Even when a child does something wrong, it's crucial for parents to help her see the distinction between how she has behaved and who she actually is—to separate the actions from the identity. If a child walks away from a bad episode thinking, *I'm disgusting, I'm worthless,* it can be disastrous. And the same is true when someone has been wronged by others. If she identifies with being broken, damaged, or ugly, then it's all over; but if she's able to maintain a positive identity, she will not be destroyed.

Changing or improving one's identity is generally more difficult for a boy than for a girl. When a boy feels identified with his faults, it's hard for him to detach from whatever mistakes he's made or sins he's committed and move on. It's a lot simpler for a girl to say, "Okay, I did something wrong. I've got to stop doing it and get back to myself again." She tends to have a more fluid self-image; she can take on one identity on Tuesday and another on Wednesday. We see this clearly in a grown woman, who starts off with a maiden name, then one day she becomes Mrs. Somebody. Whether we see the difference as inherent to males and females, or socially and societally defined, it is what it is.

What do you do if your daughter comes home from school and says, "All the kids tell me I have an ugly nose"? If you say, "Aw, no, look at that perfect little nose, you have the cutest nose in the world," she knows you're lying, and worse, you've lost her trust. So what should you say? The message should be that you love that "ugly" nose. In other words, ugly or not, you're still you. You're still a precious child. Don't model your identity after your nose, or anything else the other kids tease you about. This will provide your child with a strong immunity to other people's judgment.

Let's ramp it up a little. Say a kid comes home from school and admits he was playing with matches. Then, oops, something happened. His desk caught fire and the school burned down. Terrible, tragic. But must the child's identity also go up in flames? Should he now forever be known as a pyromaniac? No, not even in a case like this. (May God save us from such events, but you get the picture.) If children identify with their misbehaviors, it can end up damaging them for a lifetime. If we give them a strong identity, we're protecting them from a lot of misery.

The message to a child should be the same message that we have continued to receive from God throughout our history, even after thousands of years of misbehavior: we are still His. And the very least we can do is to reciprocate.

25

Integrity: The Name of the Game

Keep it simple, value truth, and allow however much time it takes.

There are certain weaknesses that children naturally outgrow, but dishonesty doesn't seem to be one of them. In fact it's more likely to get worse with time—and become more difficult to fix—rather than disappear.

Dishonesty is more than simply lying. It's a type of shrewdness, or slyness, an attitude that assumes nothing is completely true, and that everything is a little twisted. It's how the immature brain relates—and not because it's necessary to lie to protect oneself. It's just a simple, habitual unwillingness to tell the whole truth.

Honesty is seeing things as they really are. Exaggeration is the need to embellish and dramatize reality, because it's too plain for one's liking. Instead of saying something is big, people say it is enormous or humongous. Or "I've told you a million times!" instead of just several times. Exaggeration is an inability to let things be as they are.

Some children know when they're exaggerating that it's just for fun. If so, there's no need to discourage it. However, when they start to believe the exaggeration, don't participate in it. A child might say, "You *never* do this, and you *never* get me that." You immediately get defensive and respond, "Never? That's not true." The word *never* is never true. It's a distortion of reality, and therefore dishonest. When children say, "You're so mean," you answer, "No, I'm not mean. I'm just not giving you another ice cream." We need to watch out for these subtle but dangerous traits and rectify them while the child is young.

It's a moral issue, but it's also a personality trait that won't go away. Dishonesty can work itself deeper and deeper until it becomes an indistinguishable part of a person's character. Say a child does something impressive; you ask how he figured it out, and instead of acknowledging who taught him, he responds, "I just know." Without actually saying he learned it by himself, he still gives himself the credit.

Someone probably said, "Wow! You're so smart!" and he wants to pocket the compliment. It's dishonest. Adults do it all the time, because nobody corrected it when they were young. We want to cultivate in a child the ability to say, "I don't know. Can you tell me?" It bespeaks humility and honesty.

There's a story in the annals of the Chassidim about a man who heard a wonderful explanation for a very difficult passage in the Talmud. When he went back to his *yeshiva*, he successfully delivered to his colleagues the explanation he had heard. He knew he should say where he had heard it, but never got around to it. For the next few days, everyone was saying how smart he was, and he reveled in their praise. Eventually he couldn't forgive himself for having allowed a false impression to persist.

Another story is about a salesman who was in the middle of prayer when a customer walked in and said, "I'll give you thirty dollars for that cow." He wasn't supposed to speak during that part of his prayer, so he couldn't answer, even though he wanted to accept the offer. The buyer thought he was refusing and raised the bid to forty dollars. When the salesman finished his prayers, he told the buyer to pay only thirty dollars. In his heart, he had already said yes to the first offer. That's integrity.

There's a certain honesty that is not a question of lying or not lying. It's a question of being true to what's true. You can admit the truth, and you can speak truth in your heart. Admitting the truth means to stop lying. Speaking truth in your heart means being authentic. It has nothing to do with lying.

One of the virtues of life in the old days was that a person didn't take on unnatural roles. If your father was a butcher, you were likely to be a butcher too. Perhaps it was narrow and restrictive, but people knew who they were and where they belonged. They didn't play games. Today, there's an unfounded message that you can be whatever you want. It's not true. If you're four foot eleven, you're not likely to play professional basketball.

When you notice your children starting to play games with the truth, you must step in and do something about it. Keep life simple, and keep the kids uncomplicated. Don't exaggerate, underestimate, overestimate, distort, or tell half-truths. Be authentic, real, and truthful.

And if a child does stray from the truth, don't make it about you. If you say, "How dare you lie to me," are you saying that lying is wrong, or that lying to *you* is wrong? When a parent says, "I hate when you do that," the child thinks, *You hate it, and I like it. Now we both know where we stand.* What have you taught the child, other than what your likes and dislikes are? There's a difference between an emotional issue, a personality issue, and a moral issue. Teach right from wrong, but keep it free and clear of emotional reactivity. If a child tells a lie, here's an option to consider: "Wow! That's so clever, you're really smart. But you're not supposed to lie. No one is." The subtle message is that everyone lies sometimes, but no one is *allowed* to lie.

To teach integrity, it's best to bring it up in a nonconfrontational manner. If you catch your child lying red-handed, don't reprimand him on the spot. Nobody likes to be in that position, and nothing you say would have a lasting impact. It would be best to find a time later in the day, or the next day, when both you and the child are calm.

Threatening a time out is not a moral lesson. What has the child learned? That if he lies, he'll get in trouble and have to spend twenty minutes in his room. For him, it's worth it. Where's the moral lesson? It's like getting a parking ticket. If you park in the wrong place, you're going to get a ticket, but what's forty bucks? It may be worth it to you.

Certainly, telling a child that you've lost all trust in her will not help her become honest. On the contrary, now she doesn't need to be honest at all—once you've given up, why should she bother? We should never give up on our children. Just because they've lied before doesn't mean they'll keep lying. We have to maintain the right attitude so they will mirror our trust and become trustworthy.

Don't expect perfection, just movement in the right direction. In the same way that knowing that your spouse is *trying* to make you happy is enough to keep the relationship on an even keel, parents simply need to encourage their children to keep trying. Saying you don't trust them anymore is the opposite of motivation.

Don't expect immediate results. Know your goal. You want your child to tell the truth in all matters. Don't expect it to happen in a month just because you told them to. You may need to say it a hundred or a thousand times. Don't lose your patience. You're helping to develop a person, and that's a noble, long-term task.

Don't despair if he or she lapses. If a child hasn't lied for a long while and then lies again, remember, that is how a person grows. For forty years, Moses kept teaching us the same commandments. He didn't give up. When children see you're persistent, they know that what you're telling them is serious. Change will happen.

26

Taking It Seriously

When is the practice of mindfulness a must?
When it's a daily meditation on the education of your child.

Once, when I was in my early teens, an older gentleman ran into the store where I was shopping and began rather frantically asking everyone within earshot for help finding an address. He was obviously distressed and pressed for time. No one said a word. He looked directly at me, and I shrugged my shoulders.

The man launched into a scathing lecture in Yiddish that I still remember to this day. "That's how you answer me? Shrugging your shoulders?! If you don't know, say, 'I don't know,'" he chided me. "How rude!"

I got defensive and a little angry, holding myself back from telling him, "Back off and leave me alone!" But he was right. Shrugging one's shoulders in response to a question *is* rude, not to mention dismissive and disrespectful. Many people wouldn't think about it that way, or even notice; but a refined person will pick up on how inappropriate I was.

More significant than the rebuke itself was the fact that although he was a complete stranger, and obviously in a big hurry, he would not pass by the opportunity to teach a child a lesson. That was powerful. Why was I so important to him? Because a child's education is important. He didn't say, "Kids will be kids" or assume I'd straighten up some day. He recognized something wrong and took responsibility to address it.

Raising a human being is serious business. The more seriously you view a child's development, the better he will respond to your expectations. A child is a human being, a *neshama*, a soul. He absorbs everything. We need to be vigilant about the impressions he gets, striving to leave positive imprints while eliminating negative ones.

It's a core principle in Judaism that taking time every day to contemplate our children's education and upbringing is as much a *mitzvah* as any other ethical, moral, or ritual obligation. Just as we concern ourselves about a child's physical health, so should we devote at least fifteen or thirty minutes daily to think about building character, refining behavior, and fostering emotional and spiritual growth. It's not necessary to come up with a new idea or plan every day. But do take note of those little red flags—like stubbornness, selfishness, aggressiveness, or dishonesty—and pay attention to patterns—like a lack of obedience or a chronic lack of interest in school or synagogue. Most of these issues won't improve on their own. Address them with alacrity.

The fact that you're continually aware of and paying attention to your children's development shows them they are important to you. They will feel it. If you take their education lightly, you'll set a negative tone. And be consistent. If you tell a young child to break a *Shabbos* prohibition in order to get something from the car, even if he's technically exempt, you can't magically hope he'll still observe *Shabbos* when he's older. Conversely, parents who perform the *mitzvah* of ritual handwashing on a small baby's hands are paving the way for spiritual growth. Even for a baby, success is in the details.

But don't make every moment oppressively serious. Strive for balance. It's not right to hover over your children's every move and tell them exactly how to behave in every aspect of life. Be caring and careful, not controlling.

When Children Rebel

Some parents are concerned about how they rate on the scale of successful parenting. They judge themselves by how their children turn out academically, socially, or religiously. They may fret over what others think of their parenting skills as well. Even if these parents "succeed," their children might be miserable. Our children must know and feel that they come first. They need to sense that you want them to do the right thing for their sake—not because of some extraneous standard, but because they're so precious to you.

Children learn best from our modeling, not our lecturing. They'll pick up on the right way to treat their parents by observing the way their parents treat each other, in a manner that is worthy of respect and emulation. Children also notice the way we treat people outside the home, whether it's a teacher, a rabbi, a nanny, or a mail carrier.

The implicit message should be "Everything you've seen me do, now make it your own." And we should demonstrate enough integrity to make that a reasonable expectation, especially as children get older and more independent and notice more of what's going on around them. In Jewish families, once a child has reached the milestone of *bar mitzvah* (age thirteen for boys) or *bat mitzvah* (twelve for girls), they're then obligated to observe Jewish Law as an adult. At this stage, they begin to take responsibility for what we hope will turn out to be consistent with our best expectations.

This is also traditionally the stage when they are most likely to rebel.

When children want to rebel, and take their rebellion seriously, they often make a point of rejecting whatever is most important to their parents. If there's some *thing*, some value or standard or achievement, that appears to have been more important to their parents than they are themselves, they'll punish them by disregarding everything the parents hold dear. "All my parents care about is [x, y, z]," we hear them say. So they think the parents need to be reminded that their children are more important than all those *things* and have been all along.

Children tend to be most resentful when their parents enroll them in religious programs such as *bar* or *bat mitzvah* lessons to study customs and laws that they don't practice themselves. "Why are you sending me off to learn something *you're* not doing? Shouldn't we be on the same page?" They feel alienated and, on a subconscious level, disrespected by their parents. It's very different when parents express enthusiasm for a child's religious studies and actively engage in the practices themselves along with their kids. In many Jewish communities, regular father-and-son learning sessions have been instituted for exactly this reason. At home, families might invest in their libraries and read books together, or discuss the weekly Torah readings and other inspirational and practical teachings at the table. Even in the midst of a rebellious phase, it's an opportunity to keep it real and meaningful, and it pays tremendous dividends.

Kids are idealistic. They want to change the world. They want the real deal, not the halfhearted version. They're not asking for things to be easier. Even when they complain that they're expected to follow rules that other people don't, they're not saying they want to do less. They're saying they want to do more and be better, but they need help. They want to understand.

Today's parents have gotten into the habit of settling for less. They worry that if they expect too much, children will be turned off, so they lower the standards and oversimplify. It doesn't work. In truth, no one wants less. Less is not impressive. They want better. They want to be challenged. They also want to know they can make a difference and do things that make the world a better place. No one wants to be insignificant. Give them more of the real thing, and it will have an effect. Just as you can't drink wine and not get drunk, you can't learn the profound teachings of the wisdom tradition and not become more Godly and refined. Show them and share with them the beauty and relevance.

If children protest that they're not interested in what we have to offer, they're simply saying that we're not giving them enough of a challenge. Their rebellion is a signal, a catalyst for change. Take the learning to a deeper level—it's always more compelling, more enjoyable, and more inspirational than surface learning. If they don't feel the pleasure, it's because we haven't shown them what's really there. When our children see our excitement, they'll want more of the same.

Fathers & Mothers & Daughters & Sons

Frequently Asked Questions

***How do I teach impulse control? My child is what they used to call* willful*, which actually means* impossible.**

There's nothing wrong with your child other than that he's not yet an adult. You can't expect him to outgrow his childish ways in an instant. Regard parenting as an opportunity, not as a crisis or a call for panic. Every instance of resistance and misbehavior is an opportunity to teach, to pursue the noble goal of raising a human being.

Without impulse control, people become self-destructive. We need to help children get comfortable with the idea that it's okay to want something and not have it. Today, the average person—religious or not—has little sense of what it means to have self-control. People eat, do, and say whatever and whenever they want. The issue is not just crime or cheating or other obvious transgressions; self-discipline actually begins with learning to moderate our desires for what is *permitted.*

A seventeen-year-old once asked a rabbi how to observe *Shabbat.* The rabbi answered simply, "You do what you find most meaningful."

The youngster walked away completely baffled and disappointed. "You're telling me I can do what I want? I know I can do what I want. I've *always* done what I want. I came to a rabbi to find out what God wants." He was looking for solid Torah guidance, not psychology. That rabbi thought that by telling the boy to do whatever he feels is significant and inspiring would empower him. Instead, it turned him off.

In fact people do whatever they want, think, or feel is right. While it's difficult to empower children in the twenty-first century with the ability to say no to themselves, it's not impossible. And it won't repress their true natures or damage their psyches. On the contrary, it offers them mastery over themselves. Everyone is born with an evil inclination—a *yetzer hara*—that stokes the desire for things we would enjoy but cannot, or should not, have. What stops us from being able to subdue those inclinations is an unhealthy obsession with *self*.

If you can get a child, or even an adult for that matter, past that capital "I" at the beginning of every sentence, it's a worthy accomplishment. Parents want from children what God wants from us. To know that doing whatever we want is a dead end. We must show our kids that the pleasure of being needed is much more satisfying than the *angst* of being needy.

Be a model of what it is you're trying to convey. Let your children see what a life of service and self-discipline looks like. Tell them stories that reinforce the values you want to teach. Even for teens, stories from real life, fiction, or the news of the day can be effective channels for communicating values. Point out what happens to people when the "me monster" takes over, and share stories of people who have succeeded in putting aside their "me monsters" and actually doing what's right. When you give an intelligent, idealistic child the right information, nothing in the world can stop the goodness that results. Find every opportunity and means to inform and inspire.

Here are the two crucial points we need to teach our children. First, all sins are pleasurable, otherwise no one would ever commit them. The things we desire feel good, taste good, and smell good. A child needs to know that if we commit a sin, no matter how good it may feel, that pleasure itself is unholy.

Second, even if we commit a sin, we remain ourselves. If God tells us not to do something and we do it, we're still beloved. A person who sins is still the same person and should never identify himself as a sinner. The reason we don't want to sin is to maintain our connection with God; and that connection can always be restored, because there's much more to us than the sins we commit. If you give your child the impression that only bad people sin, you're making a serious mistake.

Sins are temporary, but *mitzvahs* are permanent. To date, we've accumulated some five thousand years' worth of *mitzvahs* that have been absorbed into the world and are still standing up for us, while the sins of previous generations have been paid for and are long gone. We're not victims of our sins. We shouldn't be afraid of sins; we should be afraid of God.

To teach your children right from wrong, tell them the truth. Don't try to tell a Jewish child that nonkosher foods taste bad or cause stomachaches. What will happen if that child eats the forbidden fruit, likes the taste, and doesn't get sick? The Rambam, a twelfth-century Torah scholar, said that pork is the healthiest meat, except that Jews are not allowed to eat it. The truth is the truth, no false impressions. Teach them that there are pleasures God wants us to have, and there are pleasures He doesn't want us to have. If it's pleasurable, why not do it? Because certain kinds of pleasure are wrong. Now your child is prepared for real life.

How do I redirect a selfish child?

In psychological terms, one could argue that selfishness stems from weakness and insecurity. When people feel they are lacking something, they have to be selfish to make up for the lack.

In truth, selfishness is a moral issue, and a psychological explanation may miss the point. Selfishness is the natural egotistical perception with which we were born—the assumption that life is only about oneself. It's not a reaction to insecurity; on the contrary, it's about feeling entitled to have whatever you want. You like yourself so much, you couldn't care less about others.

We're all selfish by nature. Raising children means elevating them to a higher dimension of reality than their natures, thereby empowering them to become healthy, well-developed human beings. Psychology erroneously assumes that we can't change our natures. Our sages teach otherwise: that we're given a certain nature in order to improve it. A person's nature is just a starting point, not a life sentence. We are never stuck. The solution to selfishness is to rise above your nature, and there are infinite possibilities for growth. If you have a healthy, happy, intelligent, capable child and he's selfish, it's a moral issue. This aspect of his behavior is still on the same level as when he was born, except that now he's smarter and shrewder and more skilled at getting what he wants.

The strategy is to show the child the *pleasure* of being selfless, of serving others. You want your child to grow up sharing because he has developed a taste for it, not because it's an obligation. So when you take a toy away from your child and force him to give it to his friend, you've taught him to hate sharing. The right message is, "You should share because your friend needs to feel welcomed and comfortable in your home. Do whatever it takes to make him feel welcome, comfortable, and happy. If you don't share your toys, he'll think you don't want him here, and that's not nice for him. He needs you to be his friend. Give him what he needs."

Bring it to your child's awareness repeatedly, so that it becomes second nature. Before a friend comes over, say, "Your friend is coming over. What are you going to share with him?" And after the friend leaves, check in on what happened. "What did you share? How did you make your friend happy?" The pleasure of being selfless is real. To help your child get a taste of it, you have to model it yourself by finding pleasure in serving.

The point is not that children have to share, but that human beings must rise above their selfish nature and take pleasure in other people's enjoyment. Otherwise, the child has not been raised. He's just been fed. You may have taught him how to tie his shoes and how to cross the street safely, but you haven't raised him yet. You've just maintained him.

There's a famous story about a miser who hated giving *tzedakah*. Any time a charity collector came by, he'd only offer a single coin, so small it was insulting, and nobody would take it. The Alter Rebbe, however, accepted the coin, and thanked the miser profusely. It was the first time the stingy man felt the joy of giving. Suddenly, and from then on, he wanted to give more.

Childrearing involves gradually introducing higher and more refined standards of pleasure. Every step in the direction of getting them to appreciate the pleasures of kindness, generosity, and charity is a major improvement. Until children can begin to see beyond themselves, they're not healthy children. A healthy human being is fully capable of forgoing his own needs for a cause more valuable than life itself.

My child is a sore loser. What can I do?

A teacher I know once complained about how she can't play games with her second graders, because no one knows how to lose. We need to redefine winning as being a *mensch*. If you behave like a *mensch*, you have won.

A *mensch* plays honestly, pleasantly, with excitement, joy, and a benevolent heart, which means much more than winning as it's commonly understood. In fact small children understand this better than older kids, or even better than adults, because for them, fun is what's supremely important. As people get older, their egos develop, and they become more competitive. We have to emphasize this to our children, and (first and foremost) to ourselves.

How do I deal with bullying in my child's school?

When a child comes home from school and says she's being bullied, your reaction will teach her invaluable lessons about how to handle crises in life.

A distressed parent might consider any one of a number of strategies: report the situation to authority; inform the bully's parents; confront the bully himself; enroll the child in self-defense classes; or send the child to school with protective armor. It bears asking, what would the child learn in any of these scenarios? How do we empower our children to rise above life's challenges? How can we make a difference in school and/or in the world?

First, acknowledge the truth, let your child feel her feelings. "Bullying is real. Some children are cruel and nasty. I don't know what happened that made them this way . . . we'll have to talk about it some more and figure out a solution. But you're okay, right? Are you hurt? Do you feel sad?" Your message is no, it is not okay to bully, but yes, you're going to be okay. And then help her move on emotionally.

We need to defend our children from the victim mindset. It can turn into a lifelong personality trait. Some adults feel like the world is out to get them, and that life is unfair. Their problems are everybody else's fault. How do we guide our kids past those feelings of victimhood?

If your child starts to think that's what life is all about, you have to correct it. But you can't deny the event, or imply to the child that nothing serious happened, and it's all really okay. Something did happen, and she's not okay right now, she's hurt. Yes, she will be okay, but that's an attitude, not current reality. Separate the fact from the interpretation.

If a child were to come home and say that someone bullied her, and the parent were to respond by trying to assure her that it's nothing, it may well push the child to exaggerate in order to convince you of the seriousness of the matter. Before dismissing an accusation, you have to validate the truth. You have to know your child.

If your child comes home irate, saying, "That whole school is totally messed up!," don't get into a discussion about the school being mismanaged. If you disagree with your child's teachers, be very careful not to insult or degrade the teacher in your child's eyes. You might find an opening to bring up something positive, like, "Well, I'm glad at least that you've been getting good marks in math" (or history, or Deuteronomy, or gym—whatever perks her up a bit). And regarding the complaint itself, it could be enough to say something like, "Your teacher said what? I never heard anyone say that before." That's being critical without being a critic. It leaves room in her brain for evaluating the situation without tearing the teacher down. You want to lift your child above the system, above the fray. She needs to get it that she is not a victim.

While it's unacceptable that your daughter is coming home unhappy, it could also be important for her to consider how the bully feels. For the whole society to come down on bullies wouldn't be a solution. Wouldn't that make us all bullies? Ask her what she thinks about what the bully needs that she's not getting, whether it's serious disciplinary action, a good friend, or a listening ear. It may or may not resolve the bullying issue, but you have empowered your child to rise above the obstacles and take steps toward fulfilling her own purpose. It's a moral issue, not a personal issue.

There's a powerful Chassidic adage that goes, "The world says, if you cannot crawl under an obstacle, try to leap over it. However,

I say, leap over it in the first place!" In other words, jump over problems almost as if they never existed. It's not denial; it's an advanced demonstration of victory over any challenges that life may pose.

Instead of going into crisis mode, help your child rise above the situation with joy. This attitude can be applied to every aspect of life, be it one's health, livelihood, or other obstacles. We're never fazed when we remember that God assists us every step of the way.

What if my child is the bully?

We want to teach our children the difference between being aggressive and being ambitious, between being competitive and being achievement oriented. Is it possible to accomplish something without being aggressive? Of course it is. Teach them to ask themselves if they want a life where they have to fight the system and everyone in its path.

If a child thinks success can only be achieved through aggression, he needs help. This faulty outlook sees the world as adversarial, where people have to push hard to get anything done, even if it means breaking rules or applying force. How we think about life affects our children. Show them how one can be ambitious and still believe in the good of the world. Practice seeing abundance within reach, and they will see it too. As a result, they'll simply work hard to secure every opportunity. It's about attitude.

When an older child grabs a toy, or anything else, from a younger one, did he think to ask the other child first? Maybe the younger one would have given it without resistance. The assumption that the younger child wouldn't have agreed without force is at the root of the problem.

A philanthropist bought a building to establish a *yeshiva*. Astoundingly, people asked him how he planned to deal with students who trashed the building. Why did they assume that's the norm? The tone this attitude sets transforms students into enemies. Better to set the standard high, and expect that children will reach it. Instead of strict discipline, schools need to keep the children interested, involved in what they're learning, busy, and engaged. Parents need to do that at home as well. The bullying will diminish.

There's a lot of sibling rivalry in my home. What can I do?

The first thing you need to do is teach them about sibling rivalry, because they often don't realize that is what's going on. They think they're upset over the toy. They don't realize that it's not the toy, it's the rivalry. So you have to find a gentle way of helping them recognize and admit that there's some kind of unnecessary competition going on. That's not an easy concept for a child, but if you can make the children aware of that, it will soften the conflict.

Parents should not become referees, and kids shouldn't get into a habit of running to them to complain. But how do you manage it, particularly when children are close to each other in age? If you can explain to each of them separately what jealousy means and why it's wrong, that's a step in the right direction.

Another important idea is to assume that each child is special and gifted in some way—and therefore if the child is frustrated, acting out, or misbehaving, it's because she's not being challenged enough, relative to her talents and abilities. She's bored. Try giving each one a special role where he or she becomes the leader or teacher in that situation; and then in the next situation make another child the responsible party, in an area where he or she has special talent. At times, they may not want the responsibility, but they'll still like the compliment. The fact that you think they can do it, and that you're willing to trust them, feels good. That in itself is an improvement that will move them to a better place.

What we generally do when children are fighting is to condemn them both. Nobody can have the toy or get to play. The message there is that no one is good. That's not very helpful. Instead, go in the opposite direction. Highlight their strengths. Tell them how they can learn from each other. Raise them above the issue. Don't make them less important than the toy they're fighting over.

While they're arguing, don't intervene. Wait for a calm moment when they're in a good mood and explain to them where their talents and responsibilities lie. You can say, for example, "You're the older one. Your rank is higher. Therefore it's your role to be the one who shows how to be kind [or patient, or understanding]." Then to the younger one, say, "You're good at [thus and such]. So you can show your brother or sister how to [...]" As always, it's best if you can model these qualities in ways they will notice.

So separate them not physically, but in their respective identities, and encourage each one to take a leadership position in the area with which he or she identifies. Besides putting an end to the sibling rivalry, you'll be making a *mensch* out of the child. The sibling rivalry will actually become the catalyst that moves them forward—leveraging the negative for a positive purpose rather than refereeing a fight.

If there is a real mean streak in one of the children, you have to address the issue—not with the fight, but with the person. In other words, you don't have to intervene every time there's a fight. But you do have to pay attention to the development of your child's character.

How should we handle* chutzpah*? My wife and I are so polite and soft-spoken.

Sometimes we just don't understand our kids. "I can't relate to them, I can't talk to them, it's like we don't live in the same universe." How did this happen? Whose fault is it?

First of all, don't blame it on the generation. That's what happened in the 1960s, when young people started experimenting with drugs. Their parents were mystified, couldn't imagine that they themselves were guilty, so they made it all about this alien culture that had captured their kids.

It is imperative when we see a fault in our children that we find it in ourselves. If we remain stubbornly convinced that we have no such weakness whatsoever, then we are cutting ourselves off from them. You are not of a different species. We are all human beings, with the same problems. The difference is probably just that children haven't yet learned how to hide their faults.

Therefore, no matter what bizarre or inexplicable behavior your child may display, assume you have something resembling those same characteristics. It may not be to the same degree, but the fault is in there somewhere. We need honesty and courage in evaluating our own tendencies, and must above all remain connected to our children.

Upon recognizing that we also have that trait, knowing that we're not a total disaster, then we'll realize that we have what it takes to help them—frequently, by first correcting the problem in ourselves. In that way we gain something concrete to offer them, other than a reaction of horror. It's only when parents don't want to admit that they have the same faults, that they stop reaching out, and the result is that children pull away. Their parents refused to meet them halfway.

My child is an angel at school but not at home.

Is your child out to make your life miserable? No. At school he or she feels challenged and productive, but at home, he's bored. What could be more fun than driving your mother crazy when you're bored?

If a child comes home and the unspoken message he receives is "Put your things away. Go to your room. Be quiet. I'm busy," then you're both in trouble. Drop whatever earth-shattering thing it is you're doing. Take out five minutes to say hello, ask him how he is, make him feel welcomed and loved. Then you can dismiss him and carry on with your day. It will save you a lot of grief.

When we internalize our sacred roles as parents, we don't feel as though our children are out to get us when they give us a hard time. They are not a liability. Instead of being afraid of or appalled by our children's faults, identify with them. Make them your faults too, and then from the inside you'll be able to move your child to a better place.

Imagine a kid comes home from school after being beaten up by the world out there, utterly discouraged and seeking shelter from the storm. He walks in, and the first thing he hears is, "Don't step on the floor with your filthy shoes. I just mopped it." It doesn't require a lot of time to make eye contact when he walks in. Make sure he's getting your personal attention. Put down the phone, close the laptop, and give him a hug. "Hi, I missed you; how was school?" Mean it, and be excited to see him. You don't have to worship your child—not constantly, anyway—but be there for him consistently. It will make all the difference

Should I apologize to my child when I make a mistake?

Your children will learn sooner or later that nobody's perfect, but parents need to be on a pedestal. And if you fall off, they should put you back up. It's simply inappropriate for parents to apologize to their children. Do not reverse roles. It is not the responsibility of children to judge, forgive, or correct their parents. Keep the parent and child roles appropriate, and that way they will have parents, and you will have children.

What ought to happen if a parent scolds her child for something, then finds out she didn't do it? Simply acknowledge the new information, but do not apologize. "I thought you did something wrong, but you didn't. I am so glad you didn't!" The point is, it's not that the parent was wrong, but that the information she received was incorrect. This works, because the parent has straightened out the record, and the child doesn't feel unjustly chastised or punished.

Refrain from telling your child that you lost control. She doesn't want to hear that. Telling her, "I lost my mind" or "I get upset so easily" is akin to telling her that you have your own problems, so she'd better find her own way to survive. It does not help her to know that her parent is neither smarter nor stronger than she is, and that she can't rely on her parents even for emotional security, let alone safety.

Should we tell our child about our emotional needs?

It's not uncommon to hear parents say, "You think you have problems? Do you have any idea what I'm going through, what I have to put up with?" The fact that you have problems doesn't mean you need to burden the children with your issues. They are neither your peers nor your therapists.

It's fine to be open and honest, even describing your feelings, your aches, and your pains to the children. But don't saddle the children with your neediness. They're not equipped to handle your needs. They haven't yet learned to manage their own.

So, can you be honest about your emotions? If you're sad, absolutely. It's okay to cry in front of your children. If you're worried and anxious, you can tell them. By all means, be candid. But telling your child how desperate you are for help is not helpful. In other words, don't hide your feelings, but don't hang them on the kids. When you're happy, you laugh. When you're sad, you cry.

That's life. Be open, natural, and transparent, but don't turn it into a catastrophe, and never burden your children with your needs.

How do we handle our marital conflicts in front of our child? We can't pretend all the time!

Imagine a husband comes home two hours late. Even if his wife is upset, in two days she won't remember it. But if children see their parents arguing, they don't forget it. It's better to calm yourself down and keep the peace at home. The objective is to stay focused on the big picture.

Ideally, parents shouldn't show any animosity between themselves in the presence of children; so do your best to solve whatever conflicts may arise while they're not around. It is best to talk when you're calm, and still more effective when you take the time to contemplate the situation beforehand rather than waiting till you're already upset. Once the argument starts, it's much harder.

The same way that parents choose their battles with their children, adults need to choose their battles with their spouses. Not every spat is reason enough to get upset; avoid those energy drains and learn to let them go. To the husband who comes home late, say something like, "We were expecting you two hours ago—we were beginning to worry!" Or "We were ready to eat two hours ago, but the children didn't want to eat without you. How sweet!"

Children respect their parents if they show respect between themselves. In addition to speaking to each other with the utmost esteem, it is essential that fathers instill veneration for the mother in their children. A father who hears a child speaking less than respectfully to his mother should intervene to ensure the mother's dignity and respect. The same is true the other way around.

Stop and consider the ways you and your spouse speak to each other. Do you really want your children to hear you speaking that way? If not, adjust your tone. Your children will benefit tremendously from hearing their parents speak kindly with each other. Parents are always modeling, every minute of their parenting life.

Consider what the future will be like when your children are already grown and out of the house and starting families of their own. Would you want your grandchildren to hear you arguing? If not, don't do it. It helps to pretend that you have the perfect spouse. How would you talk to her? How would you treat her? Husbands and wives should treat each other the way they would if they were perfect.

When food is brought to the table, do you just take some, or do you offer to serve your spouse first? If children are supposed to shoulder their parents' burdens, such as carrying their bags and fetching them water, shouldn't the husband do that for his wife as well? It's not that the wife cannot do so herself, but rather because it's a privilege for a husband to do something for his wife—and likewise, children for their parents.

Each moment is an occasion to show respect to a spouse. A wife can find many opportunities to model respect for the children by complimenting her husband, telling him when he does something well. It's even good to say, "I could never have done this myself."

Men thrive on compliments, because their emotional tendencies are such that they often need reminding that they're necessary, capable, and significant. And needless to say, husbands must also find opportunities to express appreciation for their wives. Women are generally more aware of their significance, to the extent that they may even assert that they don't need praise. But they certainly don't want to feel as though they are taken for granted. A husband who voices his appreciation helps his wife immensely; a wife who compliments her husband makes his life more livable.

How should my spouse and I deal with our different parenting styles?

If your spouse has a parenting style that neither resembles nor supports yours, remain flexible rather than dogmatic. The latter only creates separation. Be open and adaptable enough to accept the possibility of another way of parenting. Some forms of discipline may not appeal to you but may work for the children. There are times when mother says, "Do this," and the children don't; but when father says it, they listen. Or vice versa.

If you are kind and your spouse is strict, that could be the perfect balance. Work with, not against each other. Highlight and praise each other, and support his or her differing perspective in the presence of the children. Help the kids become aware of your spouse's positive attributes and contributions. It will ward off untold potential troubles.

What if my spouse sets a bad example?

First and foremost, show your children that you accept and support your spouse as he or she is. It's a very important lesson for them. Model the importance of overlooking a loved one's weaknesses or idiosyncrasies. As you do so, show them your dedication to speaking respectfully. Even if your idea of respect is different from your spouse's, don't be judgmental, and certainly don't tell your children that their other parent is wrong, or that you can't tolerate the way the other parent speaks.

There are couples who speak so loudly to each other, it's as if they're shouting. They probably don't see it as disrespectful, because it's not meant to be disrespectful—it's just the way they speak.

If your wife seems to be speaking disrespectfully to you (i.e., differently from the way you would speak), realize that this might be normal for her. Is she actually being disrespectful, or is she just not in line with your standards? Keep in mind that standards change from couple to couple and from family to family.

If a spouse is being disrespectful, don't reject or reprimand him or her. Your spouse needs your acceptance, not your criticism. It could be an expression of deeply held anxiety or the result of some momentary annoyance. Don't try to act like a psychologist, a police officer, or a rabbi. That's what it means to be a good spouse. If you want to have a conversation about changing this sort of behavior, do it later, when you are calmer, and not in front of the kids.

Our child hates **davening** *(daily prayers). What should we do?*

When a child says he hates praying because it's so boring, empathize with him. "I know what you mean. Saying words you don't understand and repeating them three times a day is difficult, and not being able to see who you're talking to makes it even harder."

Explain some of the stories and meaning behind the prayer he is saying. "I once read that *mincha* (the afternoon prayer) accomplishes something different from *maariv* (the evening prayer), even though they are similar."

Once your child's interest has been piqued, offer to help him understand further, through parables, or by reading a collection of commentaries together. You'll see how much more interested he'll become.

The child is pointing out something real. He's expected to recite a set of prescribed prayers every day for the rest of his life. However, since his third-grade teacher first announced the obligation, not a word was said about what those prayers are all about, except, "Have you *davened* yet?" So his prayer stays at a third-grade level. We need to match his intellectual understanding of *davening* to his level of maturity. The Rebbe Rayatz once wrote when he was nine years old that he couldn't stand the fact that during prayer, he was saying words he didn't understand. So he sat up late at night until he understood every word.

Imagine a seventeen-year-old who doesn't know what the Hebrew prayers mean. He looks up the English translations and finds words like "blessed, hallowed, sanctified, glorified." Now he's even more confused. He needs help understanding their applications and significance. What's the purpose of prayers? How were the prayers compiled? Who came up with the format?

An older gentleman once told me, "I tried to *daven*, but I don't know what I'm doing, so I really don't see the point of it."

"Well," I replied, "you're retired, are you not? What is something you have in abundance? Time. You may not have much money or knowledge—yet—but one thing you have a lot of is time. Whatever you have the most of, that's what you use to serve God. So what God wants from you now is to dedicate an hour of your time to Him."

When you pray, you are saying that time belongs to God, even if you do not know what every word means. You're dedicating your time because that's what you have. Whether you are seventeen or seventy, you can make some time out of your day sacred. *Davening* means "this hour is dedicated to God. I will do nothing else." That's your prayer, your offering. And as a parent you can say, "Let's carve out some time to learn more about the *davening* together."

How do I redirect my child's focus away from wasting time (on the internet, games, or other stuff) that takes him away from what he should be doing?

Someone once asked the Lubavitcher Rebbe why he seemed to advocate utilizing technology and engaging in the world in ways his predecessors had rejected. Had there been a shift? The Rebbe answered, "Once you learn to reject something, you become its master. Then you can use it for good. But if you can't live without it, then it's the master of you, and no good can come of that."

In other words, first, you have to dismiss it and make it a nonissue, not a thing of importance. Once you can live perfectly well without it, you can use it appropriately, because now you're in charge. This applies to everything children might develop an interest in, whether sports, clothing, or whatever. The key is to make your child a master, not a slave.

A boy comes home after playing baseball with his buddies when he should have been doing homework. He's sure his father will be angry when he finds out. Instead, his father shows interest and offers his son some ideas on how to improve his game. In this way, the father is helping his son by putting him in charge. The boy stops worshipping baseball, because now he is above the game of baseball, not under its sway. He's good at it, but it isn't his god anymore. Before long, his father will be able to tell him to spend less time on baseball and more time on homework. It would never have been as effective had his father told him playing ball is a worthless waste of time.

The key is not to turn what your child loves into an enemy. Avoid starting a war, where you are in an adversarial role toward something he enjoys. The same applies to his friends. You may object to your child's friend but be careful how you express your disapproval. If a child who doesn't have many friends finally finds one, don't turn around and say, "I don't want that kid in the house." Now you're discrediting what your child deems most interesting and important, which to him simply means you don't care.

There are times when that friend is such a negative influence, you really do have to put an end to the friendship. Don't attack the friend right off the bat. Children feel protective of their peers. Take an interest; ask your child to bring him over. Get to know the friend a little better, and show some genuine kindness. Then you're in a position to tell your child, "Maybe we should spend a little less time with this kid and do something else instead." Particularly with older children, they're likely to accuse you of condemning the friend without even giving him a chance. Join them first, then edge your child away from him if necessary. Don't parent from a distance, and certainly don't criticize from a distance.

It begins from within yourself. Be confident in what you represent. Know what your own life is about. Be inspired yourself, and that will inspire your children and give your relationship a head start. When a child shows a particularly deep interest in something, show some interest as well, whether or not you are inclined to approve. Ask about it. Understand it. Enjoy it, to whatever degree, and then if you still deem it appropriate, say, "All right, enough of that." Then you're not the enemy, but the parent; you're the wise adult, not the competition.

How should I speak with my child about intimacy?

Parents should be able to tell their children everything about intimacy. If they're asking a general question, then give a general answer. If they already know the generalities and want details, give them specifics. However, if you are not able to explain something to them in a normal tone of voice, then it's best you don't. Certainly refrain from saying, "It's none of your business" when they ask; and remain calm even if they react with, "That's disgusting!"

When asked about how to teach young children the parts of the Bible that have mature content, the Lubavitcher Rebbe said that we should teach them exactly as it says, and in the same tone we would use to teach everything else. However, if you're going to stammer or alter your voice because you're uncomfortable, then don't.

In the old days, people were able to talk naturally about such matters. Maybe it was because they lived on farms and saw animals being born. Intimacy was part of life, not a topic to be set aside for later discussion. We should never say to our children that it's time to have "the talk." Or that there's "something you need to know." The same applies when teaching a daughter about getting her period.

The more natural and normal, the better. Don't make a special occasion out of it. In other words, if you'll be embarrassed, then it'd be best to let another trusted adult do the teaching. Even so, there's no need to carve out special time. There are plenty of opportunities to talk about life (not about "it") with your children.

Parents should assume that by nine or ten years of age, their children already know something about intimacy, whether it's from studying the Torah, a conversation about modesty, or discussions about health. Since these discussions can feel awkward, even paralyzing for grownups, be careful not to overdo it. Don't tell them how intimacy is a *mitzvah* and how great it is. You don't need to embellish or treat it differently than anything else.

Rashi, the famed Torah commentator of the Middle Ages, was unabashed when teaching five-year-olds details about intimacy. Why at five years old? Because when they're six years old, it's already too late. It is best to introduce intimacy at a young age with verses and perspectives from the Torah. Then, to a child, intimacy is the Torah and not a dirty story.

For example, the way to explain murder to a child is to base it on an example from the Torah. The story of Cain and Abel, the world's first murder, presents the topic in context and gives it a moral, holy, Torah feel. If we wait until a child learns about intimacy or murder from secular sources, like movies, it might be too late to say, "The Torah says not to do that." To the child, intimacy or murder will then have become concepts separate from the Torah.

The same is true with all areas of life. It's important to teach our children to eat properly, because it's the first place a child learns impulse control. The way a child eats has an effect on other appetites as well. Teach children to eat mindfully, and it will manifest in other aspects of their lives, including intimacy.

How do I protect my child from sexual abuse?

Sexual abuse is one of the greatest fears of every parent. The potential damage is indescribable. Of course, we all teach our children that no one is allowed to touch them inappropriately. It's an important message. Yet most children don't know what inappropriate means. They can't even spell the word yet. How then do you explain what an inappropriate touch is? Some say inappropriate touch means being touched against one's will. If so, how then do you say to a child that it's possible someone could touch her, and she might like it, but it's still abusive and inappropriate behavior?

To complicate matters, the vast majority of perpetrators are people the children trust and love, often a family member. If we teach our children that what these people have done is so horrific that the people must be severely punished, will the children have the courage to speak up? With a stranger, he or she might be inclined to report an inappropriate incident. But with an uncle, a cousin, or a neighbor, children are less likely to speak out. They may want to protect the abuser; or they may have been threatened and coerced to stay quiet.

Fundamentally, you need to give your children a vocabulary with which to express themselves. When you send them off to camp, don't tell them that there are bad people out there who could do perverted things to them. Your child is not going to tell you, "You know those perverts you were talking about? Well, I found one (or he found me) and we did some perverted things together." It would be too painful, too scary.

However, if you tell your children that certain behaviors are modest *(tznius)* and certain things are not, they can understand that. Use language they already know. Explain to them that there is a type of physical touch that can feel good but is not allowed. Tell them clearly which parts of the body are off limits. It's not modest for someone to touch you there. It's not modest for someone to show you that. That way, if anything happens, it'll be easier for them to say that a counselor wasn't modest. Even if they feel guilty, a clear message and familiar vocabulary will dispel the fear and empower them to speak.

When a child speaks up and confides in an adult, the nature of the response can make all the difference in the world. You may feel sheer rage toward the abuser and feel compelled to act on your fury, but don't show that to the child. The child needs to hear that it was wrong, it should never have happened, and to stay away from that person, but that life goes on.

What damages a child most is if she identifies with the abuse, and *becomes* it; if she feels that she was involved in something so disgusting, she has become disgusting herself. This may prevent her from telling you what happened. She doesn't want you to think she is disgusting.

Often, a child tells her parents about an incident because she doesn't know what to make of it. "I'm not sure. I want to know what just happened to me. I'll tell my mother and watch how she reacts, and then I'll know." By telling her parents, the child will determine the scope of the situation. If the mother or father freaks out, the child thinks, *Oh, no. It really was horrible.* Now the child is damaged.

However, if the parents simply say, "Really, he did that? Okay, you can't be friends with him anymore." Then the child thinks, *Oh, that's it?* Now you've saved the child's life. How you react is crucial. Tell your child that what happened was not right, and then, without threats or drama, deal with the problem. But do your best not to make it your child's problem too.

My child is watching inappropriate things. What should I do?

If you're like most parents, your immediate reaction is probably something like, "What's wrong with my child? What's wrong with me?!"

The fact is there's absolutely nothing wrong with your child. There's a picture on the computer, so he's looking at it.

One father beat up his son, smashed the computer, and only then managed to ask, "What should I have done?" At that point, apart from having done a whole lot of damage, he hadn't accomplished much.

It would have been far better had the father looked at the computer screen and said, "What are you watching? Oh—some people without their clothes on." And then walked away. That's it. He would have taken all the mystery out of it, and there'd have been no fun left.

Then the next day, he could have sat down with his son and said, "So what happened yesterday? You saw people without clothing? It was interesting? Okay, fine. Are you going to do it again? Seems a little weird, no?"

You have to make fun of sins, not be impressed by them. Every sin is ultimately stupid. That's why after sinning, people tend to feel foolish. Teach your children not to look up to sins, but rather to look down at them. Look up to *mitzvahs* instead.

It can be effective to make it less personal and tell your child a story about someone else, and let that remind him about modesty. Tell him you know a guy who walked in on his kid and said, "Oh, what are you looking at? Naked ladies? They're not being *tznius*, and you're looking at them? You're better than that." Then ask him what he thinks. If he says pornography is disgusting, you can say, "Obviously, nobody taught them about *tznius* (modesty). We know better."

How do I help my child deal with death?

A woman who was a student in our Bais Chana Institute once confessed that she hadn't cried in fifteen years. She said the reason was probably that when her mother died, her father talked her through it so well, she never had to cry. He made it so logical and reasonable. She simply didn't need to mourn the loss, or so she thought.

If a child loses a parent, God forbid, we must allow the child to grieve. We must in fact *help* her grieve. Don't tell the child that you understand, because you don't. The purpose of visiting people who are grieving is *not* to tell them that it's okay, but to share in their pain. We are not there to give speeches about how everything is for the good.

In the old days, there were professional mourners whose job was to cry hysterically at funerals. These mourners, usually women, acted as helpers, giving fellow mourners permission to vent and cry. They let the survivors express their feelings.

A man once told me that he couldn't get to the funeral when his father passed away. I said, "Wow, I'm sorry, that's really horrible." In other words, I empathized with him. "Thank you," he said. "You're the first person who told me that." Everyone else had said, "It's okay." Notwithstanding their good intentions, those people had invalidated his feelings.

The purpose of validation is to help release the emotions and not to get stuck in them. Death is horrible. The reason death is so difficult is because it's not life. If life were not wonderful, death wouldn't be so terrible. It's very sad, and it's okay to cry.

How do I know if my child is doing well?

To know whether your children are doing well, you should first ascertain whether they are excited about life. If they are, that's good news. You have to make sure that your children wake up in the morning and love it.

From the Torah's perspective, our job is to create happy children. To work with happy children and help them do good is much easier than working with miserable children. So you're halfway there.

In certain institutions, if a child is happy, everyone comes down on him. It's as though being happy means the child has too much free time. Therefore the default assumption is that he must be doing something wrong. Terrible.

When your child comes home unhappy from school or camp, you've got to do something about it. It doesn't matter what it is that's making him unhappy; unhappy is unacceptable. If you sent a happy child to school who then comes home miserable, that's not okay, not even for a single day.

Some claim that bullies are making children unhappy. If so, that's generally not so hard to fix. Be your child's advocate. Make sure the playground is well supervised. Make sure the bully gets the loving guidance he needs. But if the whole atmosphere is an unhappy one, then it's just plain wrong and you can't pin it on one bad actor.

If a classroom is filled with tension, nobody learns and nobody grows. That's why children look forward to the summer. When a child goes away to camp, the once-miserable child suddenly becomes happy. This means he or she feels excited and capable. The Lubavitcher Rebbe once said that children learn more in a month of camp than a whole year in school. Children are naturally happy, and the school environment should reflect that. If not, it becomes your job to advocate for your child, as well as the other children in the class. School should be a happy place.

But back to the question. Generally speaking, you can tell if your child is doing well if you are doing well. There have to be times when you look at your child and you don't see any faults. For that moment, he doesn't need any improvement in your eyes. You simply adore him, and that is wonderful.

If there's too much focus on problem solving and not enough on pleasure, as though parenting were one big burden, it's not good for anyone. You can't function like that. No matter what is going on with the child, there must be times, at frequent intervals, when you can sit back with total acceptance and have no criticism, no complaints, no worries, no expectations. Your child is just perfect in your eyes. Expecting the best for our children also means expecting nothing from them, from time to time. If a child hears nothing but demands and rebuke, then no matter what those expectations are, they'll be too much.

Your children should sense from the way you look at them that you adore them. They should feel it when they walk into the room. No matter what is going on in the house, your face has to light up when your children walk in. You are thrilled to see them.

Sometimes we worry about a child and shed a tear. We have to be careful to keep those tears private. The child doesn't need to know about them.

All a child should see is your thrill, your delight. Yes, there are moments when you must have unyielding expectations and demands. Yet they must be outweighed by the moments when you just can't get over your child's perfection. He is exactly who he is meant to be, and you are his perfect parent.

Acknowledgments

First and foremost I am indebted to my loving, beloved, and devoted husband, Binyamin, the greatest blessing in my life, whose unfailing support has empowered me to complete this life-giving project. This book is above all to his credit.

And Yosef, my precious child, has been the inspiration and the motivation for this labor of love. My fervent hope is that this book and the teachings herein will guide Yosef on his journey, in peace and joy, as he reaches toward fulfillment of the purpose for which he is created.

Immense gratitude is also due my cherished family and step-family, Cathy, Hayley, Lindsay, Maggie, and Leor, and our grand-daughters, Noa and Shira, who have made our world a brighter place and illuminated our lives with endless blessings.

My esteemed editors and mentors, Simcha and Frumma Gottlieb, have selflessly shared with us their talents, literary crafts-manship, dedication, and sagacity through thick and thin. Thanks to them this book has reached unimagined heights.

Friends, community, colleagues, and the Rebbe's emissaries too numerous to name have always challenged, encouraged, and inspired me, and continue to do so on a daily basis. I thank them all. The friendship and vital participation of Zalman and Brochi Friedman have also made an enormous difference throughout the process of developing this book.

Worthy of special note are Yoni and Rivki Katz, who were among the first to bring Rabbi Friedman's teachings to the masses; Mushka Friedman for her Hebrew and Yiddish translations; Lori Brown, my trusted personal assistant; Malka Grossman, for her editorial expertise; Patricia Spadaro and Nigel J. Yorwerth of Yorwerth Associates for their tireless, versatile, and astute publishing experience and coaching services.

In the crafting of this book I am but the transcriber, compiler, shaper, arranger, and consolidator. The wisdom, wit, erudition, and insight belong to the mind and heart of Rabbi Manis Friedman. He is a faithful messenger bearing ancient, unimpeachable truths; at the same time he is an innovator who is never afraid to go out on a limb for those who seek truth.

Every aspect of this work—from Rabbi Friedman's lifelong cultivation of philosophical integrity and his inimitable modes of expression, to the sense of responsibility we all feel for the efficacy of every word on every page—has been guided by the teachings of the Lubavitcher Rebbe, Rabbi Menachem Mendel Schneerson, of righteous memory. One could ask for no greater role model in this life.

May all these efforts help to hasten the ultimate realization of oneness, compassion, and enduring peace among all humankind.

Rivka Goldstein

Glossary

ahava: Love.

ahavat Hashem: Love of God.

Alter Rebbe: The "Old Rebbe"—Rabbi Shneur Zalman of Liadi, 1745–1812, founder of the Chabad Chassidic movement, author of *Tanya* and *Shulchan Aruch HaRav*.

Baal Shem Tov: The "Master of the Good Name"—Rabbi Israel ben Eliezer, c. 1698–1760, founder of general Chassidism.

Beit Hamikdash: The Holy Temple in Jerusalem—the focal point of the divine presence in our world, and the "gate of heaven" through which our spiritual efforts ascend. The first two temples were destroyed by conquering invaders more than two thousand years ago. The third and permanent temple is anticipated with the imminent final redemption.

Chabad: An acronym for *chochmah, binah,* and *da'at*—the three aspects of intellect as elucidated in Kabbalistic/Chassidic philosophy.

Chassid: Originally "pious one"; in contemporary usage, one who studies Chassidus, has a mentor/disciple relationship with a Rebbe, and strives to follow in his footsteps. (Plural: *chassidim.*)

Chassidism: A way of life rooted in the teachings, principles, customs, and the sense of purpose that emphasizes love of one's fellow man. Chassidism began with the Baal Shem Tov and has evolved through the generations of Chassidic masters who succeeded him.

Chassidus: The inner dimension of Torah—sometimes referred to as "mysticism"—but that actually seeks to reveal, clarify, and internalize our knowledge of God in ways that deepen and enhance the quality of everyday life.

chuppah: Wedding canopy.

davening: Prayer, as formalized in the Hebrew liturgy.

Feter: (Yiddish) Uncle.

Gemara: The Talmud—the vast written compendium of Judaism's Oral Law, as given to Moses. Compiled over hundreds of years culminating in the fifth century CE, it includes ethics, history, biblical philosophy, customs, rabbinic folklore, and more. It serves to this day as the basis of all codes of Jewish law.

Halacha: The specific, practical details of divinely mandated behavior in all aspects of everyday life.

Kabbalah: The esoteric, abstract, "hidden" teachings of Torah that delve into the secrets of Creation and the unseen dynamics of Godliness within worldly phenomena.

Kashrut: The practice of eating only kosher (permissible) foods, based on biblical commandments, as stipulated in Jewish Law.

Kibbud Av v'Eim: The biblical Fifth Commandment, "Honor thy father and mother."

l'chaim: "To life!" An affirmation of blessing and good wishes; a toast traditionally offered over glasses of wine or other strong drink.

Lubavitcher Rebbe: Rabbi Menachem M. Schneerson, 1902–1994, son-in-law of the Rebbe Rayatz, and the seventh Rebbe in the Chabad Chassidic lineage of leadership. With his brilliant scholarship, love and empathy for all, and the inspirational campaigns that built thousands of educational and social service centers throughout the world, he transformed the spirit of world Jewry and fostered increasing well-being and brotherhood among all mankind.

Mashiach: The righteous redeemer, a descendant of the royal lineage of King David, who will teach Torah to all and lead the Jewish people as well as the nations of the world toward the ultimate revelation and realization of holiness, morality, kindness, justice, and peace.

mashpia* and *mekabel: The pairing of an empathic mentor or spiritual benefactor with the recipient of his or her guidance. The dynamic interaction between giver and receiver lies at the heart of all relationships, whether master and disciple, teacher and student, or husband and wife; the influence and energy flow both ways.

mensch: (Yiddish) A mature, responsible, goodhearted, and trustworthy person.

mikvah: Immersion in the ritual bath that washes away spiritual impurity and restores the original innocence of body and soul. In addition to other detailed specifications, according to Jewish law the *mikvah* must contain a certain minimum volume of water that flows from a natural source.

mitzvah: Often referred to as a "good deed," a *mitzvah* is a divine commandment that manifests and amplifies the intrinsic bond between a human being and his Creator. There are 613 *mitzvahs* in the Torah.

Modeh Ani: The first prayer said upon arising in the morning, expressing our gratitude for the renewal of the soul and the opportunity to serve God another day.

neshama: The soul, the essence of which is the spark of Godliness that bestows vitality and luminance to the physical body.

Rebbe: A spiritual leader whose wisdom, dedication, and insight into the particular sensibilities and mission of every individual imbues his chassidim with faith, trust, and devotion to the service of God—the Moses of his generation.

Rebbe Rashab: Rabbi Sholom Dovber Schneersohn, 1860–1920, the fifth Rebbe in the Chabad Chassidic lineage of leadership.

Rebbe Rayatz: Rabbi Yosef Yitzchak Schneersohn, 1880–1950, the sixth Rebbe in the Chabad Chassidic lineage of leadership, who brought Chabad to the United States in 1940.

schtick: (Yiddish) Any talent, style, habit, or eccentricity for which a person is particularly well-known. Originally (but not necessarily) used to describe a comedic routine or gimmick.

Shabbos: (Often pronounced *Shabbat.*) The seventh day of the week, from sundown Friday to nightfall Saturday; a day of rest. God "rested" on the seventh day of Creation and asked His people to devote the Sabbath day to study, prayer, and joyous festive meals together with family and friends. All types of work that represent creative engagement with worldly activity, such as doing business, are avoided on Shabbat.

shadchan: A matchmaker who introduces a man and a woman to each other who are potentially compatible. The *shadchan* often helps guide the couple through the dating and courting process and facilitates their decision as to whether they will become husband and wife.

shalom bayit: Peace in the home—the sanctity, mutual respect, appreciation, generosity, and kindness between a husband and wife that creates the loving and joyous atmosphere conducive to raising a happy family.

sheitel: A wig. Among other Jewish laws and customs of modesty, a married woman covers her hair in fulfillment of her commitment to the privacy and faithfulness that defines an intimate relationship between husband and wife.

shidduch: A match made by a *shadchan.*

Sh'ma Yisrael: "Hear, O Israel"—the centerpiece of Jewish prayer, recited each morning and evening to proclaim the oneness of God and affirm our individual and communal dedication to His service.

shtetl: (Yiddish) A small town or village, historically in eastern Europe or the Russian Pale of Settlement, where a Jewish community resides.

shul: A synagogue.

Tanya: The groundbreaking, foundational book of Chabad Chassidus, written by the Alter Rebbe and first published in 1796. A basic manual for divine service, it offers a profound, readily understandable clarification of the structure and dynamics of the human personality and the Godly soul.

tefillin: Small leather boxes containing biblical verses handwritten on parchment, worn on the head, and on the arm adjacent to the heart, during weekday morning prayers. They include the text of *Sh'ma Yisrael* and signify the wholesome harmony between intellect and emotion.

Tehilim: The Book of Psalms, songs of divine inspiration composed primarily by King David, the "sweet singer of Israel." *Tehilim* also incorporates other songs composed by men of kindred spirit—among them, Moses and King Solomon.

teshuvah: Often translated as "repentance," *teshuvah* is better understood as "return" to the essential goodness and holiness with which one was originally blessed by God.

Torah: The Five Books of Moses as revealed by God on Mount Sinai. This definition is frequently extended to include all twenty-four books of the Hebrew Bible, as well as the explanatory teachings of the Oral Torah that have been passed down through the generations from the revelation at Sinai.

tzaddik: A perfectly righteous person who has conquered the base, animalistic inclination toward selfishness and amorality that resides within us all and distracts us from our true purpose in life.

tzedakah: Charity or, more generally, acts of benevolence and generosity. The Hebrew root of the word—*tzedek*—means justice. The implication is that it is only just that we should share our wealth, because whatever wealth has been granted to us is not ours alone.

tznius: Modesty; a sense of privacy and decorum that eschews exhibitionism in behavior or dress.

yeshiva: A school dedicated to the intensive, diligent study of Torah—sometimes, but not necessarily, with the goal of rabbinical ordination.

Yom Kippur: The Day of Atonement—the holiest day of the year, marked by at least a full 24 hours of fasting, prayer, introspection, and divine forgiveness.

Download two FREE GIFTS now:
The Joy of Intimacy* and *Doesn't Anyone Blush Anymore
e-books by Rabbi Manis Friedman
at www.itsgoodtoknow.org/ebookgift

Learn more about Rabbi Manis Friedman and his work

Rabbi Manis Friedman regularly speaks and teaches at events worldwide. The most popular rabbi on YouTube, he offers free online tips and resources as well as ongoing releases on a wide range of topics, including relationships, dating, marriage and family, emotional well-being, spirituality, life's challenges, and much more.

Sign up for Rabbi Friedman's free email newsletter to get exclusive content, updates, and special offers at:

www.itsgoodtoknow.org

Stay connected:

itsgoodtoknow.org
info@itsgoodtoknow.org
facebook.com/manisfriedman
youtube.com/manisfriedman
twitter.com/manisfriedman

Rabbi Manis Friedman is a world-renowned author, teacher, and speaker, well known for his provocative and incisive wit and wisdom. His international speaking tours, seminars, and retreats take him around the world, and he has been featured on CNN, A&E Reviews, PBS, and BBC Worldwide as well as in such publications as *The New York Times, Rolling Stone, Seventeen, Guideposts,* and *Publishers Weekly*. He is the author of *The Joy of Intimacy: A Soulful Guide to Keeping the Spark Alive* and *Doesn't Anyone Blush Anymore?* He is the most popular rabbi on YouTube and has hosted his own critically acclaimed cable television series syndicated throughout North America.

Rabbi Friedman is the dean of Bais Chana Institute of Jewish Studies, which he cofounded in 1971, and the founder of It's Good to Know, a nonprofit life-learning foundation based in New York City. He lives with his family in St. Paul, Minnesota. To learn more about Rabbi Manis Friedman and his work, visit ItsGoodToKnow.org.

Photo by Mendel Mish@FunNFocus

Rivka Goldstein was granted a full scholarship from Harvard University and graduated with a master's degree in theological studies. She has taught world religious traditions at the University of Phoenix South Florida Main Campus and at the Miami International University of Art & Design. She currently teaches writing as a spiritual journey at the Chaya Aydel Seminary in Hallandale Beach, Florida. Rivka is also a life coach, helping men and women navigate the world of dating, marriage, parenting, family, career, and self-worth. A native of Singapore, she currently lives in Hollywood, Florida, with her family. To learn more about Rivka Goldstein and her work, visit AskDodaRivka.com.